JOEL BEALL

PLAYING
DIRTY

Rediscovering Golf's Soul in Scotland
in an Age of Sportswashing and Civil War

Back Nine Press
Chicago, Illinois
www.back9press.com
Instagram and X: @backninepress

9 8 7 6 5 4 3 2 1

First Edition

Playing Dirty /
Written by Joel Beall

Back Nine Press (USA)
Pages cm

ISBN 978-1-956237-33-7 (hardback)
ISBN 978-1-956237-34-4 (ebook)

For Zahya, my partner in crime.

For Mom, who raised me right.

For Dad, who instilled a love for the game and introduced
me to Scottish golf.

For all golfers: it's what we do.

Contents

Introduction

He introduced himself with a tumbler of truth, what he later revealed was a triple pour of 18-year-old single malt Scotch. Bold hospitality for 11:30 in the morning. I appreciated but declined the offer; I had an interview in the hour ahead, and beyond that a tee time at Balcomie Links awaited in Crail, a 20-minute journey on thin ribbons of pavement threading through sprawling Scottish pastures. Appointments that demand the sort of sharp mind that dulls in the company of fine whisky. But the man insisted, his salt-and-pepper bangs nodding to the glass in his extended right hand. A stranger passing this type of drink at this time of day was looking to celebrate or hoping to unload a pain that can no longer be carried. All that matters is he's got something to say, and he needs someone to hear it.

"Hess," they called him—just Hess. It was shouted by half a dozen patrons who spotted him holding court at our corner table, whose name echoed through the front room of the Dunvegan. The stately St Andrews pub, which sits no more than a shanked wedge from the Old Course, is as much of an institution as the links itself. Hess was medium height, stout, encased in a washed-out navy polo shirt that was perhaps a size too small, those bangs occasionally needing to be wiped away from his droopy eyes that were frantically dancing, jumping to the doorway anytime someone walked into the bar. It seemed he was giving these would-be customers an ocular pat-down before granting them a passage they didn't know they needed. Yet his appearance and diverted attention belied a zealous spark in his voice, a New England English fused with Borders Scots that left vowels unfinished, as if the words themselves were too eager to escape into the pub's ale-scented air.

"You look like you needin' a friend," Hess said, helping himself to an empty chair. "You're surrounded by 'em here. You jus' don't know 'em yet."

Hess stretched his arms out before settling in to travel back in time, detailing his life story over the next 30 minutes with an ease and smoothness that signaled this was not his first time reciting the spiel. Born in Worcester, Massachusetts, but spent most of his life in Europe, the son of a military engineer, was never anywhere long enough to miss it when his family ultimately left for the next town. Sports were his anchor, though every season meant new teammates, fresh introductions, relationships built on quicksand, and he wasn't much of a student, transferring universities twice and flunking out of another. Hess went through a number of occupations, proudly pointing out he earned some money working in real estate ("Don't need schoolin' to open doors to empty houses") and opening a personal training service outside Bristol, England, but happiness remained elusive and purpose kept slipping through his fingers.

"Being around the services, they had structure, identity," Hess remarked. "Me? Had nothing worth going after."

When he was in his late 20s, one of Hess' younger sisters was getting married to a boy from Edinburgh. The day before the wedding Hess' future brother-in-law put together a golf outing at a course just outside the city. Hess didn't play golf; his dad never had the time to introduce him to it, but Hess was bored and didn't feel like sitting in the hotel room, so he walked with the outing. One of his cousins let him take some swings, and he was able to make solid contact within a few hacks, and was surprised how much he enjoyed trying to hit the bejesus out of a ball. More importantly, Hess was struck by how happy everyone seemed playing a game no one was particularly good at. That was the joy he had been chasing but hadn't found. "Enchanted, like that," Hess said, snapping his fingers.

The next week Hess went to a range in Bristol nearly every day, using four clubs his brother-in-law let him borrow. Weapons of self-discovery disguised as sporting equipment. By the end of the month, he offered to clean the range for free in the morning for two buckets, and the owner did him one better, letting Hess hit as many balls as he wanted. Hess proudly stated he broke 100 within the first six months of playing and was down to the mid-80s by Year 2. One of his workout clients recognized Hess had the bug and brought him to Scotland for a boys' weekend in Gullane, where he played 90 holes over three days. The specific courses blurred together in memory, but what remained crystal clear was the revelation: in every clubhouse, on every tee, in every pub afterward, he found his tribe.

By the time he returned to his Bristol apartment on Sunday night, Hess began packing. The country up north beckoned. He had found his purpose.

"That was almost a quarter of a century ago," Hess said. He still dabbles in personal training and real estate, as well as "consultation," which he never elaborated on. In most countries, work defines who you are. Not in Scotland, and not for Hess. Work is simply a means to fund a habit he has no intention of quitting. "Goin' after the white ball, in as many whirls as it takes. That's what to do," Hess said. He bounces around Scotland in an RV, although he has a flat in Glasgow. For the next month he was staying outside of Anstruther, just down the road from St Andrews. Hess said he's been a plus handicap until the past few years, now hovering around scratch, which he blamed on both a loss of distance and the "gawd damn new handicap system." He plays at least once a day and often twice. Including in an hour at the Old Course, "the Old Lady," as Hess called her.

Ah, I thought, that's why we are cheers-ing, which I then articulated to Hess just to double-check. "So we are drinking, we are celebrating you getting to play the Old?"

Hess' demeanor, which had been so warm and avuncular, changed to slightly indignant. As if I hadn't heard a single damn thing he had just said. "That's why you're here?"

And I wanted to tell him. That I was here, in Scotland, to have my faith restored, while fearing what I was fighting for had already been lost. But that seemed like a lot to lay on a stranger, even over Scotch. I nodded my head. Yes, I am here for the golf. Hess leaned forward, his chin dipping in the kind of understanding that runs deeper than words. His hand found my shoulder, a gentle benediction, before he rose and turned toward the bar. "We're drinkin'," he declared, eyes fixed on North Street where centuries of golfers had walked toward the links, "because we get to golf."

•　　•　　•

Two summers earlier, a few blocks beyond Dunvegan's well-worn threshold, I met two fellow scribes outside a chapel, where St Andrews' ancient cobblestones genuflect before castle ruins. There are no church services during the summer, so on this Sunday the pews were empty, the pious instead finding worship in the pubs that lie in the chapel's shadow. We had come to pay homage at the graves of Old and Young Tom Morris before the 150th Open's final act. While visitors stream here daily, smartphones ready to capture their brush with golf's saints, our visit carried a different weight. In that cemetery, amid centuries-old stones, we sought not Instagram moments but sanctuary—a breath of air in a year that had left us gasping. Golf's civil war had drafted us all, despite our press badges and pretense of objectivity. There's no neutral ground when the ground itself is contested. Standing there among the dead we could feel it in our bones: this was not the end of something, but a terrible beginning.

Our journey led us to the remnants of a fortress that first stretched skyward in 1158, closing its gates two centuries before America drew its first breath. These stones stood against a backdrop that Scotland crafts better than any artist: rolling hills tumbling into the moody North Sea, all beneath clouds that hung exactly as they should, low and gray and timeless. No map was needed; generations of reverent feet had carved a path through the untamed grass, a whispered direction to the Morris family plot. For the uninitiated, Old Tom Morris wasn't just golf's father—he was its architect, prophet, and greatest practitioner. While dominating the game as a player, he simultaneously served as greenkeeper, craftsman of clubs and balls, teacher, and designer of courses that still test the game's best. To grasp his impact, imagine Babe Ruth not just conquering baseball but building its greatest parks, crafting its equipment, teaching its future stars, and shaping its very soul. His son, Young Tom, seemed destined to extend this legacy, claiming four Opens before fate cruelly intervened at age 24, leaving golf's greatest dynasty to wonder what might have been.

At Young Tom's headstone, we huddled in reverent silence that felt less like an absence of sound and more like a presence. Three golf writers, wordless in an age where words were our shields and swords. Then a voice—and though these men are my brothers, to this day I don't know who the voice belonged to—began to breathe life into the weathered words etched in that white stone marker. The epitaph emerged like a hymn, as if Young Tom's story might offer wisdom for the battles we knew awaited us beyond the walls:

Deeply regretted by numerous friends and all golfers
He thrice in succession won the champion's belt
And held it without rivalry ...

Then the voice paused, ever so briefly, but a pause that carried a weight of impalpable gravity ...

... and yet without envy
His many amiable qualities
Being no less acknowledged than his golfing achievements.

It sounds sacrilegious, weaving sport into sacred cloth. But Alister MacKenzie wrote that golf and religion are two of the things the Scottish take seriously. That morning, I came to understand MacKenzie never saw these as separate faiths. That's why, as golf's civil war erupted, I found myself drawn to St Andrews like a pilgrim seeking truth. If we were to wage this battle for golf's soul, if this crusade demanded our blood and ink, I needed to return to the game's holy ground—to this kingdom where golf first drew breath, where its spirit still dwells—to test my own belief against something eternal.

The next day drew me back alone to Young Tom's stone, as if some unfinished prayer needed answering. A tour group materialized through the morning mist, and someone asked the question that has haunted golf's faithful for nearly 150 years—the terrible tale of Young Tom's end.

In September of 1875, Young Tom was playing a match with his father in North Berwick when he received a telegram that his wife had gone into a difficult labor. The Morrises raced against tide and time across the Firth of Forth, but they were too late: Young Tom's wife and newborn were dead when they arrived. Young Tom carried this weight through winter's descent until Christmas Day. Some say the bottle got him, but others know the truth:

"He died," I told the group, "of a broken heart."

·   ·   ·

Two years later, golf remains trapped in an existential crisis.

The mess was spurred by the arrival of LIV Golf, a fledgling league attempting to rival the top circuit in the professional game, the PGA Tour. LIV officials promised to shake up a tired game when the entity launched in 2021 by bringing team formats to an individual sport, cutting competitions from four days to three and hosting more international events than the American-centric tour. The tournaments themselves aspired to be social functions rather than sporting events—"Après Golf," was the term—with DJs blasting music and extracurricular attractions performing as the competition unfolded. Most noteworthy, in a sport without guaranteed contracts and where half a dozen players will crack $10 million in earnings per season, LIV was offering nine-figure signing bonuses and no-cut guarantees. To note, Phil Mickelson reportedly received $200 million for a four-year deal with LIV Golf; Tiger Woods is atop the PGA Tour's all-time money list with $120 million over a 30-year career. And it wasn't just stars like Mickelson or Dustin Johnson receiving hundreds of millions; some players with just one or two career wins were receiving upward of $75 million. Contrast that to the tour, where the league average was $2.3 million in 2023.

LIV officials assert these differences would disrupt the sport while proving additive to the existing product. The problem, however, has nothing to do with what LIV is or aspires to be. The league is bankrolled by Saudi Arabia's Public Investment Fund, the kingdom's sovereign wealth fund, and the brainchild of Saudi's Vision 2030. Proponents call "2030" a blueprint to diminish Saudi Arabia's reliance on oil by expanding its economic portfolio and updating and rebuilding its public offerings, and one of those avenues is an investment in athletics. Critics have argued these interests are far more menacing than mere societal ambitions. The current Saudi regime has continually and ruthlessly silenced dissidents. Civil liberties—especially for women and LGBTQ communities—are almost nonexistent. According to the New York Times, a 2017 purge consolidated bin Salman's authority over every branch of the government. The kingdom has played a vital part in Yemen's ongoing military conflict which has left 250,000 people dead. For Saudi opponents, the kingdom's thrust into golf is a thinly veiled attempt to Westernize and "sportswash" its image.

Now, the idea of a competitor to the PGA Tour had lurked in the shadows for decades; the tour itself came to pass after players split from the PGA of America in 1968 to form the Tournament Players Division. More recently, former World No. 1 Greg Norman and media tycoon Rupert Murdoch attempted to create a "World Golf Tour" in the mid-1990s featuring the top players competing in an eight-event series. Other iterations of a world tour have come and gone without much fanfare. The LIV framework began to arise in earnest in the fall of 2019, to the point that current PGA Tour commissioner Jay Monahan issued a warning in January 2020 that any player who sided with a rival league would face suspension and possibly a lifetime ban. Still, until the spring of 2022, LIV was discussed as a provocative hypothetical but one whose reality and viability were routinely dismissed.

To the tour and many of golf's constituents, there was a fundamental fault with the competition LIV Golf had created. At its heart, golf is appreciated for being the purest rendition of meritocracy, where spots aren't given, and you only make what you earn. LIV Golf was the antithesis of this spirit, offering paydays to players most fans would not pay to see. LIV itself was incapable of taking a step forward without stepping on its own foot, its short existence marked by mistakes and parody and incompetence. Players rumored to defect brushed aside criticism of Saudi Arabia's appalling human rights track record with claims that they were simply "trying to grow the game." Reporters were tossed out of press conferences for questions LIV officials didn't like. The league's logos and team names appeared to be lifted from a kindergarten classroom (with one team accused of copyright infringement). Mickelson, the de facto front man, almost sabotaged the entire league when admitting to a writer that the Saudis were "Scary motherfuckers" who murdered journalist Jamal Khashoggi and executed gay people … but was partnering with them because Mickelson believed it was the best way to leverage the tour to his monetary demands. James Piot, who is a professional, was listed as an amateur at the league's launch event while player Hudson Swafford was listed as "Swafford Hudson" on the LIV website. A pairings party accidentally revealed "Patrick Reed" on the video board a day before reports of Reed joining LIV trickled out. In the league's first season, most of the events were attended only by hundreds of fans, with many venues receiving protests due to Saudi's human-rights issues, and during one of LIV's big events the final holes of the television broadcast were dropped by more than 80 percent of TV affiliates in favor of other previously scheduled programming.

Except, as time went on and the money grew, a handful of in-their-prime stars like Brooks Koepka, Bryson DeChambeau, and Cameron Smith eventually left the confines of the PGA Tour thanks to deals that would put Scrooge McDuck to shame. It was an exodus that signaled LIV Golf was succeeding against its own missteps, for it had blank checks and a forever runway to take flight, and it was willing to take others down in order for it to rise. The established tours—not able to match the financial offerings of LIV because they operate as tax-exempt non-profit 501(c)6 organizations—attempted to use legacy over leverage with their players and lost; by the Tour's own metrics, six of its 10 most popular players jumped to LIV.And money wasn't the only dagger. The only reason rogue leagues were fun thought exercises was because the tour had fallen into stasis. The idea that professional golf was diluted—which in turn, dilutes fans' interest—came well before its LIV battle. With the PGA Tour hosting 40-something tournaments in a calendar year it can be trying, and sometimes straining, to find significance in each event. At times the tour seemed allergic to creativity, the golf mostly looking the same as the golf played the week before that looked like the golf coming the week after. As a response, the PGA Tour had a revolt of sorts by the remaining top players, a movement that ultimately led to organizational restructuring that conferred more power to the best players than ever before. Those players were mostly placated, with the tour asking sponsors for more prize money and funneling its financial reserves to players through bonus pools, despite some players continuing to leverage the league for all its worth. In itself, this was not necessarily bad. The rollout and responses for both sides were flawed, to say nothing about moral entanglements ... yet, in a distilled form, it was capitalism. Professional sports, after all, is a business.

The trouble is that their profession is also millions of fans' passion, and though not all parties were guilty, it appeared that most of the game's central actors cared more about getting paid or taken care of rather than about where their actions could be taking golf as a whole.

The emergence of the Saudi-backed circuit has resulted in breakups and alliances and caused suspensions and lawsuits. It has caused a game known for its civility to become uncivil, and has brought the politics of human rights into a space supposedly reserved for sport. It has spawned reactions that span the emotional spectrum, from intrigue and excitement to angst and dread and everything in between. Which is why, ultimately, the schism has inflicted the most pain on fans. This has become a sideshow with the worst type of actors, and as bad as the play has been, where it could lead is worse. Fans' attention is divided between an entity that doesn't know what it's doing and doesn't offer much in the way of competition, yet does boast some marquee names, against the traditional power with true competition and true consequences that is losing the very stars needed to pull people in. Forget additive; that is the very definition of subtraction. The schism has diluted the product.

That's an important delineation, *schism*. Competition in any business is healthy. It can usher in positive change, spur innovation, and force the entities in question to be better, because that is what is required to survive. But schisms ... schisms can be terminal.

•　　•　　•

In the summer of 2023, the PGA Tour and Saudi Arabia's PIF reached a framework agreement, one that signaled the parties had reached detente. Whether this brings long-term peace remains in question. A congressional probe was opened by the United States Senate's Permanent Subcommittee on Investigations in response to the surprising partnership between the tour and PIF. According to Senator Richard Blumenthal (D-Conn.), the deal "raises concerns about the Saudi government's role in influencing this effort and the risks posed by a foreign government entity assuming control over a cherished American institution." The alliance could be reviewed by the Committee on Foreign Investment in the United States, which analyzes mergers regarding potential threats to the nation's security.

In a bid to address antitrust concerns and reduce dependence on Saudi investment, the PGA Tour secured a $1.5 billion deal with Strategic Sports Group, a consortium of private equity investors. PIF responded by shattering the fragile peace, signing world No. 1 Jon Rahm to LIV Golf in a seismic December 2023 move. Yet 2024 proved challenging for both tours—the PGA Tour struggled with declining viewership while LIV Golf failed to capitalize on Rahm's star power, remaining largely irrelevant to mainstream golf fans. Heading into 2025, optimism persists for an agreement between PIF and the PGA Tour, though the path has been littered with unfulfilled promises and broken timelines and dashed expectations. That doesn't mean LIV Golf wins its battle against the PGA Tour should long-term peace remain evasive. It just means the battle continues, which, for the rest of golf, sure feels like a loss.

• • •

There are hundreds of gravestones in the cemetery of St Andrews Cathedral. Most lack the dactylic stanza that was bestowed to Young Tom, their stones marked only by a date of birth and date of death and a dash in between. All those years, all those experiences, somehow packed into a symbol and forgotten by history.

That has been the recurring image in my head during golf's civil war, because while the focus has been on the entities fighting at the top, it is the rest of the game that's had to shoulder the cost and toll of the battle. For the better part of two years, the PGA Tour, LIV Golf, players, and most of the constituents involved with both have taken for granted the privilege of fan investment, of their attention and time and passion. It's not capital or leverage or legacy that's important; what makes any of this matter is the men and women and children that invest themselves into this beautifully stupid game. The stakeholders think fans are ancillary fixtures, and yet the fans are the ones that give what's going on consequence and meaning, and why companies are willing to spend millions to associate themselves with an ecosystem that emits an emotional pull. Professional golf's epitaph will ultimately flow from the pens of those who loved the game enough to believe it was about something more than money.

So far, the sport has banked on the belief that golfers are obsessed with golf. It is a sickness that has no cure. Golfers especially have a high tolerance for pain; the game leaves you humbled and embarrassed and hopeless and somehow those sentiments dissipate at the chance to do it all over again. The game's power brokers assume this devotion was bottomless—that we'd endure any indignity, swallow any bitter pill, just to keep our fix alive. But even addiction has its limits. There is palpable fatigue from those inside the game and out regarding professional golf's hostilities, and the sport has already reached the point where many just want peace, no matter how it's achieved ... but what is peace if there is no accounting for what is lost to achieve it?

What golf is experiencing is merely the new reality that all sports will face. Saudi Arabia has ambitions to purchase franchises in the National Football League, the National Basketball Association, and Major League Baseball; one of the reasons the Saudis are still interested in a tour partnership is the Tour's new private equity group has ties to every major sporting league in the United States. The interest is mutual; with franchises now commanding billions of dollars per team, there are only so many entities that can meet the asking mark, and plenty of these owners—billionaires in their own rights—already have business connections with Saudi Arabia. The leagues themselves, while publicly trying to distance themselves from sportswashing, are intrigued, especially if legacy media deals begin to taper off in the streaming era. It's not just American sports; the regime has plans to bring the Olympics to the kingdom, and given the International Olympic Committee's shameful past of accepting bribes for hosting bids, you don't have to squint too hard to see that wish coming to fruition. Golf is not the Saudi endgame; it is the storm that hangs on the sporting horizon.

Which is why I decided to spend a summer in Scotland, the homeland of golf. The siren song I heard that day in the cemetery still calls, and it's time to answer it.

In Scotland, golf exhales. Here, far from the boardroom battles, the game still breathes as it was meant to—pure and democratic. The courses, those ancient strategists carved by wind and time, somehow always find room for one more dreamer chasing daylight. Links and life intertwine without ceremony: fairways spill into village squares, first tees lurk behind bus stops, flagsticks wave to fishermen. Duck into any pub and you'll find half the day's tee sheet has preceded you, scorecards spread across tables like battle maps, pints marking the spots where glory was found or lost. This is golf's last pure kingdom, where wealth is measured not in gold but in twilight rounds, where every weary wanderer can find refuge. Where the past feels present and the game never gets old, because good things never do.

Scotland is where golf's truth still whispers, if we're quiet enough to hear it. The game remains wonderfully, stubbornly itself. Not perfect, mind you; nothing wrapped in human hands ever is, but Scotland golf is as unadulterated of a product as we get. It reminds us that all that is good with this beautifully dumb sport can continue in the face of the unknown. Whatever happens with the PGA Tour and Saudi Arabia ... well, professional golf tournaments come and go, but Scotland golf is forever.

The fracture in professional golf cuts deeper than the superficial battle between tours and kingdoms, or even the painful rifts between former friends and colleagues. A more fundamental separation has emerged: the growing void between golf's glittering professional façade and its beating heart. As the elite game drifts further from its foundations, players quietly abandon the pretense that competition matters more than compensation, their moral compass swinging from "What enriches the game?" to "What enriches me?" Those steering the sport have shown, through actions both subtle and stark, that preserving their authority and appeasing well-compensated players outweighs nurturing the passionate community whose devotion makes any of this possible.

This struggle transcends defining golf merely as a product—though that term signals how far we've strayed. It's about whether the sport can resist being reduced to another commodity for consumption, packaged and sold to fans who deserve something more meaningful. At its core, this is a battle for golf's essence and its soul. Waxing poetic about Scottish golf might seem trite, yet there's truth in that romance—truth that professional golf desperately needs to reclaim. The game longs for players who carry this understanding, who recognize their role as stewards rather than entertainers. It yearns for storytelling that honors golf's life force, for venues that whisper of its origins, for supporters who value excellence above marketability, and for leaders whose vision stretches beyond the next financial quarter.

Consider this both a love letter and a clarion call—an unflinching analysis of professional golf's precarious state paired with a celebration of the game's enduring spirit, still vibrantly alive in Scottish links, towns, and people. In places where golf's rhythms conduct daily life, existing not as a commercial enterprise but as a cherished inheritance belonging to all. My journey seeks to bridge the widening gap between the game's current trajectory and the timeless nature that exists over there. To remind us what golf once was and instill hope of what it could be again before the sport swallows itself whole.

I want to help you find what Hess has found.

CHAPTER 1

Royals

King James II • MBS and Vision 2030 •
Four friends • Sportswashing • Walking the dog

The earliest documented evidence of golf comes from a royal edict by James II, King of the Scots—a ruler often overshadowed in history. James ascended to the throne at the tender age of seven, following the assassination of his father. His nickname was "Fiery Face," which sounds formidable, but it referred to the prominent crimson birthmark on his left cheek, which his contemporaries associated with a volatile temperament. His early reign was steeped in bloodshed as rival factions exploited his youth and inexperience.

Perhaps these tumultuous beginnings shaped James' fixation on military strength. As an adult, he developed a keen interest in modern warfare, particularly the emerging power of artillery. Once James consolidated his authority and quelled the uprisings, he traveled across Scotland, engaging with his subjects and earning a reputation as a popular monarch. Yet the specter of his violent youth lingered;

conflict was all he had ever known. James sought to expand Scotland's territory into Orkney, Shetland, and the Isle of Man, though these efforts largely faltered. Nevertheless, his ambitions burned brightly. He believed Scotland's potential was only limited by the readiness of its forces. In James' eyes, his militia's archery skills had deteriorated, distracted by frivolous pursuits. Convinced that recreational activities were weakening the nation's defenses, James issued an Act of Parliament on March 6, 1457, banning golf.

> Item, it is ordained and the decreed that the lords and barons both spiritual and temporal should organize archery displays four times in the year. And that football and golf should be utterly condemned and stopped. And that a pair of targets should be made up at all parish churches and shooting should be practiced each Sunday ... And concerning football and golf, we ordain that [those found playing these games] be punished by the local barons and, failing them, by the King's officers.

James' obsession with munitions and expansion proved to be his undoing. In 1460 he attempted to rid his English neighbors from Roxburgh Castle in the Borders region. During the siege he imported a multitude of cannons from modern-day Belgium. But one of the weapons, named "the Lion" exploded upon firing with James standing nearby. He died instantly.

James' golf prohibition remained after his passing, and it was strengthened through similar bans in 1470 and 1491 under the next two monarchs. However, records show these decrees did little to dampen the growing fervor for the diversion among the working class. Far from being the pastime of privilege and wealth that it is often seen as today, the game in its earliest recorded form was an act of defiance. Golf was an outlaw sport.

•   •   •

The man behind professional golf's reckoning is not a golfer. He doesn't care for sports, period. To understand where the schism is going you need to understand how it started, and with whom. Mohammed bin Salman (often referred to as MBS) ascended to his position as crown prince of Saudi Arabia in 2017, marking an unprecedented shift in the kingdom's leadership dynamics. At just 35 years old when appointed, he became the youngest defense minister in the world and the first millennial to hold such significant power in the region. His father, King Salman bin Abdulaziz Al Saud, technically holds the throne, but bin Salman's aggressive modernization agenda and hands-on governance style have made him the kingdom's undisputed operational leader.

"Saudi Arabia for the past 30 years was like watching a silent movie: one elderly king after another flickered across the screen saying nothing and doing nothing," says Karen House, a Pulitzer Prize winner and former publisher of the *Wall Street Journal* who's extensively covered Saudi Arabia for four decades. "Saudi Arabia since 2016 is an IMAX movie on fast forward. Everything MBS does is big, bold, fast, loud, riveting."

The urgency behind these sweeping changes stems from Saudi Arabia's existential economic challenge: diversifying beyond oil dependence. The kingdom's petroleum exports have historically accounted for roughly 80% of its budget revenues and 90% of export earnings, creating a precarious economic monoculture. Vision 2030, bin Salman's flagship initiative, represents the most ambitious economic restructuring in the nation's history. Beyond standard diversification efforts, the plan includes revolutionary projects that capture global attention: The Line at NEOM, for instance, represents not just an architectural marvel with its parallel mirrored skyscrapers running 75 miles, but a complete reimagining of urban living. The project promises to house 9 million residents in a zero-carbon environment with flying taxis, a hybrid of artificial intelligence and human innovation, and a lifestyle that bin Salman describes as a "civilizational revolution." Other megaprojects include the Red Sea Project, a luxury tourism development spanning 28,000 square kilometers, and NEOM's Trojena, which will offer indoor skiing in the desert—all part of a broader strategy to transform Saudi Arabia into a leading global destination for tourism, technology, and innovation.

One of Vision 2030's tenets is a "vibrant society," and a vessel selected to reach this ambition is sports. It's been a relatively successful venture, bringing in boxing, wrestling, and tennis exhibitions along with Formula 1 races to the kingdom. The country has leaned hard into football, "winning" the right to host the 2034 FIFA World Cup (amid accusations FIFA changed its bidding policy to rig the election in Saudi Arabia's favor), signing star Cristiano Ronaldo to a $200 million deal to play with Saudi Arabian soccer team Al Nassr, and the Public Investment Fund purchasing an 80 percent stake in Newcastle United, a professional football club in the Premier League. Part of this sports enterprise is Golf Saudi, led by Yasir Al-Rumayyan, who resides in bin Salman's inner circle and serves as governor of the PIF. Al-Rumayyan is considered a passionate golfer, and his imagination for what the sport could do for Saudi Arabia is wide. There are things at the grassroots level, like growing participation in Saudi Arabia to developing a national team and elite players, along with big-picture items such as the development of courses to aid tourism and hosting professional competitions. It is this last point that sparked the Saudi International into existence in 2019, a tournament that was sanctioned by the European Tour.

By all accounts, bin Salman doesn't have a personal appetite for athletic pursuits. The reason they're a core value in his vision, however, is he understands their appeal, especially to his own people. Bin Salman is extremely popular among younger demographics in Saudi Arabia, thanks to introducing once-unimaginable change. Women are allowed to join the workforce and drive cars and be in social settings without the permission of male figures. Movie theaters reopened in 2018 after a 35-year ban on public cinema. The Saudi religious police—a feared institution that ran with unchecked power—has been stripped of authority, bestowing a sense of freedom and openness unknown to those under 40.

The other half of the sports equation is that bin Salman realizes first-class athletic spectacles are the hallmarks of a modern, booming culture, and sees their economic potential. It's through this channel that Al-Rumayyan convinced bin Salman of golf's capacity, for it is a well-known recreation of some of the world's leaders and power brokers. That capacity quickly grew from the Saudi International to a potential stake in a new golf circuit: the Premier Golf League. However, the PIF decided rather than backing another entity it could just create its own league (using a similar framework to the PGL), and thus LIV Golf Investments was formed.

Now, from an investment standpoint LIV Golf is small potatoes compared to other Vision 2030 projects. LIV Golf has somewhere in the neighborhood of $3 billion in funding; for context Neom has a starting budget of $500 billion and the aforementioned 75-mile buildings are expected to cost $1 trillion and take 50 years to construct. However, the golf endeavor has heightened importance in the kingdom's push to a better tomorrow. For one Al-Rumayyan views it as his darling, and few if any voices carry his weight in bin Salman's circle. Beyond sports, LIV Golf functions as a sophisticated networking platform, facilitating connections with global business executives and government officials.

But a point that cannot be overstated—and arguably fuels the desire to make Saudi Golf ultimately succeed—is the combination of disrespect, retribution, and thirst for power that lies at the heart of bin Salman's reign.

"Despite sweeping social and economic changes that have liberated society, political life has moved in reverse," House explains.

Crown Prince Mohammed bin Salman's rule has been marked by severe human rights violations and the systematic suppression of dissent. His regime has imprisoned numerous human rights activists, including prominent women's rights advocate Loujain al-Hathlawi, who was detained and reportedly tortured for campaigning against the male guardianship system. While some symbolic reforms like allowing women to drive have been implemented, women still face significant legal and social restrictions under the male guardianship system. LGBTQ+ individuals face potential death penalty, imprisonment, and social ostracism, with no legal protections or recognition of their rights.

The Saudi-led military intervention in Yemen, launched in 2015 to counter perceived Iranian influence through the Houthi rebels, has resulted in what the UN calls the world's worst humanitarian crisis. The conflict has led to over 150,000 deaths, widespread famine, and the displacement of millions. Bin Salman's regime has faced international condemnation for indiscriminate airstrikes on civilian areas and the blockade of humanitarian aid. The 2022 mass execution of 81 men in a single day highlighted the kingdom's increasing use of capital punishment, while the brutal assassination of Jamal Khashoggi—dismembered with a bone saw according to Turkish intelligence reports—demonstrated the lengths to which the regime would go to silence critics.

According to the *New York Times*, the November 2017 Ritz-Carlton purge marked a decisive power grab by bin Salman. The detention of hundreds of influential Saudis, including Prince Alwaleed bin Talal, one of the world's wealthiest investors, allowed bin Salman to extract billions in assets and eliminate potential opposition. Detainees reported severe physical abuse, with at least one death in custody. This consolidation of power gave bin Salman unprecedented control over Saudi Arabia's key institutions: he now oversees all security and intelligence agencies, controls the world's largest oil company Saudi Aramco, and directs the $930 billion Public Investment Fund (PIF). His authority is absolute, constrained only nominally by his father King Salman, whose declining health has further cemented bin Salman's grip on power. The nickname "Mr. Everything" reflects his totalistic control over Saudi policy, from economic reform to foreign relations.

So when Saudi Golf—and as an extension, Vision 2030 and bin Salman—was rebuffed when attempting to become part of golf's political matrix with the PGA Tour, European Tour, and others, the project was not scrapped. That is not what bin Salman does. "He doubles down. He is not accustomed to losing," House explains. "When he fails at something, his inclination is to try harder."

If golf's current ecosystem wouldn't let the Saudis in, they would create their own. And if the existing framework was destroyed in the process, all the better. It sounds ambitious, taking down an entire system from scratch. And it is. That is the undercurrent of Vision 2030, what spurs the kingdom into a better tomorrow.

But to those who dispute the formidability of LIV Golf, Golf Saudi and bin Salman, who hear grand ambitions of luxury resorts and megacities in the desert and 75-mile buildings and laugh, it's worth noting bin Salman's true passion: video games. According to House, it explains both bin Salman's fantastical aspirations and serves as a warning to his doubters.

"The reason he believes he can do anything is that, in the world of video games, anything is possible," House says. "He's in love with video games where all things are possible and believes that if you put your mind to it, that's what real life is like too."

·   ·   ·

The young men nursed their drinks—two Tennent's lagers, a cider, and Scotland's beloved Irn-Bru—as they perched in their open car trunks at the Elie Golf House lot. Their feet swung above the scattered gravel while their gazes wandered between each other and the ground, my seemingly simple ask hanging heavy in the air: *What brought you guys together?*

My softball question had sparked an uneasy silence. Here they were, savoring rare sunshine at Elie's pristine links after two rainy weeks, when my innocuous query had turned unexpectedly profound, as no one had ever examined the foundation of their friendship before. I silently cursed myself—*This is why no one likes journalists.* Finally, Michael Wilson, the eldest, broke the tension. He realized their bond lay in their ordinariness; what seemed unremarkable to them had caught my attention precisely because of its authenticity.

"Over here, this is how golf is," said Wilson, waving his cider around the group to emphasize the point. "It's radical, really, compared to how we do things in this country. There's still a bit of a hardened social hierarchy in Scotland. Not much mobility among classes, you rarely rise or fall from where you were born. For the most part it's not malicious or spiteful. You just stay where you are."

"Golf though? The great equalizer. No one cares who you are or what you do. Be good fun, try not to play like shit, but if you do, be fast about it."

Michael's insight wasn't mere improvisation, though he later confirmed it was spontaneous. As a schoolteacher and former theater club director, he had a gift for articulating deep truths simply. His observation wasn't just philosophical musing or naïve romanticism about the game—it was evident in the faces of his friends gathered around him.

There was Michael, the educator; Jack, a retail construction worker; Finn, a supermarket delivery driver; Robert, a nurse that was transitioning into a computer programmer because "women don't respect nurses." They had met at an open competition at Burntisland, a vista-heavy parkland course tucked between sands and winding topography, something that looks like it belongs on the west coast of Oregon rather than this section of the world. None of the men had played Burntisland before the competition; despite being the 10th-oldest club in the world, formed from the opinions of Tom Morris and Willie Park and boasting a redesign by James Braid, Burntisland's location—about an hour from Edinburgh and an hour from St Andrews, in a sleepy parish on the northern shores of the Firth of Forth—means it's often missed by both voyagers and most Scottish natives not familiar with the area. They were paired together that morning at Burntisland and noticed how easy they got along. They discovered they all lived near Edinburgh, with Robert and Jack separated by only a few blocks. No one remembers what they shot that day, although Jack pointed out "score isn't much a thing we concern ourselves with," and repaired to a tavern down the road by the water after the competition to continue the good time. They ended up closing the bar down that night, with Finn sleeping in his car. That was 12 years ago, and they've been golf buddies ever since.

Golf buddies ever since. Simple words that belie a profound truth about connection in our modern age. As adulthood crowds us with careers, families, and constant relocations, meaningful friendship becomes increasingly rare. Enter golf—more than just a shared passion, it's an arena where trust is built through etiquette and integrity, where conversations flow naturally between shots, and where joy and defeat are experienced in equal measure. But golf's deeper magic lies in its ability to strip away pretense. Over eighteen holes, masks slip. The course becomes an unfailing truth serum, revealing character through shanked drives, missed putts, and weather-beaten rounds. A lie detector test that without fail can cut through the bullshit. The course becomes a conversation, a confessional, a crucible that transforms strangers into confidants. Whether it takes a single round or several seasons, a golf friendship, once forged, endures. While other activities may build similar bonds, few match golf's quiet ability to reveal who we truly are, and bind us to those who witness our unvarnished selves.

Their weekly rounds over the past decade, made possible by synchronized work schedules, nurtured more than just golf partnerships. The friendships deepened beyond the course: Robert stood as Finn's best man, Michael became godfather to Jack's son, and when flooding devastated Finn's family home, Jack was there with hammer in hand. Their bond strengthened through golf travels—to the misty Highlands, the wild western coast, and England's storied links. Such trips underscore a fundamental principle about Scottish golf: its accessibility transforms the game from mere sport into a catalyst for lifelong connection.

Scotland has the most golf courses per capita of any country in the world, boasting over 587 courses to a population of 5.4 million. From its gems to its depth, the standard, caliber, quality and elegance of Scotland courses are unrivaled (which we'll revisit in a second), although those sentiments are tangential and secondary to the fundamental truth: More than 99.9 percent of them have some form of public or visitor play. That is not a hyperbolic figure; Loch Lomond Golf Club and Renaissance Club are the only *completely* private aberration across multiple top 100 Scotland courses lists. Contrast that with the United States, where a quarter of all golf facilities are private.

The disparity is amplified when looking at the premier, bucket-list sites. Using America's top 100 ranking from *Golf Digest*, zero of the top 10 courses are public, and just one in the top 40 is municipal. There are 15 venues that have some public entry, although 13 are resorts and most require accommodations on site to play the courses.

Narrowing the focus to the best public courses somehow underlines the barrier between the rich and middle class. Two of America's golf meccas—Pebble Beach and Pinehurst—are technically open to everyone, but so are courtside seats and commercial space flights. The green fee at Pinehurst No. 2 hovers at $500 and at Pebble near $700, and that's not accounting for the stay at each resort. They are not alone: Using *Golf Digest's* separate best public ranking, the average green fee for the top 10 courses—Pebble, Pacific Dunes, Kiawah Ocean Course, Whistling Straits, Shadow Creek, Pinehurst No. 2, Bethpage Black, Bandon Dunes, TPC Sawgrass, and Erin Hills—is $570, Bethpage Black the lone course that comes in under $330. They are public in name only.

This is not a golf problem. It's an American golf problem. Much as the governing bodies and powers that be try to grow the game (or at least preach about attempting to grow the game), golf remains a privileged activity. In Scotland? Golf is not an aspirational sport. It is the pastime of the people, because the people can afford it.

Residents of St Andrews can purchase a season-long Links ticket—giving them access to the Old Course, New, and five other courses for an entire year—for $400. I'm not an exclamation mark guy, but ... $400!!! In this economy! Those who live in the surrounding northeast Fife area can sign up for $700, with those in Scotland outside of Fife able to buy $1,000 passes. Incredible as a deal as it looks (and is), these figures are the norm.

According to an audit by the Scottish Sports Council, more than 96 percent of Scotland courses and clubs offer annual memberships or passes for less than $2,500. This includes the best of the best:

The four clubs that play out of North Berwick West Links—in my humble opinion, the most enjoyable course in the world—charge $700 for a yearly membership. Royal Dornoch charges $500 in annual dues. Cruden Bay is $325. Nairn starts around $450. My personal favorite, Brora, beginning at a whopping $375.

Even Scots without memberships or reciprocals usually have a national discount. Elie is an Old Tom Morris links touched up by James Braid that resides less than 30 minutes from St Andrews. It's an open-yet-punishing routing that's a hell of a lot of fun with stunning views of the Firth of Forth and cliffs of Kincraig Point. Any course ranking of merit has Elie among the best 25 courses in Scotland; it is a masterpiece. In America, a tee time at a course with the quality of Elie would cost well north of $300. Michael and the boys paid less than $100 each.

Unlike American courses, where pristine conditions demand constant irrigation and grooming, Scottish links largely rely on nature's care. Apart from the greens, Scottish courses rarely supplement rainfall with artificial watering, allowing the land to breathe and transform with the seasons. The results can be dramatic: summer rains paint the links in brilliant emeralds, while dry spells transform them into golden, windswept expanses with firm, fast fairways. This natural approach stands in sharp contrast to American expectations, shaped by Augusta National's perpetual perfection and the PGA Tour's parade of meticulously groomed venues. Such artificial standards demand extraordinary resources—water, labor, chemicals—costs that inevitably cascade down to the everyday golfer's green fee. Scottish golf embraces nature's imperfections; American golf tries to control them, at a price.

Because of the low barrier to entry, Scotland clubs welcome members across the social spectrum, from surgeons to shopkeepers. No profession better illustrates the contrast between American and Scottish golf than the caddie. The American caddie faces near-extinction—present at less than six percent of facilities and available to just one percent of golfers. Decent wages are mostly limited to elite clubs or resorts, and U.S. caddying largely survives as seasonal work for students or aspiring pros. At most prestigious American clubs, an invisible barrier separates caddies from members, as loopers are unable to afford membership at their workplace. This division between those who carry bags and those who own them reveals a deeper truth about American golf's stratification.

The Scottish caddie inhabits a different world entirely. Here, the profession commands respect, and the traditional divide between caddie and member dissolves: many caddies belong to the very clubs where they shoulder others' sticks. Recently that has included Robert, who has spent his mornings as a caddie in the seaside town of Lossiemouth as he takes online classes during his career switch.

"I went to Florida once for a wedding, and we played some games," Robert says, now with a cigarette dangling from his lips. "The caddie experience—how do I say this?—the formalities, the power dynamic between who I was paired with and their 'tenders, it was like having a butler. It was laughable! I'm nobody, and I gathered my playing mates weren't special.

"There is no division [in Scotland] between player and caddie. You are equals, partners, navigating the dares and tricks the game has in store."

Finn latches onto *butler* after it stumbles from Robert's description and spends the next couple minutes improvising a theoretical Robert as a golf servant, a scene apostrophized by Finn handing Robert another Tennent's on top of a box of Wilson golf balls acting as a de facto silver plate. Michael and Jack are bent over laughing, Robert, not so much, remarking he'd rather pour the Tennent's over Robert's head if it wasn't a sin to waste good beer.

Michael later explains the group is in a new phase of their kinship. Michael moved to Glasgow with his wife over the winter, while Robert is looking to relocate, spending the weeks around Inverness and his weekends all over the map trying to figure out where he might go. Jack's still in Edinburgh although for the first time in his career his job is taking him to other parts of Europe, which has been good for his bank account and bad for his golf.

But the boys have made a pact: Three times a year, minimum, for weekend trips. ("Somehow the wives have encouraged us, which makes ya wonder what they've been up to all the time we've been playing," Jack says.) On this sojourn they would be playing Elie,

Lundin, Anstruther, Ladybank and Scotscraig, and in the parking lot Robert does his best to pitch everyone on an Inverness trip in late August. Before packing up and heading to their shared bed and breakfast, Robert's presentation is successful. Glasses are raised and clinked; *Inverness, here we come.* They know what brought them together and what will keep them from drifting apart.

•　　•　　•

Steampunk Coffee occupies a converted warehouse tucked behind High Street, the flagstoned commercial backbone of North Berwick—a postcard-perfect seaside town where Edinburgh's well-heeled escape for weekends of golf and beach walks along the Firth of Forth. The café embodies the artisanal coffee revolution that has swept through Scotland's East Coast, though with a distinctly local charm that sets it apart from Edinburgh's more self-conscious establishments. Inside, rough-hewn stone walls dating to the 1850s contrast with sections painted in muted sage and terracotta. Weathered leather armchairs and industrial metal stools cluster around reclaimed wood tables, while Edison bulbs cast a warm glow through antique brass fixtures. The café's mascots—a rotating cast of local dogs, from Highland terriers to weather-beaten border collies—weave between customers' legs, adding to the living-room atmosphere. Outside, a lovingly restored 1972 VW Type 2 bus the color of burnt orange marmalade serves as both an Instagram backdrop and a weekend street-food kitchen. The seemingly random placement of a rusted 1953 Raleigh bicycle above the gleaming La Marzocco espresso machine speaks to the café's carefully curated chaos. Unlike many third-wave coffee shops, there's no pretension here—just expertly roasted beans and baristas who treat your oat milk cardamom latte order as seriously as any single-origin pour-over.

While researching this book about Scottish golf's evolution, I conducted hundreds of interviews in the traditional haunts of the sport's storytellers—walking fairways, lounging in wood-paneled clubhouses where the portraits of stern-faced former captains watch over proceedings, perching on barstools in pubs where the tap list is carefully considered. But my conversation with Professor Joshua Ralston demanded a different setting, though he protested missing a rare sunny day on his beloved North Berwick links. However, the complexity of his insights into the Saudis' role in golf's cultural identity crisis demanded the kind of focused attention that's difficult to maintain while trying to avoid a slice into the beach bunkers.

Ralston is a reader (a professor) at the University of Edinburgh in Christian-Muslim Relations, and is considered one of the world's leading authorities on Middle Eastern geopolitics. He has also spoken extensively about Saudi Arabia's foray into golf since the onset of the professional game's schism. There is no one better to discuss the very complex, complicated and loaded subject of what Saudi Arabia is doing with golf, and why.

Saudi Arabia's aggressive expansion into global athletics is publicly framed as a multi-pronged initiative to diversify its economy, modernize its society, and develop its cultural footprint. However, critics and observers consistently return to a more cynical interpretation: *sportswashing*.

This phenomenon, while seemingly straightforward, represents a sophisticated strategy where sporting events and investments serve as vehicles for reputation management and ideological promotion by states, corporations, and individuals with compromised public images. It's a practice that fundamentally challenges sports' cherished notion of political neutrality—the idea that athletics transcend political divisions and unite people across cultures. Instead, sportswashing weaponizes sports' universal appeal and emotional resonance for propaganda purposes. The strategy operates on three interconnected levels: distraction from criticism and controversy, minimization of documented wrongdoing, and normalization of controversial actors within the global community through the legitimizing power of sport.

The term *sportswashing* entered the lexicon in the 2010s, coined by human rights advocates and media critics analyzing Azerbaijan's $660 million hosting of the European Games amid reports of journalist

suppression and political prisoner detention. Similarly, Russia's estimated $51 billion investment in the 2014 Sochi Winter Olympics and
the 2018 FIFA World Cup came under scrutiny as attempts to project soft power while obscuring domestic crackdowns on dissent and
international aggression. However, the practice's historical roots run
far deeper. The 1936 Berlin Olympics stands as perhaps the most infamous example—a carefully choreographed spectacle where Nazi Germany temporarily suspended its most visible anti-Semitic policies to
present a sanitized image to the world while simultaneously promoting its ideology of Aryan supremacy through athletic competition.
This historical context has informed contemporary criticism of Saudi
Arabia's estimated $15 billion investment in golf and other sports.
The stark contrast between golf's traditional values of integrity and
fair play (to say nothing of its nonexistent golfing heritage and challenging desert environment for course construction, requiring massive water resources in one of the world's most water-stressed regions)
against Saudi Arabia's documented behaviors has only intensified this
scrutiny.

However, Ralston has posited that chalking up Saudi's efforts as
mere sportswashing is somewhat problematic. In his estimation, this
diagnosis lacks nuance and context. At worst, it is a poorly disguised
upshot of racism.

"I think the sportswashing fails to take Saudi Arabia's internal
and regional reasons for engaging with sports seriously on their own
terms," Ralston says. "It operates with hypocritical language so that a
Saudi investment in golf is irrational and crazy money, while Fenway
Sports Group (one of the largest private-equity investors in the PGA
Tour) or other investors are given the benefit of the doubt. It also fails
to account for how we on the receiving end of funding are benefiting."

According to Ralston, accusations of sportwashing against Saudi
Arabia hinder our capacity for a broader understanding of the politics
of sports. More often than not, the term has been univocally deployed
against non-Western countries as a pejorative term, rather than parallel phrases like "soft power" or "public diplomacy," which are often
portrayed as legitimate actions of states. Ralston also points out to

what he perceives as double standards. "For instance, what counts as a being of perpetrator of injustice?" he asks. Ralston points to the criticism Qatar received for its treatment of migrant workers when it hosted the 2022 World Cup. But, Ralston says, "Most owners of major sports clubs and hosts of major sporting events are perpetrators of some kind of injustice." Staying with the migrant theme, Ralston cites attempts by the United Kingdom's Home Offices to deport asylum seekers to Rwanda. The British government regularly promotes the Premier League and the English national team as tools for soft power. Moreover, Rwanda is an economic and business partner with both the British government and EPL clubs, such as Arsenal. "And yet, neither public discourse nor academic literature focuses on how football sportswashes both the Home Office and the Rwandan government," Ralston says. "In fact, if someone points out such facts, they are accused of minimizing the ethical issues in Qatar and Saudi."

To Ralston, what's more interesting is how Saudi's sportswashing relates regionally in the Gulf State, to the kingdom's own understanding of itself as a country and its relationships with its neighbors, Qatar and the United Arab Emirates. "Decades before Saudi Arabia was ever significantly involved in global sport, the UAE and Qatar had both made themselves some of the most powerful investors in football," Ralston says. "Abu Dhabi's purchase of Manchester City and the broader conglomerate of City Football has paid massive dividends. City is widely considered the best club in the world and Abu Dhabi's name is inherently linked to them. Their stadium is named Etihad and the kit has endorsement deals with the airline, while Visit Abu Dhabi or the Emirates campaigns are ubiquitous presences every time City is on television. Qatar has also been widely successful through football, owning the biggest club in France, Paris St Germain, and becoming the first Arab country to host the World Cup (in 2022). Saudi Arabia's interest in football lags well behind both countries.

"With golf, Saudi Arabia can be the leading regional and global player. The creation of LIV and possible investment in a new PGA Tour or global league gives Saudi Arabia not just a seat at the table, but a leadership position on the board. In football, Saudi Arabia is like a tour pro with a few minor wins. In golf, they are looking to be like a hall of fame golfer with multiple major wins and a world number one ranking. Why buy a club or a player when you can buy an entire sport?

"This is in part why involvement with golf has been so controversial, at least when it comes to the men's game. The PIF's investment in golf is not like their purchase of Newcastle: largely playing within the confines of the league and tradition. Instead, they have been a disrupter."

As he acknowledges, these stances have earned Ralston criticism, with some accusing Ralston of whataboutism or false balance. "It sometimes comes across like I'm defending Saudi, which I'm not," Ralston says, "but more trying to explain in better terms." After spending time with Ralston, going through his writings and exchanging emails, I would attest that is his intention. He's also not an MBS apologist. "I do not think that he is unduly critiqued, as he is an authoritarian dictator," Ralston says. "What I do think is unfair is how he and Saudi are critiqued without further examination of the many ways that the United States, Europe, and other Western countries are already allies with Saudi Arabia. If we are to critique MBS and Saudi, we need to also critique ourselves."

From afar, it may seem like Ralston and I disagree on the sportswashing element. That's not necessarily the case. Those who accuse Saudi Arabia of sportswashing without understanding Vision 2030 or the economic aspirations are trying to assemble a puzzle without all the pieces. There's clearly an Arab bias when it comes to some of these criticisms; look no further than Qatar. The German team threatened to boycott the 2022 World Cup over Qatar's labor practices, although Bayern Munich—the most successful and popular club in Germany—had no problem taking Qatar's money for jersey sponsorship. And by the accepted definition of sportswashing, Saudi golf has failed on two fronts: to distract and minimize. If anything, more attention has been brought to the kingdom's human-rights issues because of its journey into golf and sports.

While Professor Ralston's analysis is compelling, I don't fully subscribe to the argument. The Public Investment Fund's multi-billion-dollar investment in LIV Golf defies conventional business logic—pouring astronomical sums into a league populated by a mix of declining stars, mid-tier talents, and relative unknowns, whose broadcasts struggle to outperform animal blooper shows in viewership. But viewing LIV Golf through a traditional return-on-investment lens misses the point entirely. For PIF and Mohammed bin Salman, LIV Golf was never conceived as a standalone business venture. Rather, it serves as a sophisticated diplomatic instrument, a bridge-building mechanism targeting the corporate and political elite who populate golf's ecosystem. The strategic decision to partner with the Trump Organization properties underscores this calculated approach to relationship-building through golf's established networks.

Bin Salman's candid remarks to Fox News anchor Bret Baier in September 2023 reveal this naked pragmatism: "If sportswashing is going to increase my GDP by way of 1 percent, then I will continue doing sportswashing ... I don't care ... I'm aiming for another 1.5 percent. Call it whatever you want, we're going to get that 1.5 percent." This startling admission strips away any pretense about Saudi Arabia's true motivations in golf investment.

The same clear-eyed analysis must extend to the PGA Tour's $3 billion private equity infusion. While this investment has largely escaped the intense scrutiny focused on Saudi involvement, the underlying motivations of these American financial institutions deserve equal examination. As subsequent chapters will reveal, these private equity players aren't simply betting on golf's commercial potential—they're strategically positioning themselves to engage with Saudi wealth through the more palatable vehicle of an established American institution rather than through LIV Golf directly.

Despite LIV Golf's failure to fully distract from Saudi Arabia's controversies or minimize its human rights issues, it has achieved perhaps its most crucial objective: normalization. This process began subtly, with early defenders pointing to PIF's extensive portfolio of U.S. investments—from Uber to Meta, Starbucks to Electronic Arts.

The Tour's shocking June 6th framework agreement with PIF accelerated this normalization, capitalizing on widespread exhaustion with golf's civil war. The sport's stakeholders and followers increasingly prioritize peace over principles, demonstrating how sportswashing succeeds not through complete vindication but through the gradual erosion of resistance.

I've included Ralston's perspective despite my disagreements because it adds crucial depth to this complex debate and because these ethical quandaries will only intensify as golf—like all professional sports—becomes increasingly entangled with global wealth and power dynamics.

The "where do you draw the line" question has dominated golf's discourse for three years, and with good reason. Ethical consumption in sports fandom is virtually impossible. The industry is riddled with moral compromises: from athlete misconduct to owner malfeasance, from commercialization to political exploitation, from tainted money to misplaced priorities. Golf's own history of exclusion based on race, class, and gender makes this particularly thorny terrain.

I don't know where to draw the line when it comes to golf, but I do know which side of it I want to be standing on. A regime characterized by extrajudicial killings, systematic oppression of women and LGBTQ+ individuals, exploitation of migrant workers, multi-generational imprisonment of dissidents' families, and a consistent ranking among Freedom House's "worst of the worst" in terms of civil and political rights transcends moral relativism. Even in a world of infinite shades of gray, some choices remain starkly black and white.

•   •   •

We were in St Andrews for all of 12 minutes when my long-haired chihuahua Bruiser christened the Road Hole, marking the ancient stone wall between the Jigger Inn and fescue rough. After our odyssey—Dublin to Belfast, a ferry to Scotland, then the long drive to the Home of Golf—I couldn't fault his urgency. (A note on our maritime route: UK air travel with pets requires Byzantine paperwork; boats merely require a pulse, though I may have inadvertently skipped a security check.) Forget that we had stopped multiple times for Bruiser to relieve himself throughout the day, including before our walk down North Street before stepping onto the Old Course. He was clearly out of his element. He's also not a golf guy, on account of being a dog, so he had no idea he was literally pissing on history. Still, I watched in horror and was afraid to look up, expecting the police—or worse, the R&A—to escort us out of town, if not excommunicate us from the sport entirely.

Instead I looked up to find a comedy of canine irreverence: three dogs marking their territory nearby, while a ginger labradoodle performed unspeakable acts upon a rubber carrot. We had found our place and people.

The Old Course is closed on Sundays, a prohibition that stems back to the 16th century when religious leaders stressed that golf went against honoring the Sabbath. Hundreds of years later, locals petitioned the keeper of the green, Old Tom Morris, to overturn the rule. "If the golfer doesn't need a rest," Morris replied, "surely the course does." There is golf at the other St Andrews links on Sundays, just not at the Old, as profit is set aside in a bow toward history. She remains open, however, her confines transforming into a public park. People have picnics and informal kickabouts, and there's the occasional sight of Frisbees tossed misguidedly into the wind coming off the North Sea. Mostly, she's a dog park. Nowhere is off-limits. There's an unspoken agreement to avoid the bunkers. Same with the greens, although few pay attention to that last one. The only rule is to pick up after yourself, and your mutt.

The terrain can handle the traffic thanks to a fine-grained sandy soil that drains well and compacts with ease. Conversely, what happens on Sundays has little to do with the resilience of the ground.

"Imagine doing this back home," says Ken Lee, a Chicagoan that was spending a month in Europe with his family, including their spaniel, Charlie. "Most clubs would use deadly force."

Lee's not wrong. I've lost count how many times I've been yelled at for walking a course I wasn't playing in the States, including one I worked at and another where my apartment was 300 yards or so from a fairway. Those ivy walls and brass gates aren't accidents, and often serve as figurative structures; American golf does its best to keep society at arm's-length.

The Home of Golf? It takes its arms and wraps them around you, releasing only to wave you through. To the Scottish, land so venerated shouldn't be kept behind closed doors, and accessibility extends beyond who gets to tee it up.

It's not just St Andrews or Sundays that share this belief. Scotland's relationship with its courses extends far beyond golf. Every links serves as public parkland, a practice rooted in the centuries-old "right to roam"—formalized by the 2003 Land Reform Act. While golfers enjoy certain privileges, the courses remain communal spaces, asking only that visitors avoid the greens and respect ongoing play. The land belongs to all, and both courses and golfers honor this covenant.

"There's this wonderful sense 'We are all in this together' in everything we do," says Alex Cowie, a retired military police officer and St Andrews resident. "Golf is for the people—all people—not just golfers. Life in smaller towns here can revolve around the clubs, but the inverse is true. The course reflects its surroundings."

"There's a greater purpose with courses and clubs and all of us that frequent them, and it's to make life for the area and its people better for it."

I'm not sure how many courses I was able to walk Bruiser on this summer. I do know, for the two weeks we spent in St Andrews, nearly every day we would cruise down North Street, make a right on Golf Place, and let the Old Course explode beneath our feet. Just a man and his dog, sitting on the steps between the 18th green and 1st tee, watching golfers do what was once forbidden, now free to all.

JOEL BEALL

CHAPTER 2

Intentions

Crail and Oliver • LIV's origins •
Nairn and a father's ashes• Greg Norman •
Prestwick • Aim

The old Frenchman's pursuit of his hat has come to an end, a chase that started off the front of Balcomie's 3rd tee box some 150 yards away when the wind lifted Oliver's Titleist cap from his balding head and concluded with the cap, perhaps exhausted, taking shelter inside the lip of a greenside pot bunker. This was followed by a full-extension bellyflop from Oliver into the sand, which from a distance looked a lot like an in-his-prime Ken Griffey Jr. robbing a double in the gap. Only after our laughter had subsided did we spot the guilty rake, the true engineer of his spectacular tumble. "I've always been shit in the sand!" he howled as he dusted pebbles and beach from his chest.

Oliver asked if I ever sparred in a breeze so wicked. *Yes, just last week, here*, I thought. That was on July 4th, the only time my wife, bless her heart, accompanied me for a round, and Crail was ostensibly the place to do it. In terms of ambience, Crail is on the short list of Scottish haunts. It's not particularly difficult and there are a few pedestrian holes, yet its brilliance shines through—especially the par-four 5th, a dare across the rocky bay that Ryder Cup captain Sam Torrance called the toughest par four in Scotland. Crail gets what most golf courses fail to grasp: the game should spark joy. But on Independence Day, the fresh-faced lad at Crail's front desk tried to warn us, his hospitality wrestling with bewilderment at our stubbornness: "Are you quite sure about this?" he'd asked, his politeness barely masking his certainty that we'd lost our minds. When Scots suggest the weather's too brutal, you're either about to experience something legendary—or catastrophically foolish. My usual 280-yard drives withered to wounded ducks barely reaching 200, putts oscillated like they were having seizures, and any ball daring to climb above waist height got Mutombo'd back to earth. My wife's poncho wrapped around her like she was Egyptian royalty. When the storm finally drove us indoors, it felt less like surrender and more like heavenly intervention—saving not just the round, but quite possibly my marriage.

But I held my tongue. In Scottish golf, getting thrashed by the elements isn't just common—it's sacramental, like a rider's first dance with arena dirt. The magic of golf in this kingdom lies in that paradox: weather can be biblical, yet the golf remains divine. It's the ultimate test of golf addiction. Casual players see ominous skies and flagsticks bent in half, feel their shirt plastering to their spine, and sensibly mutter, "Maybe tomorrow." The true obsessive witnesses this same apocalyptic scene and grins like a madman, thinking, *now this is living*. And right now, Oliver needed affirmation.

Oliver, who had moved to San Francisco in the 1990s before returning to France, had spent the past two months in Scotland after his daughter had a bike accident that caused rib, arm and leg injuries. She's in school at the University of St Andrews, and like her father ,is golf-obsessed. It was touch-and-go for a few weeks, Oliver said, with infections and internal bleeding giving the family scares. Oliver's wife and their two other adult children, both sons, came because they didn't know if it would be the end.

She was still in the hospital daily, but was able to check-out 10 days prior, and was staying at a house that Oliver has rented. That's why Oliver is out at Crail; before they get the all-clear to go home, Oliver's daughter has requested a round with him. The doctors have been noncommittal if that's a possibility. Still, for two hours a day, when his wife or sons take watch in the morning, he sneaks to Crail to shag balls or play 13-14 holes. He says he does it to stay sharp and be ready. "No matter how old you get, you still want to impress your girl," he says. Oliver can't totally unplug—a few days ago he aborted a round when his wife was worried about their daughter's rising temperatures—yet there are moments when reality recedes, when it's just golf. They may not be long, he says, but for now it's all he's got.

•　　•　　•

LIV Golf has a sea of entry points for criticism. That includes its origin story, which is not its own.

In 2010 a British corporate finance attorney named Andy Gardiner scribbled down a 100-page manifesto, a vision to transform professional golf into a team game. He spent the next decade networking and forming alliances to bring his idea to fruition, eventually finding a financial partner in Saudi Arabia that had the means and audacity to take on the system. After whispers of a shadow organization meeting with PGA Tour players and agents throughout the previous season, Gardiner formally introduced himself and his "Premier Golf League" in February 2020 in a series of puff-piece interviews that played up his business and diplomacy acumen. His proposal: a 14-event schedule of 54-hole tournaments with shotgun starts the first two rounds—with 10 tournaments in the United States, with stops in Europe, Asia, Australia, and the Middle East. Teams of four players would simultaneously compete for an individual and team prize, with a captain deciding before each round which two players' scores would count for the team. Players and agents were pitched that the league would eventually have a $10 billion valuation (yes, billions with a *b*). Other aspects included potential relegation and promotion, match-play playoffs with higher seeds choosing the team they play, eight-month seasons and $392 million in prize money per season (across individual and team payouts). He wanted to work with, not against, the establishment, although players and agents involved in those talks said the opposite.

Gardiner tried to downplay the requisite sportswashing questions, asserting he had up to 60 different backers. That included the Raine Group, which almost single-handedly made Gardiner's presence formidable, yet multiple sources have confirmed in the past years that Saudi's Public Investment Fund was the primary financial engine. When pressed on the PIF's role, Gardiner repeated the same answer to multiple outlets: "The Public Investment Fund of Saudi Arabia is incredibly passionate about golf and its future, and I'm delighted to have them involved."

The PGL was to start in January 2022, and the tour deemed the threat credible enough that Jay Monahan issued his own threat. "If the Team Golf Concept [one of the other names used by the PGL] or another iteration of this structure becomes a reality in 2022 or at any time before or after, our members will have to decide whether they want to continue to be a member of the PGA Tour or play on a new series," Monahan wrote in the winter of 2020. That kind of brimstone isn't wasted on a half-baked pitch.

Only in the spring of 2021, whispers began to emerge that PIF decided to breakaway from Gardiner, and the rumors became official in the fall when Greg Norman was named CEO of LIV Golf Investments, with a targeted start date of a new league—shockingly, also boasting a worldwide schedule with 48-player, 54-hole events with a team concept and shotgun start—just months later. Several executives left the PGL and took similar roles with Performance 54, the group in charge of directing LIV Golf's operations.

The PGL tried to continue. There was a launch of a website filled with non-sequitur mission statements, reading very much like the offspring of a middle-school sonnet and a marketing pitch conjured by a C-list advertising firm that failed to run the pitch by actual golfers.

Incredibly, those statements and website are still live, and feature such gems as:

For the love of Tiger's red shirt, Augusta's green jacket and
Samuel's Ryder Cup

Imagine the rivalry. Imagine the revelry. And yes, we hit a few
into the trees

That mere mortals can try where legends have triumphed

For the love of the shanks, hooks, slices and thins

All contest. No cut

Just the thought of it makes the heart beat faster

In the same poetic tenor, we'd be remiss in failing to mention a hilariously unhinged open letter weeks before LIV's first event. Aside from calling out LIV for copying its format, the PGL tried to appeal to PGA Tour players:

> "Your profession is approaching an historic crossroads. The 'International Series,' funded and owned by LIV Golf Investments, represents an existential threat, not only to the PGA Tour's dominance but also its mode. Change is not only inevitable, it is happening—and no amount of purse rigging, head-burying, ban-threatening, alliance-making or 'moving-on' will derail it."

The letter also went after Rory McIlroy, who had early been dismissive of the PGL given its Saudi ties:

> "The Policy Board has, however, refused to discuss our proposals. Based on a presentation by Allen & Co, it disputes the

PGL's ability to generate $10BN+ of value. As Rory McIlroy recently messaged, 'We had Allen and company present to the board in Orlando about the PGL proposal. They don't think 10B by 2030 is feasible at all. They said you'd need to create 20 Ryder Cups a year from now until then to get to that number. In the corporate finance world, this is technically known as 'bullsh**.' But, then again, Allen & CO has never spoken to us, nor had access to the information it would require in order to produce an accurate valuation."

And Monahan:

"You should not fear the wrath of Jay Monahan, he is not on the Policy Board and works for you," the letter reads. "You should exercise your rights. Despite it being 'your' PGA Tour, you do not own it (nor will you own LIV or the Super Golf League). You could own half of the PGL.

"Act now or spend a lifetime wondering: 'What if...?'

Alas, like every open letter known to man, nothing came of the plea. The PGL didn't get off the ground, because apparently it's tough to run a golf league without players, teams or money. They tried to partner with the DP World Tour, only for the PGA Tour to create a strategic alliance with their Euro counterparts. They tried to pivot toward the PGA Tour, asking for the PGL to exist under the tour umbrella in the fall season in exchange for 50 percent ownership of the league. For some reason, the tour wasn't interested in helping out the people who tried to take them down.

In certain golf circles, Gardiner is viewed as a tragic figure—the architect of his own vision who now watches from the shadows as others commandeer and twist his creation. Yet sympathy feels misplaced. For all his corporate savvy and legal expertise, Gardiner overlooked the most fundamental rule of dealmaking: when you dine with the disreputable, expect to be served as the main course.

His retreat into silence sparked rumors of a PIF-mandated gag order, though these proved baseless when, in February 2024, news broke of an eight-figure legal battle over LIV Golf's alleged theft of the PGL blueprint. Some interpreted LIV's wholesale adoption of Gardiner's framework as laziness or arrogance. This misses the mark. It wasn't about sending messages or displaying creativity; it was simply the reflexive action of powers accustomed to taking—and getting—what they want. Like an apex predator, they move with neither malice nor mercy, leaving others to count the cost in the quiet aftermath of inevitability.

•   •   •

I floated down the brick steps of Nairn's clubhouse—*floated*, that's the word. You know the feeling, when a course seeps into your bones and writes itself into your memory even as you're still discovering it, when every fiber of your being thinks, *Man, how great is this?* By the time my feet returned to the ground the adventure turned as quick as the Scottish weather, for what started out as a scorecard in my back pocket was cupped in my right hand, serving as a map for a man's final resting place.

As a preface, throughout this book I will desperately try and heroically fail to minimize hyperbole when it comes to course talk. One of the beauties of golf books is they double as road maps for future trips, and should this eventually be a compass to you I want to make the most of your precious time. I say that to say this: There's no apology for the ornamented prose heaped on Nairn. It's just that damn good.

The links is 15 miles east of Inverness, nestled in an ancient fishing and market town where the River Nairn spills into the Moray Firth. The country roads off the A96 are hugged by heather and gorse, nature's warning of what awaits. Nairn has been designed by Andrew Simpson, then tweaked by Old Tom Morris, then by James Braid, then by Ben Sayers, then by Braid again, and underwent a facelift in 2018 by Tom Mackenzie for the 2021 Amateur Championship, but like a true links it is molded by forces greater than man: wind, land, sea.

The course presents a fascinating contradiction, the terrain both flat and rumpled like a crumpled tablecloth. The water stands meaningly at guard to the right of six of the first seven holes. This is no mindless bomber's paradise but a thinking player's examination, defended by strategic bunkering, natural sandscapes, rolling dunes, sneaking burns, and fairways that demand precision. There's no gentle handshake to start your round—the opening hole stretches beyond 400 yards and often plays into the prevailing wind, followed by a second that can be stretched to an imposing 480 yards.

Still, when the wind is down, it achieves that highly sought-after but rarely attained dynamic of being challenging but playable, where birdie and triple are in plain sight on every shot. The par fours and threes are a nice blend of varying distances (including a handful of drivable fours), with the fives changing from reachable to three-shot puzzles depending on the box and breeze. The greens are wickedly nuanced, their contours whisper rather than shout as they are imperceptible until they are under your feet. Nairn stands apart among Scottish links for its composite Bent grass putting surfaces, distinct from their American cousins but delivering some of the truest rolls in Britain. The visual composition is without fault, the rolling emerald fairways and greens dotted and framed by sand, water, heather and gorse, and when the wind blows the fescue rough ripples like wheat fields at sunset, creating a symphony of movement across the links land.

Should you require further prodding, between the 9th green and 10th tee stands a testament to Victorian ingenuity: a stone icehouse from the 1800s, repurposed into what might be golf's most charismatic halfway house. The main clubhouse, with its well-worn leather chairs and oak-paneled bar, is as comfortable as it sounds. If you give the club a heads up, Hugh Sutherland, the club's archivist, will happily take you on a tour of Nairn's history (which includes the 1999 Walker Cup and 2012 Curtis Cup) with an extended library of books, records, photographs, trophies, pictures, artifacts, and more that puts most other golf museums to shame.

There may be links with better routings, stretches of holes that are more dramatic and photogenic and interesting, links that are ranked higher on the various industry lists. Arguing and comparing the merits of courses is what we golfers do. But after a summer of discovery across this ancient kingdom, as I distilled countless rounds into my 12 most cherished Scottish sanctuaries—my First Team All-Scotland, if you will—Nairn demands its place among the chosen. Everything that stirs the soul about Scottish golf is here, waiting to be found.

(Yes, 12, and Lord knows whittling it down nearly broke me. The exerted time, energy and passion, late-night deliberations and culling of contenders; I've invested less emotional capital in most romantic relationships. And let's be clear: I'll defend these selections with more vigor than I'd muster for my own kin. Blood may be thicker than water, but neither runs as deep as the burns crossing these chosen fairways. I will share the list later in the book.)

My company for the day aided Nairn's cause. Alister "Ali" Asher, a former Nairn captain and owner of 12 bakeries, was gracious enough to serve as host. I later learned that Ali had earned the prestigious "Scottish Baker of the Year" award in 2014—a fact his modesty had kept concealed. I played with Michael Green, owner of a local curling rink, a teacher, Martin, whose last name I butchered so bad in my notes he must remain Martin, and a fourth member of our group was the spouse of a Ladies European Tour (LET) player and I fail to mention him only because I'm not entirely sure he knew I was writing a book. They were the type of guys who feel like long-time friends within 15 minutes of introduction.

Although this shouldn't come as great surprise. Perhaps you have heard the curious claim that in Scotland—should a stranger knock at your door, asking to you use the restroom—one is legally bound to allow them through. The "fact" is so widely believed that *Telegraph* readers in a 2008 poll voted the mandate as the fifth-stupidest British law. (For those scoring at home, "It is illegal to die in the Houses of Parliament" and "It is an act of treason to place a postage stamp bearing the British monarch upside-down" were the winners.) Thing is, the Scottish toilet order is not in the country's constitution, nothing more than folklore. Its persistence, however, speaks volumes about the nation's character, that hospitality is the currency of Scotland as much as it is the crux of being a Scotsman. Folks go out of their way to make you feel welcome and comfortable and included.

"It's funny, we don't really know how nice and gracious we are until visitors from other countries tell us," Martin says. "It's how you grow up here. You're taught to look out for others before yourself. Didn't comprehend until later in life that, touching as a lesson as it is, it doesn't work if others don't carry their weight. But everyone does. Everyone looks out for each other."

That afternoon at Nairn, the clubhouse buzzed with excitement around Calum Scott, their 20-year-old member who had just claimed the silver medal as Low Amateur at the Open Championship at Troon the previous week. Members shared tales of young Calum and his brother Sandy's childhood antics—their determination to challenge the adult players, occasional tantrums and all. There were a lot of handshakes and hugs, and not just with Calum. This humble club, this town of less than 10,000 had produced a proper golfer that tied Brooks Koepka and Max Homa and beat Rory McIlroy at the Open, and everyone toasting Calum felt they played a small role in it.

Feeling like an outsider amid this intimate celebration, I quietly slipped toward the side door, only to be intercepted by a fellow American, Steven Mooney, near the clubhouse stairs. Looking to be in his late 40s or early 50s, he approached with an unusual request: Where would be the most fitting place to scatter his father's ashes?

His father George had succumbed to Covid-19 in the pandemic's early days, the virus accelerating his battle with lung cancer. For three decades, George had made annual pilgrimages to Scotland for golf, having fallen in love with the country while working as a safety supervisor on an oil platform off Aberdeen. George mostly came with his friends, but two summers in a row he brought over Steven. George wanted Steven to be part of the annual tradition, but Steven—who's also in the oil industry on the sales side—found himself traveling more often than not during the summer, and when he started his own family he found it hard to justify the flight and accommodation expenses.

While father and son still played together frequently after George's retirement, they never managed to return to Scotland together.

Nearly four years after his father's cremation, Steven felt the links would be a more fitting resting place than a mantelpiece. He'd waited for the perfect moment, initially hoping to bring his own sons, but their interest in golf hadn't yet developed. When a London business conference presented itself, Steven arrived a week early to fulfill this mission. He'd already scattered portions of his father's ashes at St Andrews and Murcar Links—where George had played his first true links course. But Nairn held special significance for Steven: it was here that he had first defeated his father.

Having focused so intently on reaching Nairn, Steven found himself uncertain about the precise location for this final tribute. His single visit and limited knowledge of the course's history led him to seek my advice about meaningful spots. After reviewing the scorecard, I asked if any moment stood out. Steven recalled only that his father's friend had announced their scores approaching the final green—both putting for five, with Steven one stroke ahead. George's attempt missed badly, while Steven's ball stopped within easy range. The memory of whether his father finished the hole had faded, but before he finished the story it was evident Steven knew the 18th green would suffice.

"I know he hugged me before that day. He was an emotional, loving guy, which is not what comes to mind when you think of a Texan rigger," Steven said. "But his hug when I beat him, that's the one I remember the most."

•   •   •

You can discern much about a boat—its destination, its course, whether it's headed for safe harbor or disaster—by observing who is at the helm. Thus, any illusion that LIV set sail as a diplomatic envoy is shattered by appointing a pirate as its captain.

In November 2021, when Greg Norman stepped into his role as CEO of LIV Golf Investments, it wasn't just another corporate appointment—it was the culmination of a three-decade vendetta against golf's established order. Prior to its launch, Norman asserted LIV would complement the professional landscape while bringing in a revolution to the sport. Put aside those conflicting ideologies and focus on his alleged desire to work within the system; for those who knew Norman's history, this posturing rang hollow, masking a deeper, more personal crusade.

The seeds of Norman's insurgency were planted in the 1990s, when the PGA Tour faced scrutiny from the Federal Trade Commission over potential antitrust violations. Norman, ever the opportunist, saw not a crisis but a chance for conquest. He wanted to start an eight-tournament series beginning in 1995, the fields consisting of the top 30 available players from the World Ranking and 10 sponsor exemptions. The idea, Norman touted, was to make professional golf more intercontinental, although the true mission was clear: First prize for each tournament would be $600,000, with last place getting a guaranteed $30,000. For context, that winner's check was double that of the 1994 U.S. Open's first-place payout and triple what the R&A was awarding at the Open.

"Norman's gall and greed stunned much of golf," wrote Thomas Boswell in the *Washington Post*, adding the WGT was a "brazen display of self-interest" and an "ugly idea, both crass and alien to golf." Then PGA Tour commissioner Tim Finchem warned players they were facing suspension for defecting.

Still, Norman had the ear of other players, calling a meeting at his Shark Shootout event in November 1994 at Sherwood Country Club outside of Los Angeles. Norman believed he held all the cards. He made his pitch to the rest of the Tour's best, touting that he had the financial backing of Rupert Murdoch and FOX Sports. But Norman hadn't counted on Arnold Palmer. Then in his mid 60s, Palmer delivered a lesson in legacy that transcended dollar signs, reminding the room that both he and Jack Nicklaus had faced similar temptations but refused them, choosing the sport's health over personal enrichment. Palmer stood and walked out, taking Norman's dreams with him.

"The King had spoken, and everyone listened," Nick Price, then-World No. 1, told Golf Channel's Rex Hoggard in 2023. Added Paul Azinger: "The consensus didn't stick with [Norman] when he got out there in a public forum. The guys that he thought were onboard totally flipped on him right in front of all of us. We all said no."

Norman still worked to get his project in the air, including an attempt for other players to sign a petition of sorts, but no one else was willing to hop aboard. Finchem—a lawyer himself who worked in President Jimmy Carter's administration—flexed the Tour's legal muscle and ultimately no legal action was taken. In 1996, the tour introduced the "World Golf Championships," a series of limited-field, no-cut events promising big paydays to the top players ... the same premise as Norman's series, fueling his bitterness. Tour leadership had quelled Norman's insurrection.

But to think failed rebellion would lead to repentance is to not know Norman, a man who published his autobiography before ever winning a PGA Tour event. Time hardened his resolve. "The players should keep their eyes open ... to opportunities that allow [them] to do what you want to do as an independent contractor," Norman told *Golf Digest* that fall. "Seve and I were staunch supporters of that, of growing the game of golf on a global basis. The tours should keep their eyes wide open."

In a way, how Norman's narrow-minded, rapacious conflict against the tour has come to fruition is aspirational. After decades of nursing his grudge, he finally found backers with deep enough pockets to wage his war—though the Faustian bargain required Norman to become a mouthpiece for the Saudi regime. It's why, three years in, he remained the head of LIV. Despite numerous speaking gaffes, including downplaying *Washington Post* journalist Jamal Khashoggi's murder by Saudi Arabian authorities by saying, "We all make mistakes." Despite making a fool of himself with an open letter threatening PGA Tour Commissioner Monahan (again, open letters never, ever work) and his flub with LIV's World Ranking qualification process, unceremoniously rescinding LIV's application after it had already been denied for failing to meet the OWGR standards. Despite making grand promises regarding his league or player moves, most of those promises would never come to fruition. Ultimately, none of that matters. The reason he's the captain of the LIV ship is because LIV wasn't built to reach shore; its objective is to sink the PGA Tour.

The cost was whatever integrity and standing Norman had left in the game. The R&A didn't invite him to its champions celebration at the 150th Open and Augusta National declined to extend him access to the Masters despite other organizations' leaders being present (forcing Norman to acquire badges on his own). Should there ever be peace between the PGA Tour and Saudi Arabia, Norman will be gone, evidenced in the side agreement released by Congress during its hearing into the framework agreement that dictated Norman would be terminated. It will be the final indignity for a man who sought to reshape golf only to be remembered as the sport's most persistent antagonist.

Conversely, Norman's had displayed a conspicuous absence of principle well before LIV, both professionally and personally. Throughout his playing career he had the reputation of being frosty off-camera, only to turn up the charm once the lights went on. His first manager, James Marshall, once said of Norman, "I don't think I've ever met anybody with quite such a big ego." Norman's never been beloved by his Australian patriots, calling himself a victim of "tall poppy syndrome," where those of success are cut down by the populace. "No, Greg, it's people telling you you're a wanker," popular golf voice Michael Clayton told the *Sydney Morning Herald* in 2022. "Australians are great at saying, 'Come on, mate, that's bullshit.'" His marriage to tennis star Chris Evert was well publicized; what went under the radar is Evert was the former wife of Andy Mill … Norman's close buddy. "Greg Norman at one time was my best friend and a year-and-a-half ago, I would have taken a bullet for this guy," Mill told the *Daily Telegraph* in 2009. "But I didn't realize he was the one that was going to pull the trigger."

That Norman has tried to make himself to be a martyr is not surprising. Nothing is further from the truth. He's no visionary or crusader, either, and frankly calling him a "captain" is generous. Norman is nothing more than a honeybee: something that doesn't realize the very thing he wants will ultimately cause his own destruction.

•   •   •

The Scottish golf pilgrimage has its rituals. Among them is paying homage at Prestwick, the grounds that gave birth to the Open Championship.

Allan Robertson was the undisputed best of his generation; he was the first to break 80 at the Old Course, and legend has it that Robertson never lost a match when money was on the line. So when Robertson died in his early 40s after an attack of jaundice in the fall of 1859, a landowner (and founding member of Prestwick) named James Ogilvie Fairlie and the Earl of Eglinton raised the question of who would take Robertson's title. Fairlie sent missives to places like Aberdeen, Blackheath, Bruntsfield, Carnoustie, Panmure, Dirleton Castle, Innerleven, Montrose, North Berwick, Perth, Musselburgh, and St Andrews, asking each club to send their best players for a competition where a red Moroccan strap, known as the championship belt, would be up for grabs. A whopping eight players entered, with three rounds contested over Prestwick's 12 holes on October 17, 1860. Willie Park Sr of Musselburgh topped Tom Morris, the greenskeeper at Prestwick who had designed the links a decade before. The first 12 Opens would be held at Prestwick (with a season off in 1871 after Young Tom Morris had won the belt three consecutive years); though it hasn't been back in roughly 100 years—the course's footprint too small to receive large crowds—Prestwick is just behind the Old Course for most times hosting the Open at 24.

History breathes through the club's hallways, where massive glass trophy cases chronicle the Open's humble origins. But it's the links itself that makes a visit here a golfer's pilgrimage. The opening hole, pressed against a railway line, offers a nerve-testing start with its sliver of a fairway—among Britain's most demanding first holes. The 3rd, a short par-five that doglegs right, dances with both beauty and danger: a meandering burn traces its edge while the legendary Cardinal bunkers—vast sandy chasms—bisect the fairway. Then comes the celebrated par-three 5th, "Himalayas," where golfers must trust their instincts on a blind shot over a towering dune. The inward nine tests even the steadiest hands with its cunningly contoured greens—the back pin position on the 13th proves particularly elusive—while the 15th's pinched landing area makes the already-narrow first hole seem generous by comparison. But perhaps the course's crowning glory is the 17th, a hole so masterfully conceived that C.B. Macdonald replicated it at National Golf Links of America, and which Bernard Darwin immortalized as "the most spectacular blind hole in all the world."

Leave your scorecard ambitions at home when you visit Prestwick. Personally, your enjoyment should never be predicated on score; just try to take a few good swings, cherish being outside and with friends, and should that fail, there's a bar waiting for you afterward. While this philosophy might not resonate with every golfer, it's essential to embracing Prestwick's spirit.

Some criticize the course for its quirks, and first-time visitors navigating without local knowledge—be it from a caddie or member—will inevitably wish for several mulligans. Were this layout unveiled today, critics might dismiss it as contrived; if every links employed such architectural audacity, golf might well drive us all to madness. But such critiques miss the essence of what makes Prestwick special: these aren't imperfections but character. Here stands a course gloriously frozen in time, its terrain shaped as if by ancient giants who molded these hollows and hillocks into a living museum of golf's heritage. Prestwick's unconventional nature isn't a flaw to be criticized—it's an experience to be savored.

But Prestwick will forever command a place in my being for reasons that transcend itself.

A short primer: For most of my life I've avoided crowds. A lot of that sidestepping had to do with a speech impediment, a fusion of a stumble and mumble, making words fall out of my mouth without making much sense. My body language is a disaster, too. Do you remember that Keystone Light "Bitter Beer Face" ad campaign from the mid 1990s? I was told too many times to count that that's what I looked like, forever scowling, and that I emitted an aloof vibe. I eventually discovered in my mid 30s that I had Autism Spectrum Disorder, in the range formerly known as Asperger's Syndrome. It is a mild case, emphasized by a lack of social-emotional reciprocity, and the aloofness and scowls are likely the result of underdeveloped social cues in the brain.

Conversations and social gatherings can still be problems, I can still come off as aloof, and that bitter-beer face is still plastered on my stupid head. But golf is the one place where I feel comfortable, perhaps because in golf you are together in isolation. Maybe the only other such spot is the neighborhood pub, where you can meet with the same people every week, and sometimes there is conversation, and sometimes each is left to wrestle with whatever brought them to the bar in the first place. Or maybe because autism is a lot like golf, there is no beating it, you can only hope to do your best and try again tomorrow.

Even with this refuge, I usually preferred to play alone. I've realized it's better for myself and everyone if I'm mostly off to the side. I wish I could say I was comfortable with that reality, but sometimes lone wolves want to be part of a pack. Alas, I also hated the idea of my presence ruining someone else's time, so by myself I went.

The epiphany struck me in Scotland, building quietly through three weeks of links golf before crystallizing that day at Prestwick. It was the Sunday before Open week when I joined three coworkers-turned-confidants: Will Irwin, Luke Kerr-Dineen, and Jamie Kennedy. To call them mere colleagues understates our bond; they are friends, and we form something close to a perfect foursome—their shared passion for soccer (against my benign indifference) notwithstanding. The stories and laughter we shared that day, and throughout Open week, remain too precious for print, sealed in memory's vault where the best moments of friendship belong.

Scottish golf's deep connection to friendship deserves—and will receive—deeper exploration in later pages. But that day at Prestwick offered an echo of the first Open Championship, where three historic rounds gave birth to what would become golf's most prestigious and egalitarian spectacle. Both experiences illuminate the same timeless truth: while golf may count our strokes individually, its soul lives in those who share its journey.

•   •   •

One final note on LIV intent. For all of Norman's blustering, the only real difference between his revolt in 1994 to 2022 was that others were willing to ignore Palmer's advice. While their motives for doing so vary, the enzyme behind the most important person's defection mirrors Normans': Ego, avarice, and misguided retribution.

We will get in-depth about Phil Mickelson later. His purpose was never in doubt, and almost single-handedly stopped LIV before it began when his comments to author Alan Shipnuck were published in February 2022:

"They're scary motherfuckers to get involved with," Mickelson said. "We know they killed [*Washington Post* reporter Jamal] Khashoggi and have a horrible record on human rights. They execute people over there for being gay. Knowing all of this, why would I even consider it? Because this is a once-in-a-lifetime opportunity to reshape how the PGA Tour operates."

What has been lost to history, however, are Mickelson comments that were made just days before Shipnuck published his story. In a story from John Huggan posted on February 2, 2022, Mickelson laid the framework for his imminent departure by listing his grievances with the tour:

"It's not public knowledge, all that goes on," Mickelson said. "But the players don't have access to their own media. If the tour wanted to end any threat [from Saudi or anywhere else], they could just hand back the media rights to the players. But they would rather throw $25 million here and $40 million there than give back the roughly $20 billion in digital assets they control. Or give up access to the $50+ million they make every year on their own media channel.

"There are many issues, but that is one of the biggest. For me personally, it's not enough that they are sitting on hundreds of millions of digital moments. They also have access to my shots, access I do not have. They also charge companies to use shots I have hit. And when I did 'The Match'—there have been five of them—the tour forced me to pay them $1 million each time. For my own media rights. That type of greed is, to me, beyond obnoxious."

One more quote, for good measure: "I'm not sure how this is going to play out," Mickelson said. "My ultimate loyalty is to the game of golf and what it has given me. I am so appreciative of the life it has provided. I don't know what is going to happen. I don't know where things are headed. But I know I will be criticized. That's not my concern. All that would do is dumb down one of the most intricate issues in sports. It would be so naïve to not factor in all of the complexities. The media rights are but a small fraction of everything else. And it is the Tour's obnoxious greed that has really opened the door for opportunities elsewhere."

Obnoxious greed. Forget the failure to grasp a basic understanding of how media rights work, that no athlete in any viable sporting league owns such claims. Or that he asserted the tour is sitting on $20 billion in digital assets; $20 billion for a league that, less than two years before, signed a $7 billion, nine-year contract with CBS, NBC, and ESPN. Or that sources confirmed to me that Turner Sports, which had aired all five iterations of "The Match" to that point, paid the $1 million fee, not Mickelson personally, and that Mickelson made millions from the franchise, with $9 million alone coming from his first battle against Tiger Woods in 2018. Instead, focus on the idea that Mickelson, who made almost $100 million in career earnings for playing a game and untold millions more in endorsements, felt he was undercompensated for (checks notes) playing golf.

As the next three years would prove, Mickelson was not alone in that belief. It's why professional golf's solution to the schism—which was, essentially, to throw money at the problem, was maddening. Greed and undeserved entitlement caused this mess in the first place, and those are not financial problems. They are issues of the heart, and no dollar sign fixes that. Eventually the sense of privilege returns because it is a demon that can never be fed.

•   •   •

I received an email from Oliver two months after I met him at Crail. There had been several setbacks with his daughter; rehab had not gone smoothly, and she was having trouble putting weight on her leg. She was able to return to school, although since walking remains hard Oliver and his wife have extended their stay until she's OK on her own. They take turns chauffeuring her to and from class.

Oliver said they haven't been able to golf. The hope remains, and just a few days earlier she had taken a few putting strokes in the living room. As for Oliver, he said he developed a bad case of the driving yips. He did not sound defeated. "I got a free lesson from a fellow I met on the range," he wrote. "Quick and handsy. I work to be slow. I will be ready when she can play."

CHAPTER 3

Meaning

Anstruther • Competitiveness • Ru and Cruden Bay •
True nature • Work

Andy McAuley wipes away the crumbs from his golden peach fuzz, although the grease from the meal and mist from the sea keeps the remnants of his lunch a tongue lash away from of his lips. McAuley doesn't mind. His sandwich from Anstruther Fish Bar is "The best you can get," he says with an ease and candor that only comes when speaking the truth. The line that wraps around the building and up the street shows he's not alone in his belief; the food is so good that the chipper can charge for ketchup and no one blinks.

McAuley reached out through Twitter to connect for a game. He is a Scotsman in his mid-30s who travels through Europe helping start-ups build smartphone apps. He's on the road so much that he doesn't have a permanent residence, preferring to keep his things at his retired parents' place in the South Ayrshire region along the west coast.

When he's between in-office assignments, he will come to Scotland for weeks at a time, working in his mornings and playing in the afternoons. We made a date to tour Anstruther Golf Club, a wee nine-holer less than nine miles to the south of St Andrews. Less than an hour after teeing off, I came to the conclusion that I may never leave this country.

Anstruther often serves as either a jet-lag antidote for weary travelers or a consolation prize for those who missed the Old Course ballot. While it serves both of those exigencies well, the distinctions do Anstruther a disservice; a substitute course has no business being this … indelible? Entertaining? Delightful? There's something here that transcends its role as understudy to St Andrews' grand stages.

I won't go hole-by-hole or map every hillock and hollow, for some mysteries deserve a live reveal. Don't be deterred by the scorecard. What's marketed as a par 31 that tips out at 2,100 yards cannot be conveyed by numbers. Just know the opener is a generously wide drivable par four featuring a 60-foot summit to the green, although the climb banks against the hill, meaning anything under 260 yards (or against the wind) could be left with a hundred and change in. And that a two-story granite monument in the design of a medieval castle battlement touches the 2nd green, commemorating soldiers from the town that made the ultimate sacrifice during World War I. Or that the links has its own "Amen Corner" of par threes, including a 247-yard downhiller with the North Sea's fury crashing on the left, a green the size of a coffee table on the right and a hell of a lot of gorse and uneven lies punishing any hint of timidity—such a brute that *Golf Monthly* dubbed it the toughest par three in the UK. And that the course itself sits like a jewel—the bustling town spilling out on two sides, pastoral farmland stretching northward, the eternal sea commanding the southern view, creating one of Scotland's most captivating golf landscapes.

The links before you shapeshifts with each gust and lull. Some pockets of the golf world view nature's fickle hand as an architectural failing, believing a course should maintain absolute sovereignty over its examination. But Anstruther—like all Scottish links—exposes the myopia of such thinking. Links golf isn't merely a game played on the land; it's a marriage between sport and the elements. Like any partnership, it can be both harmonious and tempestuous within a single breath, and therein lies its splendor: what poetry exists in the predictable?

This ethereal quality explains how a player can go low at Anstruther or walk off needing a stiff drink. A gentleman I briefly met in the bar afterward said he went 18 holes two days earlier, shooting 4-under on his first go-around, and 8-over on the second. "Many a golfer will survey their ego before, and need reassessing after," he said. "[The links] taunts you in its invitingness. The wind is down, aye, she can be had. Expecting little wind is a proposition I would never take."

To view the wind as adversary misses the point entirely, yet treating it as ally proves equally misguided. The wind is rather a muse, coaxing creativity we never knew we possessed. At Anstruther, it serves as nature's paintbrush, what we can create capped by only what we can execute, imagine, and feel. So forget alternative; Anstruther earns must-stop status for anyone visiting the Fife area.

Unfortunately, it was a tour made alone, as Andy was caught up with client emails and had to bail. He surfaced in time for lunch, which metamorphosed into something more intimate than a meal.

We are leaning against a white railing separating the village from the harbor, where bowriders, catamarans, and fishing vessels dance their gentle maritime waltz. Shore Street's stone façades march along behind us—a parade of whites and sandy hues occasionally punctuated by defiant splashes of blue and pink—lending Anstruther an aesthetic that could be mistaken for Amsterdam's canals or an Amalfi Coast village. But our eyes are drawn seaward, as they always are when conversation drifts toward life's weightier matters. It is clear Andy is financially well-off. Spiritually, the well is barren. He is not happy, his recent trips revealing a hollow space within his constructed life.

"My mates and I were arguing over a pint about the YouTube influencers," Andy says. "They can't stand them. I get it. Attention-seeking is not our way. To me, that's not the point. My marbles return to the conceit: Making a living sharing golf. How pure, how lucky?"

Time weighs on Andy's mind—its finite nature and how to spend what remains. When I probe whether he's tempted by the siren song of social media stardom, his answer drifts back to Scottish summers of his youth. He speaks of 36-hole matches with his brother, sometimes striking out on impromptu camping expeditions to chase down courses they'd never played. They played matches, nothing for money, yet almost every game was recorded in notebooks. Their mother kept the journals; when Andy's brother was married, he compiled them into a custom-designed leather binder, a testament to what shaped them both.

"Funny ... as lads you want nothing more than to grow up," Andy says. He doesn't finish his thought. Andy's searching for something he once possessed, to a purpose as pure as those marathon summer days. He doesn't say it and I don't point it out, but deep down, both of us know he knows where he can find it.

•　　　•　　　•

For most of its existence, LIV Golf has presented itself as little more than a circus—all gaudy spectacle and contrived excitement, its tournaments playing out on mostly empty courses to negligible television audiences. Conversely, it's been impervious to its own failures, and to dismiss LIV is a dangerous folly—a lesson golf's power brokers have learned at a considerable cost. LIV's been called a trainwreck, yet the truth is more insidious. It's a nuclear meltdown in slow motion, leaking toxins at a relentless advance that's irrevocably altering the golf landscape.

The poison can be enticing, however. Chief among them is access. If you're looking for an up-close and personal connection with your favorite player—or any player—LIV Golf has the upper hand on the major championships and PGA and DP World Tours. Part of that is due to limited crowds, which—depending on whom you ask—is by design, or a byproduct of aversion. Whatever the catalyst, the reality is there aren't many fans on-site compared to a PGA Tour event, giving the ones who are there an unobstructed and intimate view. There are no more than 150 people who roam hole-to-hole with the marquee attractions like Bryson DeChambeau or Jon Rahm.

The intimacy of LIV's presentation offers undeniable allure. Spectators are treated to a symphony of golf's subtle sounds typically reserved for broadcast audiences—the whispered strategy sessions between player and caddie, the satisfying whistle of a purely struck iron, the soft touchdown of a ball on green. The proximity transforms viewers from distant observers to immediate participants in the drama. You're close enough to read the micro-expressions that cross a player's face: the fleeting shadow of doubt before a crucial shot, the flash of frustration at a missed opportunity, the joy of a perfectly executed plan. This nearness—with fans allowed remarkably close to tee boxes, fairways, and greens—creates an almost theatrical intimacy with the action.

The concession prices are cheap. Tickets are cheaper. Autographs are easy to grab, and a fan village is not short on attractions. Even the omnipresent music—while perhaps jarring to purists—adds an energy that resonates with most attendees, creating a vibe more akin to a social gathering than a hushed sporting event. In an age when major sports leagues increasingly cater to corporate boxes and premium experiences—often pricing out the average fan—LIV has positioned itself as the people's alternative. They've cracked the code on the peripheral elements that make modern sporting events engaging to a broader audience. The tournament itself might not satisfy the golf obsessive's appetite for high-stakes competition, which is fine! Spoiler alert: Even diehards can't get up for every event of the more than 40 PGA Tour stops. And there are plenty of attendees at PGA Tour and sports events that are there strictly for social purposes. They are just looking for something to do on the weekend. It may not be for the true fan, and maybe that's by design. The case can be made that LIV does a better job of appealing to the casual observer better than most leagues, and that is a big demographic.

Yet herein lies the fundamental disconnect: for the devoted golf fan, the diehards who cherish the sport's competitive essence, LIV represents an inversion of everything that makes golf compelling.

Set aside, for a moment, the ethical quagmire. Sports—particularly golf—has long presented itself as one of society's last bastions of equal opportunity, a realm where talent, determination, and performance are the only tenders that matter. Every shot carries consequence, every tournament writes its own drama, every victory must be earned through excellence rather than entitlement. LIV Golf dismantled this fundamental premise, replacing merit with membership, competition with exhibition, and earned rewards with guaranteed wealth. They didn't cease being skilled athletes, but they surrendered something vital—the warrior spirit that defines true competitors, trading their gladiator status for the comfortable life of traveling showmen. The stakes disappeared, replaced by appearance fees and predetermined payouts regardless of performance. Perhaps one of the biggest indictments came from Brooks Koepka. He feared that his body had betrayed him long before he let on: that the Koepka, Destroyer of Worlds that had been on display at majors might be gone and not coming back. When he was offered a buttload of money, he took it before anyone was the wiser—which, for those scoring at home, was four months after Koepka said, "Somebody will sell out and go to [LIV]." Koepka did bounce back, finishing second at the 2023 Masters and winning the 2023 PGA. However, at that Masters Koepka made a stunning admission: He may not have gone to LIV had he known he still had game left in him. This encapsulates the venture's underlying nature—not a competitive tour, but a refuge for those seeking to cash out on their reputations, whether due to declining skills, waning motivation, or simple avarice.

It should be no surprise that most of the individuals that were initially drawn to LIV were injury-prone, has-beens, never-wases, those that many viewed as having character issues. Their only throughline a willingness to take the PR hit for a golden parachute. It's crucial to emphasize this point explicitly: LIV's early roster was largely populated by golf's peripheral figures—players who were already drifting toward irrelevance. To dignify LIV's events with the term *competition* seems generous when examining a field consisting of:

- Six luminaries (and that's being generous),
- Six good to above-average players,
- A dozen rank-and-file, and
- 30 names who would struggle for a tour card.

For context, it would be like a breakaway baseball circuit featuring a lineup of one former Major League Baseball All-Star, one starter, two benchwarmers, and five minor-leaguers. (Meaning, every team would be the Oakland A's.) LIV and its backers bristle at the term *exhibition*, but such a label actually flatters their product. Even the most contrived made-for-TV golf events typically showcase something intrinsically appealing: a clash of generations, a test of specific skills, a pairing of celebrities. Despite its growing roster of defectors and increasingly prominent names, LIV has failed to manufacture such magnetic moments. The fundamental dynamic persists.

LIV Golf has staked its future on its team format, positioning it as the foundation for long-term success. The organization envisions a Formula 1-style model where regionally-based clubs attract dedicated sponsors and passionate local followings. However, this strategy faces significant challenges. At LIV events, spectators appear largely indifferent to the team component, perhaps because the format remains fundamentally individualistic—team standings are simply a mathematical sum of individual scores rather than true team competition through match play. The lack of authentic team identity or loyalty further undermines this approach. Without meaningful team engagement, LIV's core concept begins to unravel, raising questions about its purpose and direction.

Fans seem confused too, and it shows; by almost every metric available, few were turning in, to the point where the league stopped reporting its own numbers. That's why LIV Golf has been a failure: for all its claims of disruption, it has not gained your care. It's the most expensive member-guest ever produced.

The most problematic aspect of LIV Golf from a competitive standpoint has been its pervasive sense of unearned entitlement. LIV defectors seemed oblivious to the fact that their massive paydays came with conditions, instead believing they deserved their windfall despite modest career achievements. This entitled mindset manifested in multiple ways: They demanded major championship exemptions without merit, expected immediate Official World Golf Ranking points despite the standard two-year accreditation process, and deflected accountability for their association with their employer's human rights record by claiming to be "just golfers." The situation reached a low when several players, including Phil Mickelson and Bryson DeChambeau, sued their former PGA Tour colleagues despite years of clear warnings about the consequences of defection.

The league's pattern of disinformation and grievance-mongering was equally troubling. Saudi Golf Federation CEO Majed Al Sorour threatened to create alternative majors. Mickelson promoted conspiracy theories about collusion between the PGA Tour and USGA. Joaquin Niemann, despite his unremarkable major championship record, repeatedly complained about OWGR points. The league's attempted shortcut through the MENA Tour partnership predictably failed. DeChambeau criticized the pace of reunification talks, which—given DeChambeau's role in said litigation—is akin to driving a car into the ocean then chewing the mechanic out for failing to drain the engine of salt water. Henrik Stenson expressed indignation when stripped of his Ryder Cup captaincy after moving to LIV, despite being informed of the consequences of such a move. Greg Norman's bold claims about recruiting top talent proved empty. Perhaps most emblematic was Talor Gooch, who suggested asterisks for potential major victories by non-LIV players, demanded special exemptions he hadn't earned, and compared LIV events to a Ryder Cup he had never experienced.

These aren't merely complaints from disgruntled golfers; they represent a fundamental misunderstanding of competitive sport's core principles. While true athletes accept defeat as motivation for improvement, LIV's participants consistently seek to change the rules rather than elevate their game, then cry foul when the rules are enforced.

The pattern is clear: instead of competing within established frameworks, LIV repeatedly attempts to rewrite them, betraying a profound insecurity about its ability to succeed on merit alone.

LIV positions itself as golf's revolutionary force, promising to modernize a supposedly stagnant sport with shorter formats, team dynamics, and enhanced entertainment value. Yet beneath its shotgun starts, loud music, and matching jerseys lies a product that fails to address professional golf's fundamental challenges. The same issues that plagued the PGA Tour—weeks that mostly look the same from the weeks before, predictable broadcasts, limited fan engagement— persist in LIV events, just with added pyrotechnics and inflated purses. Like a middle-aged man trading his sedan for a sports car, LIV mistakes superficial changes for meaningful innovation, focusing on packaging rather than substance.

The organization's desperate grasp for legitimacy becomes most apparent in its players' constant self-justification. Besides, there is nothing inherently cool about players demanding a relevance they never had, and it misses a crucial point of sports and life: Those who insist on their significance succeed in proving a lack of it.

·   ·   ·

It is late November and Ru Macdonald has returned from the DP World Tour's finale in Dubai. The weight of time on the road is etched into this voice, the familiar exhaustion of a traveler who knows that home, with its beautiful chaos of young children, will offer no respite. The fatigue melts away quickly, however, and his words become more colorful and animated when we delve into golf, his native language, and the place he learned it.

"I was still a lad, no more than 12," Ru says. "The genesis was hearing American voices at Cruden Bay. You're impressionable at that age. Made me wonder, 'Why are these people coming here?' That grew when I worked in the pro shop. All these visitors coming in, so excited to be at a place we call home, and they would always be surprised. And that was before they got swept away by the magic of the dunes."

This is vintage Ru. The game has always been his stimulant of choice. Throughout the summer, our paths intersected at various tournaments and clubhouses, although I held off the formal interview until now, as he stands on the threshold of his own odyssey, the uncharted waters no match for the purpose of his flight.

Few figures in golf possess Ru's combination of business instinct, knowledge, and strategic insight into the game. His career reads like a masterclass in golf industry versatility: from curating bespoke golf travel experiences to hosting an acclaimed podcast, managing a premium golf rental property, and steering a thriving consultancy. But it's his innovative work with the European Tour that has truly cemented his reputation. Alongside my *Golf Digest* colleague Jamie Kennedy, Ru has revolutionized the Tour's digital presence. Their creative fingerprints are all over the DP World Tour's most memorable content: from heartwarming segments featuring wide-eyed kids grilling tour pros, to the hilarious chaos of an anger management therapy session for golfers, to the ambitious challenge of pros attempting to score a hole-in-one in 500 attempts. These aren't just clever concepts—they're meticulously executed productions that have transformed how the sport views the tour and its players.

Ru's passion for golf radiates with an almost childlike purity—a rare commodity in an industry that can sometimes grind down even the most ardent enthusiasts into cynics. While many complain about dwindling access or catering to the lowest common denominator, Ru's eyes still light up discussing the subtle breaks of a green or the way morning light streams across a fairway. His wonderment is contagious; every conversation with him serves as a spiritual renewal, reminding me why covering this game remains a privilege, and I find myself carrying a fragment of his enthusiasm, seeing the sport through fresher eyes.

"When you talk about passion he is a perfect example," Jamie says. "He eats, sleeps, and drinks golf. It doesn't come from a flashy or privileged place either. He genuinely loves the game, especially in Scotland. He enriches everyone and everything around. He volunteers to help clubs and even some tour players with their social media and content. He has his fingers (quietly) in a lot of pies within Scottish golf and is genuinely excited to help people coming to Scotland to play.

"He's my text outlet for any random thought or rant I have. I probably message him every other day with something. He is a fellow golf sicko who is happy to help but in the same way, he is happy to challenge or question a way of thinking or opinion."

And to understand Ru's soul—to grasp the essence of what drives this perpetual sense of curiosity—one must understand Cruden Bay.

The small town of Cruden Bay, located on the northeast coast, a little over a two-hour drive from St Andrews, has a mystique that extends far beyond its golfing heritage, drawing literary pilgrims through a captivating—if somewhat misattributed—connection to gothic horror. Legend insists that Bram Stoker conceived *Dracula* while gazing upon New Slains Castle, a tower house and stone chateau that's perched on cliffs that plunge into the North Sea. Sroker was a frequent visitor to the area, he did write the novel's first chapters while in town for holiday. One problem—Stoker's notes on *Dracula* predate his first journey to Cruden by two years, the earliest drafts emerging in 1890, while his maiden voyage to these shores wouldn't occur until 1892. The truth, as his biographers have meticulously documented, is more nuanced. The castle served as a "visual palette" for Stoker, and it later appeared in two of his lesser-known novels, *The Watter's Mou'* and *The Mystery of the Sea*, which could explain why it's been folded into the Dracula legend. So even if you think vampire literature sucks (pun absolutely intended), at least you can impress your friends at trivia night with this obscure bit of Scottish history.

But to the golf-obsessed? Cruden Bay is a fever dream sprung to life, a course that seems to have emerged from our most fanciful golfing reveries—except you can actually play it. The links is 25 miles north of Aberdeen, nestled against a town of weathered cottages with slate roofs and tight rock walls lining narrow streets that bend towards the sea. The kind of place where peat fires smolder in every pub, no matter the season. There is evidence golf was played here as early as 1791, but the current links was visualized by Old Tom Morris and Archie

Simpson and opened for play in 1899, with Tom Simpson and Herbert Fowler recasting some of the work in the 1920s. The links began as an ambitious venture by the Great North of Scotland Railway Company, which erected a grand hotel on the property, envisioning the course as the crown jewel in their leisure empire. When the hotel succumbed to financial troubles in the 1950s, the links nearly followed it, until three local businessmen—understanding the ground they walked upon—stepped in like knights to rescue the course from distress.

Save for a few tee box additions and a revamped 10th hole, the links of then remains what it is now—a sui generis experience bred in the fires of pink sands and sky-scraping dunes, molded by reason and extraordinary vision, that tiptoed through the artificial and contrived to reach its endpoint as a natural wonder.

Cruden Bay requires an imaginative faculty more so than most links, equal parts artistic touch and unshakable resolve. It's the epitome of a good routing; Morris and Simpson appear to have been more archaeologists than designers, excavating a golf course that nature had already hidden within the dunes. Your journey through the property feels predestined, each step as natural as following a deer trail through ancient woods. The terrain is beautifully untamed, with native grasses and rugged contours conspiring to ensure that no two shots are ever quite the same, even when playing from seemingly identical spots. No hole is the same, yet they're all in concert with one another. It features one of my favorite four-hole runs in the world:

- The drivable par-four 3rd, with a rippling fairway allowing a ball to reach the green, but guarded with out-of-bounds on the left, untamed sandhills on the right and a pot bunker on the left side of the green.
- The 195-yard par three 4th, over a chasm to an elevated green, hugged by a river on the left with the old fishing village of Port Erroll on the other side of the bank, with the castle looming in the distance and the North Sea as backdrop. One of the best vistas in the sport.

- The 5th is a meaty par four that's really a four and a half, off an elevated tee box down into the bluffs that kicks off a stretch where the course weaves in-between the dunes.
- The mercurial par five 6th, often playing as a three-shotter yet in the right conditions can be had in two, but the green is guarded by a wee devilish burn.

Arriving at the 9th tee requires a climb into the mists, where you are rewarded with an arresting view of the course and those pink sands disappearing into the sea. The scene feels transplanted from Ireland's wild Atlantic coast rather than Scotland's more restrained eastern shores, with the bathtub green of the 14th below a reminder that this course is not like others. Every time I'm on this hole, I remember the wonderful quote from the writer Dr Samuel Johnson when visiting the area in the 1770s: "no man can see with indifference" the sea chasm known as the Bullers of Buchan. The same could be said for Cruden Bay itself—though not everyone bows to its charms. Some dismiss it as quirky and eccentric. But barbs in their hands fail to pierce those who love this place, because while the descriptors have merit, their connotation does not. What skeptics believe is imperfection is Cruden Bay's essence—a raw, uncompromising design that reveals its genius to those who surrender to its wild heart.

This was the cauldron that brewed a golf romantic like Ru. His father worked in the conservation of national parks, which brought his family from Islay to the Cruden Bay area when he was young. Those early days were spent at Newburgh-on-Ythan links, just 15 minutes away, where his father would drop him off until he was ready to tackle Cruden's secrets. It wasn't long until he matriculated to Cruden and immersed himself in club life, playing medal games with local members, working in the pro shop, and caddying for visitors. Ru quickly accelerated through the professional industry after university, winning Golf Tourism Scotland Young Person of the Year in 2013, and joined the Old World circuit several years later, which took him across the world. Despite seeing the best this sport has to offer, Ru has remained anchored at Cruden. He doubled down, in fact, buying a property with his brother just off the course called "Dunes," opening their doors to golf travelers that have made the journey. He can wax about the links all day: "Every time I walk up 9, and see this oasis of golf below you, it's hard not to get swept up and realize how lucky you are"—it's the community that make Cruden what it is to Ru.

"We get energized off the love of this course," Ru says. "We'd always have great chats [with visitors], who are coming from some of the best courses in the world to see our little place. We'd take pride in that, the warmth in the welcome, just by the golf course itself. It instilled a valuable lesson of making them feel wanted, to give them the great experience they hope to get."

It's what has Ru down about the pro game. The greed, the talk of money, the broken promises. It's not the golf experience he knows. He hasn't been able to detach himself from where the game has the ability to go, and he believes his sense of direction to be true. That's why he has resigned from the DP World Tour to start his own company, Linksland Golf, which will focus on content built around Scottish clubs and courses to inspire others to come and experience the beauty for themselves.

He wants people to feel the way he feels, and there are worse analogs than his love for home.

"The way you feel connected. Getting blasted by the North Sea. Alone in the dunes. Just playing yourself," Ru says. "Not bringing a fucking golf speaker [laughs]. Catching a break from the wind, and being able to take a breath. That is everything."

•　　•　　•

Two common defenses emerge whenever LIV Golf is criticized. Both are fixated on financial gain: "You would take the money too" and "You can't blame someone for making a business decision for their family." Both arguments crumble under scrutiny.

It's easy to take a flamethrower to these takes, starting with the fact that, out of the top 100 golfers in the world, 20 of them—in the words of Koepka—sold out. That's a lot that took the bag ... but not as many who passed, almost all of them were given similar offers. The math alone dismantles the narrative, but the philosophical shortcoming runs even deeper. I am not obtuse to the importance of wealth, an emphasis that feels like it only grows by the year in our culture. Also recognize that, to some, accumulating assets and resources and prosperity is not just *a* priority but *the* priority, a concern that guides and explains every decision they make. If that's the way you live your life, fine. But—and this is the important part and the part that gets lost on so many—money is not a universal True North. Dismissing this truth as idealistic reveals more about the critic's cynicism than the complexity of human motivation.

"Everyone has a price" echoes through golf's civil war like a cynical mantra, gaining resonance whenever another star like Koepka or Jon Rahm performs their inevitable about-face on LIV. These reversals—from principled resistance to lucrative surrender—are often met with knowing nods and whispers of "told you so." I once viewed this sentiment as merely cold-hearted; now I recognize it as fundamentally false, a convenient fiction that helps justify moral compromise. The truth is more nuanced than either extreme suggests. Yes, there are those who stand as moral titans, who would sooner live in poverty than betray their principles—and their resolve is admirable. But this isn't just about choosing between sainthood and selling out. The real story lies in the middle ground where ordinary people make extraordinary choices every day, turning down more money for less prestigious jobs that align with their integrity, choosing fulfilling work over corner offices, or accepting lower salaries to serve causes they believe in.

My journey with this question isn't theoretical. I've faced the crossroads where principle meets profit, where figures on a check tried to seduce me away from my convictions. Each time the decision was surprisingly simple—not because I'm particularly virtuous, but because I had clarity about what matters. This crystallized after a near-death experience that stripped away superficial concerns and laid bare what I value. In that crucible of perspective, I discovered my True North coordinates for navigating decisions. What emerged wasn't a set of lofty moral abstractions, but practical standards: the joy of meaningful work, the peace of ethical alignment, the richness of authentic relationships. None of these came with a price tag, and no amount of money could replace them.

I acknowledge that stance comes from a position of considerable privilege. I'm fortunate enough to have work that fulfills me, and crucially, I don't face the grinding anxiety of living paycheck to paycheck or relying on food stamps. But here's the reality that undermines LIV golfers' financial justifications: neither do they ... in fact, they are incredibly far from it. We're not talking about struggling athletes making tough choices to feed their families. These are multimillionaires, many with career earnings that already span generations of wealth. Even those who've weathered financial setbacks—whether through reckless investments, gambling addictions, costly divorces, or hushed-up scandals (and yes, these examples aren't purely hypothetical)—maintain lifestyles that most people can barely imagine. Let's be crystal clear: when these players jumped to LIV, they weren't desperately securing their financial futures or ensuring their children's education. They were already set for life. This wasn't about need; it was about want. It wasn't about security; it was about excess. They simply saw an opportunity to transform enormous wealth into staggering wealth, regardless of the compromises required.

Which allows us to dissect the second defense: "It's just a business decision for my family." This rationalization, deployed by defectors like Rahm, Dustin Johnson, and Harold Varner III, received surprisingly little scrutiny from the golf community. At least it carries a shred of honesty—unlike the transparently hollow "growing the game" rhetoric peddled by others. But this family-first justification reveals a stunning moral blindness, a willful ignorance of breathtaking proportions. These players, while cloaking themselves in the nobility of family values, conveniently overlook the millions of families suffering under the very regime signing their astronomical checks. The same government funding their children's trust funds systematically oppresses countless other children, parents, and families. The cognitive dissonance is staggering: how do we reconcile the sanctity of one golfer's family with the systematic suffering of thousands of others? Is proximity to professional golf the arbiter of which families deserve consideration? Does the ability to shoot under par somehow grant one family's welfare priority over another's? This selective morality—where the well-being of a millionaire's family outweighs the basic human rights of countless others—exposes the bankruptcy of the "family decision" defense. It's not about protecting one's own family; it's using them as cover for naked self-interest.

The evidence lies in Phil Mickelson's revealing comments—not his infamous "scary motherfuckers" quote, but rather his calculated admission: "Knowing all of this, why would I even consider it? Because this is a once-in-a-lifetime opportunity to reshape how the PGA Tour operates." This statement, from LIV's earliest and most vocal champion, reveals the truth: LIV was never about elevating golf or creating meaningful competition. It was leverage, a crowbar to pry open the PGA Tour's (assumed) coffers.

This betrayal cuts deep, because of the unique relationship between sports fans and their heroes. The evolution of this bond follows a predictable but poignant arc: we begin as starry-eyed children, progress through adolescence's disillusionment as we recognize our idols' human frailties, yet emerge still invested in their journeys, their triumphs, their redemptions. This emotional investment isn't trivial: it represents years—sometimes decades—of dedicated following, of early morning viewing sessions, of celebrating victories and agonizing over defeats. We know these guys aren't perfect; we've long since abandoned expectations of purity. But we never expected them to so casually discard the essence of competitive sport for a guaranteed payday.

When these players switched allegiance to LIV, they didn't just change employers—they shattered a fundamental covenant with the galleries that follow them. They demonstrated that all those years of support, all those moments of shared sporting drama, meant nothing when weighed against sufficiently large financial incentives. This revelation—that their commitment to the sport and its traditions was always conditional, always negotiable—breaches even the most cynical fan's defenses. It's not just disappointment; it's the death of something we didn't realize we still believed in.

What if LIV Golf emerged without its Saudi backing? Imagine instead a breakaway league bankrolled by some maverick billionaire—think a golf-obsessed Elon Musk or Mark Cuban—whose sole ambition was to disrupt professional golf's status quo. The same players and teams and middling courses, but stripped of its current geopolitical implications. Would such a venture be more palatable? As a golf purist, I'd still have reservations about its impact on the professional game's traditions and competitive integrity. Yet such concerns would exist purely within golf's biosphere, representing merely the latest chapter in the sport's evolution, not unlike the emergence of the PGA Tour itself from its precursors.

But this hypothetical misses the reality: LIV Golf isn't a competing business venture, as its staff and officials assert it to be. (Unless you know of other start-ups hemorrhaging billions of dollars without a sniff of profit.) It's not an innovative disruption of an aging model. It's a calculated attempt by a nation-state to weaponize sport for political gain and image rehabilitation. The Saudi regime isn't interested in golf's traditions, its competitive integrity, or its long-term sustainability. They view the sport merely as a vessel for reshaping global perceptions while normalizing what drew attention to it in the first place. LIV is a moral crisis masquerading as a sports league. Despite the players' attempts to compartmentalize these issues, to pretend they're just athletes taking advantage of a business opportunity, there's no separating LIV Golf from its architects' intentions. The golden strings that bind them remain visible no matter how desperately their well-paid puppets try to obscure them from view.

•   •   •

Durness Golf Club is out of the way, and that's the point. It's as far northwest as the mainland will go, and we know this thanks to a sign that greets us in the car park that says as much. In this country that's speckled with golf courses seemingly around every corner, the nearest golf course to Durness is a long 60 miles away down a frighteningly narrow road. The area has been inhabited since prehistoric times, and a variety of Viking artifacts were discovered in a cave not long ago, yet the current population of the village hovers around 350 and the natural beauty nods that the land has not been spoiled or tamed by man. There are a few inns, a pub that's open in the summer, and a youth hostel near a cave. It's the type of town you go to when you don't want to be found.

The Durness links is young by Scottish standards, having opened in the 1980s under the vision of three local enthusiasts, yet it possesses the timeless veneer and charm typically found in James Braid's storied designs. Its ranking as the world's 12th-best nine-hole course by *Golf* magazine in 2020 barely hints at its magnificence. The North Atlantic commands attention on almost every hole, its steel-blue waters providing ambience as the links weaves through a tapestry of windswept marram grass and ancient, polished rock. A landscape conducive to only golf and the occasional grazing sheep, though wire fences thoughtfully protect the greens and tees from wandering flocks. Just 100 players call it home, including the handful of Highlands members who make their trips once or twice a year through the countryside. In keeping with its modest scale, the club operates with two employees, one of whom is Alistair Morrison.

He is a prodigy. At 32 he has already been the head greenskeeper for a decade strong. He apprenticed at Brora, the Highlands gem roughly two hours southeast, the type of post that bestows the next opportunity of his choosing. Morrison, who grew up in Durness, decided to go home.

"It was always in the back of my mind," Morrison says. "When I saw it come available, I jumped at it. That I was young and naïve helped."

It's his dream position, working at the course that introduced him to the game, but it is hard work. Morrison's days begin before dawn, when the dew clings to the fescue and the only sound is the distant crash of North Atlantic waves. From early March through late October, he is tethered to these nine holes—mowing greens, hand-cutting cups as the sun climbs higher, repairing divots and bunkers battered by coastal winds and hackers, and trimming the native grasses that frame each hole. Between maintenance runs, he darts into the club-house to answer emails, update social media, and coordinate with vis-iting groups. During peak season, 14-hour days are the norm. While others might call it a thankless position, Morrison sees the effort as an extension of himself—though there are moments when even he ques-tions the wisdom of being a one-man army at the edge of the world.

"There's definitely attachment to it, but it requires all or nothing," Morrison says. "There aren't many people in this part of the country, yet we're the only thing in roughly two hours in any direction, so we cover a lot of area. We get more traffic than you think, and you have to justify to visitors why they decided to visit."

The weight of responsibility settles heavily on his shoulders. It can be trying in ways that scratch deeper than the surface, wearing grooves into both body and spirit. When the mowers break down—and they always seem to choose the most inconvenient moments—he has to transform himself into an impromptu mechanic, hands growing cal-loused from tools that weren't meant to be part of his daily ritual. Despite being the man in charge, a title that should perhaps shield him from certain tasks, he finds himself tending to duties well below his station. Nothing pushes him closer to the edge of frustration quite like having to bend down, again and again, to pick up discarded cig-arette butts—each one a small reminder of others' thoughtlessness, each one stealing a piece of dignity from work he otherwise holds sacred.

It can be taxing in ways that accumulate like layers of sediment, building pressure over time. The physical labor alone would be enough to test anyone's resolve, but being constantly exposed to the mercurial Scottish elements does a particular kind of number on the body. The wind carries salt and bite, the rain seeps into bones, and the rare sunny days demand their own toll in sweat and sunburn. Each season brings its unique challenges, writing its story in aching joints and weather-worn skin.

When your profession transforms into your passion—or perhaps it's the other way around—the lines between work and life blur until they become nearly indistinguishable. You can't simply leave work at work; it follows you home like a shadow, filling your thoughts during dinner and staying with you until your head finally hits the pillow. Even then, it can keep you from finding peace in sleep, as your mind races with tomorrow's tasks and unsolved problems from today.

It can be testing in ways that few outside this world could truly comprehend. No one really knows the full measure of work and time Morrison pours into Durness—the pre-dawn starts, the missed family moments, the physical toll that accumulates like interest on a debt that can never quite be paid off. This reality sometimes leads to quiet moments of doubt, when he can't help but wonder if all the effort, all the sacrifice, all the pieces of himself he's invested in this place are truly worth it.

It's toward the end of the season, and anyone who's spent time on a grounds crew can testify, even the most ardent lover is ready for a separation at summer's end. The course can become a skin that you're unable to peel off. Only Morrison can't, because he is all Durness has got. "It becomes a part of you, right?" Morrison says. "Good and bad. This is some of the best scenery in the world, but it takes effort not to let it become normal."

So the question's worth asking: Why Durness, why home, when almost any club would hand him a blank check for a job not as taxing? He doesn't require much time to respond.

"Other clubs, they're sort of a conveyor belt, you know? They get you in, move you through, move you away," Morrison says. "Here, nine-hole courses don't get the respect they should. They get downgraded unnecessarily. Durness proves that wrong. There's pride in doing that. There's pride in what this is, and where it is, at least to me."

Morrison continues to list several links to punctuate the idea, although the point has been made. His words trace the delicate threads connecting ambition to purpose, success to meaning. Other clubs may extend their hands, offering paths paved with prestige and promise, but they lack something essential—something that speaks to the deepest chambers of his heart. It's written in the way his eyes soften when he surveys the grounds at dawn, in how his shoulders square against the challenge of each new day, in the pride that fills the spaces between his words when he speaks of this place that has become not just his work, but his calling.

CHAPTER 4

Survival

Brora • Jay Monahan • Threats • Saving Brora •
Losing yourself to live

The Scottish Highlands' raw magnificence and rustic grace can be sensory blitzkrieg. Ancient pines and gnarled rowans stand over unmapped forests, their darkness giving way to crystalline glens where pink-tinged mist clings to heather. Mirror-smooth lochs reflect mountains that thrust skyward, their slopes a riot of purple thistle, golden gorse, and white cloudberries against the deep red-rust of billion-year-old Torridonian sandstone. The sparse human traces enhance rather than interrupt this canvas; villages made of battered rock-wall cottages hugging waterways rarely exceed a thousand, fostering communities where neighbors' lives interweave like Celtic knotwork. There are over 40 whisky distilleries scattered throughout the region, transforming barley and spring water and a wee bit of yeast into a nectar of the gods through arts preserved through generations. Mythologizing the Highlands can read like naïve idealization, except experience proves it exceeds the capacity for imagination.

But romanticism has its costs, for beneath the grandeur lies an unforgiving reality: Life can be hard here. The weather wields absolute power; savage winds and horizontal rain batter communities for days, while winter's grip extends deep into spring, turning heating bills into burdens and electricity outages into certainty. Young people face stark choices: remain in their hometowns where career opportunities are limited, or seek futures elsewhere. The remoteness, while viewed as an escape, can also be a trap—medical care can be hours away, delivery costs spiral upward, essential services often come with premium price tags that strain local wages. Housing, when available, commands prices inflated by holiday homes and wealthy escapists. Highlanders endure through an alchemy of resourcefulness and stubborn will, measured in the understanding that anything less won't be enough.

This stark dichotomy applies to Highlands golf. Royal Dornoch is the crown jewel, a course consistently ranked as the top in Scotland, and at times the world, a place that caused Herbert Warren Wind to remark, "No golfer has completed his education until he has played and studied Royal Dornoch."

Though new courses are often knocked in Scotland, few can challenge the aesthetics and challenges of Cabot Highlands' Castle Stuart, with a new Tom Doak course on property taking shape. Golspie and Fortrose & Rosemarkie present scenic, enjoyable treks at bargain rates. Moray Golf Club, Tain, Boat of Garten, and Spey Valley are among the best off-the-beaten-path destinations Scotland has to offer. Our love for Nairn was previously documented. Entire trips can be booked around Highlands golf and the visitor would be fulfilled.

And to me, the best of Highlands golf—of Scottish golf, of golf period—is found at Brora.

Every player has a bias toward their favorites—what a dull way to go through life without them. Courses that don't need to be the best or most entertaining or thought-provoking, just a place that ripples in the uncharted depths of your soul. Few venues resonate like this James Braid creation, just off the A9 and 20 miles north of Dornoch, hugging the North Sea with no dunes to block the elements, where sheep and hairy coos (the Highland breed of cattle) roam alongside golfers. I'd call it a dream course, but it's better than that: it's real.

The links of the Highlands are not spared from hardships, however. The area is often neglected by pilgrims; instead they kneel at the altar of St Andrews or are drawn to the golf coast of East Lothian with its concentration of championship links. Ayrshire to the west is third among visitors according to numerous tourist boards, with Aberdeen—some 75 miles past St Andrews and 90 minutes by car—considered the outer limit for explorers. With fewer visitors, most Highlands clubs miss the U.S. golfer subsidization that's foundational for Scottish courses. Labor is difficult to come by and retain, the weather shortens the playing seasons while making the links tougher to maintain. Coastal erosion has become an alarming concern; Fortrose & Rosemarkie, which sits on the Chanonry Peninsula that extends into the Moray Firth, has a GoFundMe page to help fortify its links with rock armor, while Golspie is looking into a £2 million project to keep its links from falling into the sea. Many golf clubs dance on the razor's edge of financial ruin, their balance sheets a delicate tightrope walk from season to season, hoping each year's revenue will be just enough to keep the lights on and the gates open when spring returns.

Which is why Brora president Andy Stewart was proud to announce to his fellow members at a season-opening meeting in 2020 that, for the first time in history, the club was projected to end the upcoming year with a surplus.

"The number was 100,000 pounds, which was predicated on 400,000 pounds of visitor green fees, of which I think we probably had £300,000 already booked," Stewart remembers. "Until then, the job of the committee had really been to keep the doors open to try and make the costs match the revenue. We had made an investment in our staff, to make the club more attractive to visitors. Now, we were going to be able to have a proper savings.

"So we were feeling very happy with ourselves, and at this member's meeting, one of the members said, 'Andy, uh, I've got a question. What's this Covid thing that we've just started to hear about?' And I chuckled dismissively and said, 'I don't know what it is, but I'm sure, I'm sure we'll be fine.'"

Three weeks after the meeting, Brora was facing a shortfall of a quarter of a million pounds, and with Scottish shutdown laws, perhaps even worse. On March 24, a brokenhearted Stewart sent a missive to Brora's 600 members, letting them know they were staring down the abyss.

"We need the support of all our members at this time if we are to survive," Stewart. "This is a member-owned golf club and the members will determine whether or not we exist beyond this."

•   •   •

He banked on legacy, loyalty, and morality. Jay Monahan went broke on all three.

In Monahan's defense, he didn't have many moves to make, which is why it's easy to wonder if golf's civil war could have been avoided had the PGA Tour commissioner listened to overtures from the Premier Golf League, the Public Investment Fund and others in the years leading up to the launch of LIV Golf. And there were "others;" in 2021, a group later identified as Silver Lake (a technology funding company) went to the tour with an eight-event team pitch, according to the *New York Post*, with the group promising "to invest $500 million up front to get the concept started and another $500 million to come as the concept gained footing." Silver Lake and the players would own the league, 50/50. In 2023 Phil Mickelson confirmed the pitch on Twitter; it is widely believed Mickelson was also involved with the concept. However, according to the *Post* and Mickelson, chairman of the PGA Tour's policy board Ed Herlihy nixed the idea: "If it's not 100 percent owned and controlled by the PGA Tour, it will be viewed as hostile." Other Silver Lake attempts in 2022 were likewise turned down.

In hindsight, engaging with the Saudi threat earlier might have forestalled the current crisis. However, such a strategy deserves scrutiny, particularly given Mickelson's dubious role. His simultaneous manipulation of both the Tour and the Saudis to create a new league—a chess game played with the same aggression as his approach shots—remains an underexamined aspect of this saga. Moreover, the PGL without PIF funding existed only as a theoretical construct. The suggestion that earlier PIF negotiations would have smoothed the path oversimplifies an intricate dilemma. Accepting Saudi money then—in the wake of a journalist's state-sanctioned murder—would have been as ethically fraught as it is today.

The complexity of the situation defies easy solutions; in the three years since this controversy erupted, no one has presented a convincing alternative strategy for Monahan. But—and this is a big-ass *but*—it's also why Monahan receives over $23 million per year: to make those hard decisions, and his path cost the sport dearly in time, resources, and goodwill that frankly it didn't have. While no perfect solution existed, Monahan's string of miscalculations revealed a leadership void at precisely the moment golf needed decisive guidance.

There was the declaration of victory after Phil's scary-motherfuckers blunder at the 2022 Players Championship, the only thing missing a "Mission Accomplished" banner behind the dais:

"The PGA Tour is moving on. We have too much momentum and too much to accomplish to be consistently distracted by rumors of other golf leagues and their attempts to disrupt our players, our partners, and most importantly our fans from enjoying the Tour and the game we all love so much ... So there is no better place than at the home of the PGA TOUR to reiterate our focus and promise to our fans and our players. Let's move on."

"We are and we always will be focused on legacy, not leverage."

"What's most important is if you look at the PGA TOUR today, and you've heard me say this before, we're going to grow faster over the next 10 years than we have at any other point in our history. Our players have spoken. They are 100 percent behind the PGA TOUR. They have expressed their loyalty and commitment in their own unique ways. In 2021 and 2022, we have 13 title sponsors that are entering new title sponsor agreements. We're secured through the end of next year. At the beginning of this year, we walk into our new media rights agreements with the partners I just mentioned through 2030. We have the backing of all of our partners. We've never been better positioned, and this is real."

There was the announcement banning players after they had already announced their departure to LIV in May 2022, a true *You can't fire me, I quit* situation. There was doing a televised interview with CBS Sports during the 2022 RBC Canadian Open, which coincided with LIV Golf's launch. Monahan, whose confidants referred to as "Hockey Jay" for his toughness in meetings, looked very much like someone who got pushed into the boards. Worse, when asked by CBS's Jim Nantz about a 9/11 advocacy group's statement condemning LIV players for taking the Saudi money, Monahan responded, "I would ask any player who has left or any player who would consider leaving, 'Have you ever had to apologize for being a member of the PGA Tour?'"

He urged his players to wage a public battle for the Tour while he operated behind closed doors, only to cross their loyalty with the clandestine framework agreement months later. His ties with Strategic Sports Group—a Fenway Sports-led venture where his personal and professional connections ran deep—further compromised his position. His response to LIV's emergence proved reactive rather than revolutionary; while the hasty reforms may have temporarily stanched the exodus of players, they revealed a leadership operating in crisis mode rather than from strategic conviction.

Which leads back to that 2022 Players Championship press conference, and though many point to the "moving on" quote as one of his coldest self-owns, to me another remark stands out, when Monahan was asked, "As much as you talk about moving forward, do you still consider this to be a threat, and is there any part of you that still looks over your shoulder?"

"I wake up every day assuming someone is trying to take my lunch. That's the way I operate. That's the way we operate as a team," Monahan said. "The best players in the world have told you how they feel. I mentioned our partners firmly behind this Tour. I see the possibilities for what we are going to become and how we're going to evolve. I see the incredible working relationship we have with our players."

"So long as we focus on the things that we control, which is what I've always tried to do and what we've always tried to do as a team, I think we're going to win, we're going to grow, and I'm not looking over my shoulder, I'm looking forward."

If Monahan believed what he said to be true—and by all accounts, those who work with Monahan call him a good, decent man—this is perhaps his biggest failure.

Banking on legacy as a bulwark against wealth proved catastrophically naïve. The allure of Saudi millions overwhelmed any concern about their source, as evidenced by the exodus of the Tour's most marketable stars. Consider the stark mathematics: six of the top 10 players from the Player Impact Program—Mickelson, DeChambeau, Johnson, Koepka, Rahm, and Watson—defected despite the Tour's efforts to retain them. Most telling was the futile attempt to secure loyalty through bonuses; the Tour's $20 million investment in Mickelson, DeChambeau, and Johnson crumbled against LIV's reported $850 million onslaught. This mass departure created an existential challenge: how does one sell a product when its premier attractions have deemed it inferior?

The financial hemorrhaging extended far beyond lost talent. Multiple sources revealed the Tour burned through $150 million to $200 million on enhanced bonus pools, inflated purses, and legal warfare with LIV before the framework agreement materialized. While Monahan acknowledged to his staff that mounting legal costs had become untenable—even as he and PGA Tour board member Jimmy Dunne worked to maintain the Tour's financial stability through 2027—the truth likely resides somewhere between crisis and solvency. Though inaction wasn't an option, engaging in an unwinnable arms race was a fundamental misreading of the landscape. Having a vision means controlling your destiny, which the tour does not. That lies with the major championships, tournaments that some fans and players believe are the only things that matter. The Tour excels at crafting golf's narratives, developing personalities and providing the theater where careers unfold. Yet LIV demonstrated it could replicate this platform, making World Ranking points—and their pathway to major championships—the Tour's critical advantage. However, it's not the job of Augusta National, the USGA, the R&A, or the PGA of America to clean up this mess, and that the PGA Tour is beholden to them to succeed should be an intervention. Should the majors ever sever their traditional allegiances, the current exodus would pale compared to the potential mass departure. Unless tour leadership conducts an unflinching assessment of its product and value proposition, its greatest threat may not be LIV Golf, but rather its own arrogance and complacency.

A vigilant leader would have recognized the Tour's descent into mediocrity long before crisis struck. Professional golf had devolved into a monotonous parade: an oversaturated schedule featuring interchangeable tournaments, populated by undistinguished players, at forgettable venues. This homogenization of the product alienated even the sport's most devoted followers. The emergence of a rival tour should have served as a catalyst for self-examination rather than an existential threat—competition, after all, often breeds innovation.

While Monahan cannot shoulder sole blame for golf's current conflagration, his role as steward demanded more than passive observation as the flames took hold. Yet in a stunning twist of institutional politics, his position has not only endured but flourished. The January 2024 agreement with Strategic Sports Group, birthing the for-profit PGA Tour Enterprises, saw Monahan emerge as CEO with expanded authority and a coveted policy board vote.

The price of this consolidation of power? The abandonment of the very principle he had demanded his players defend.

• • •

"When you're brought up in Brora, you tend to fall into one of three things: You played golf, you played football, you went to jail," says James Macbeath, head greenskeeper at Brora. "Luckily I only did two of the three."

The town of Brora checks in at 1,200 people, and yes, there is a football (soccer) club: the Brora Rangers of the Highland Football League. With a capacity of 4,000, the Rangers (the equivalent of a semi-pro team in the States) have the second-largest park of any team in the 18-club league. The town's beaches, which are scattered with Jurassic rock, are known as some of the best dolphin-watching spots in the country. But golf is what brings travelers to Brora, and what brings them back.

Five-time Open champion Peter Thomson made a five-hour journey from St Andrews to Brora in the mid-1990s on a caddie's recommendation. After playing, he declared it "the most natural links course in the world"—and it's easy to see why. The course unfolds across untouched farmland, surrounded by Highland hills that fade into the clouds. A serpentine burn weaves through the property, while centuries of sheep seeking shelter have created natural bunker depressions. Few Scottish courses can boast more holes hugging the coastline. Though golf has been played here since the 1890s, James Braid's 1923 redesign, focusing on new tee and green locations, remains largely untouched. At just over 6,100 yards, Brora isn't long, with punitive rough and fescue found only at the links' outer edges. The layout features a single par five, while several par fours tempt players to drive the green. Yet its challenge lies in subtlety and strategy, not brute force. The course's natural defenses are formidable: rolling knolls and rumpled fairways complicate approach shots, while small, undulating greens are maintained at nature's firm consistency. About 50 bunkers, many guarding the putting surfaces, dot the landscape. With no dunes between links and sea, the wind is an ever-present adversary. The par threes offer a masterclass in variety—two requiring long irons, one a mid-iron, and a short-but-devilish test protected by clever bunkering and a tiny target. While beginners won't feel overwhelmed, skilled players expecting to finish in red numbers will quickly come to peace with their arrogance.

Unlike most modern courses, Brora remained true working farmland until 2021, operating under a shared lease between club and farmers that let livestock roam the links freely. The course's only concession to golf's traditional manicuring: modest two-foot electric fences encircling the greens. And yes, for those wondering about the inevitable biological consequences of sharing fairways with cattle and sheep, the local rules mercifully treat animal droppings as casual water, offering free, um, "relief" from these hazards. But the herds and flocks are docile. They'll stand mere feet from you as you address your ball, utterly unimpressed by your new Pro V and far more interested in the tender grass beneath their feet. Their presence—the soft lowing of cattle, the distant bleating of sheep, the rhythmic sound of grazing—creates a symphony unique to Brora. It's golf as it might have been played centuries ago, when the game first took root in Scotland's wild places, where the line between sport and agriculture blurred.

"Wild, isn't it?" remarks Paul Kahn, a fellow visitor with his left palm extended to four hairy cows ahead of us on the 14th hole. "Drop a pin on a map and you'll find man and animal in conflict. Seeing this, can't help to think we're doing it all wrong.

"After all, they were here first."

I only played through Paul, yet on the hole he produced that gem along with this, when hearing I visited one of his go-to pizzerias in Inverness the night before: "If you return, ask for the Pooh Bear. It's a pepperoni pie on top of another pie, with honey in the middle. Only for me and my friends. You're a friend."

Brora's magnetism strikes like a slow-burning revelation rather than a thunderclap, its charm building with the relentless power of an incoming tide. The seduction begins on the journey itself—an hour-plus pilgrimage from Inverness through Highland wilderness, where civilization retreats into memory. You turn off a road barely wider than a cart path into a modest car park, where the clubhouse perches above the putting green and 1st tee. Here, the North Sea isn't just visible—it's an omnipresent force, its salty breath mingling with every swing.

The pro shop staff embodies Scottish hospitality at its finest, their warmth genuine and knowing—they understand you've ventured to experience this sanctuary, and their appreciation runs deep. The course eases you in like a masterful host, offering four opening holes that amuse rather than intimidate. The first presents itself as a potential eagle opportunity, reachable with a well-shaped drive or even a bold 3-wood. The 2nd and 4th holes seduce with delicate wedge approaches, but don't be fooled by this gentle introduction. As the course gradually bares its teeth, the edge is softened by the presence of Highland cattle grazing nearby, their shaggy forms adding to the authenticity of the setting. Then comes the 9th, a 160-yard par-three that appears to shoot into the ocean, as if the green were floating on the horizon where sky meets sea.

The back nine unfolds in the classic out-and-back tradition, and while it may not match the front's theatrical flair, the sea remains your constant companion. Here, the prevailing wind hurts, transforming seemingly modest holes into stern tests. What appeared reachable in two now demands careful calculation and respect. The brilliant bunkering forces precision over power, yet the course never descends into cruelty. It challenges without crushing the spirit. By the time you reach the 120-yard par-three 13th—called "Snake" for the burn that crosses in front of the green twice, with wooden bridges to cross where sheep have laid down for rest and a green is protected by five pot bunkers—you think, "This place is magical." By the time you climb the 16th, convincingly named "Plateau," to reach the 17th tee box, to see the course and livestock and ocean stretching to the horizon, you think, "I don't know if it gets better than this."

There is no equation for how certain golf courses capture our souls, not unlike falling in love. We can intellectually appreciate objective beauty—the architectural brilliance, the sweeping vistas, the strategic challenges. But then there are places that bypass all rational assessment and strike directly at the heart. Just as true love transcends any checklist of ideal qualities, certain courses possess an inexplicable pull that defies conventional evaluation. So when it comes to Brora, yes, I'm predisposed to Braid's design philosophy, but I can name a dozen of his courses that more rigorously test architecture principles. Scotland offers countless stunning landscapes, countless warm welcomes, countless memorable journeys. Honestly, I'm a sucker for road trips. By any measurable metric, Brora might not top the lists. And yet ...

They say extensive travel breeds humility—the more you see, the more you realize how little you truly understand. But sometimes, amid all that uncertainty, you stumble upon absolute truth. So let me speak not from scholarly analysis but from the depths of faith: There is a place where all the elements that make golf transcendent—the land, the game, the spirit—coalesce into something greater than their sum, and it is at Brora.

My perspective may be colored by the pilgrim's romance. The journey to get there, the delicious absence of tee-time battles, the solitude of often having the course to yourself, the landscape that feels plucked from a fairy tale. Yet speak to the locals—those who have watched thousands of sunrises paint the links in morning light, who know every sheep by name—their eyes still sparkle when Brora enters the conversation. To them the club is something sacred, a treasure they simultaneously yearn to share and instinctively protect. It's their eternal secret, hiding in plain sight along the North Sea, known to many but truly understood by few.

"No matter where you're from, you appreciate what you had as a kid," says Malcolm Murray, the head professional at Brora who grew up in the region. "Our childhood courses always mean something. But you go out into the world, and you realize what you had truly was special. You come back and you realize what you had."

"It's funny, we're known for being accessible," Macbeath says. "Suppose it's the Highland way. That's how we naturally are. But then other Highlanders come and provide similar feedback, and you go, Oh, I guess we have something here." Adds Murray: "I think that's been one of our successes. There is little thought about giving good service to visitors, because it's something we innately do. The shop, the maintenance, if you get a drink above [in the bar]; you're not a visitor. For a day, if you're here, you're one of us."

Stewart's love affair with Brora began on holiday visits. Arriving with his family, he found himself increasingly drawn to this remote stretch of Highland coast until, at 40, he surrendered and made it his home. The course and its tight-knit community pulled him deeper into their orbit —first as a member in 2010, then onto the committee five years later, and finally, in 2017, as club president. His day job as a lecturer in business, management, and golf at North Highland College gave him a unique perspective: if Brora could cast such a powerful spell while perpetually scraping by on bare-bones budgets, what heights might it reach with proper funding? As 2020 approached, Stewart dared to dream of unleashing the course's full potential.

Then Covid-19 delivered its cruel twist. What should have been Brora's moment of triumph —a celebration of its 130th anniversary in 2021—suddenly teetered on the edge of becoming its eulogy. Health and safety restrictions forced most of the staff homeward as the club desperately tried to preserve what little remained in its coffers. The operation contracted to a skeletal crew: just Murray, Macbeath, and Tony Gill, the general manager, holding the fort. Stewart, refusing to stand idle, threw himself into the breach as a full-time volunteer.

With the gravity of the situation weighing heavy, Stewart fired off an urgent email to the membership. Just for good measure he broadcasted Brora's plight to social media.

"The post was aimed at members that we had who paid by direct debit. I had anecdotally heard that they were thinking about stopping their payments," Stewart says. "I was a bit furious, and I explained that the golf club was in real difficulty, and that it wasn't my golf club, it was their golf club, and they needed to step up."

Stewart takes a breath, and begins to laugh. "My naïveté was, I remembered that social media posts are not restricted to Brora."

Brora's digital signal echoed across the golf world with unexpected force. Players from Tokyo to Texas, from Sydney to São Paulo, reached out with a singular question: "How can we help?" On its surface, the response might have seemed misplaced—surely, amid a global health crisis unlike anything in living memory, the fate of one Scottish golf course should rank low on humanity's priority list. But such thinking misses a profound truth about human nature: In moments of crisis, when the fog of uncertainty is thickest, we don't just fight for survival. We fight to preserve what makes life worth living.

When word spread that this remote Highland gem was fighting for survival, the golf community responded with the fierce protectiveness of family.

"It was the weirdest market dilemma," Stewart says. "We had demand, but we had nothing to supply. So we sat down, we came up with a range of options. A person wanted to donate £100 then they could have this, 200 pounds that. There were sponsorship opportunities. There were limited life memberships. If anyone wanted to give us £10,000, they could become a platinum member. The benefits of being a platinum member do not come anywhere close to the amount of money that people put in.

"But the very strange thing was that I was involved in lots of email communication with people that wanted to help."

Stewart and the club soon discovered that many donors sought nothing in return. The contributions ranged dramatically, from five-figure sums to modest amounts of just a few pounds, each person giving what they could afford. Some contributors held cherished memories of Brora, while others had never been but knew of its sterling reputation and dreamed of making a visit. Remarkably, many donors had never even heard of Brora, yet they saw in the club a reflection of what made their own golf experiences meaningful. The popular podcast No Laying Up exemplified this spirit, rallying its community to raise enough funds to keep an additional greenkeeper employed who otherwise would have faced furlough.

"It was a blur at the time," Murray recalls. "It was a realization that a lot of people have a great feeling about Brora. It was a great feeling, from many different people. Even those who sent £5, sometimes I think those mean the most."

Macbeath is a raconteur whose eloquence is never in doubt, though he struggles to capture the magnitude of the response—typical of Highlanders, whose harsh living conditions have bred a practical rather than sentimental nature. "I was flabbergasted," Macbeath says. "Humbling. Just very humbling. We have pride in Brora, and clearly many other people do too."

Eight weeks after Stewart's initial post caught fire, the club announced it had raised over £300,000. In facing extinction, Brora revealed its immortal soul.

•   •   •

To understand why Monahan, Dunne, and Herlihy orchestrated the shocking June 6th, 2023 deal with Saudi Arabia, Occam's Razor points to money. Herlihy—a partner and co-chairman of the legal powerhouse Wachtell, Lipton, Rosen & Katz—and Dunne—the vice chairman of the investment banking firm Piper Sandler and golf's premier dealmaker—saw what many others missed: golf's civil war was bleeding the PGA Tour dry. The tour had overextended itself, promising astronomical purses it couldn't sustain while hemorrhaging millions in legal fees from its battle with LIV Golf. In subsequent Congressional testimony, Tour COO Ron Price and Dunne admitted that LIV had "put us on fire" with its unprecedented spending. This revelation came during a Senate Permanent Subcommittee hearing titled "The PGA-LIV Deal: Implications for the Future of Golf and Saudi Arabia's Influence in the United States." Senator Richard Blumenthal voiced what many were thinking: the deal "raises concerns about the Saudi government's role in influencing this effort and the risks posed by a foreign government entity assuming control over a cherished American institution." The full scope of these concerns would soon become clear.

From a pure capital perspective, the deal makes sense—though it also makes the Tour's initial refusal to engage with PIF's partnership overtures indefensible. Business leadership demands clear-eyed pragmatism. The tour was never going to prevail in a war of attrition: a non-profit corporation squaring off against a sovereign wealth fund managing nearly a trillion dollars. That no one at tour headquarters seemed to game out this inevitable conclusion speaks to either staggering ignorance or blinding hubris, and it's hard to say which is more damning. Speaking of financial decisions that strain credulity, Monahan's $5 million raise from 2022 to 2023 (from $18 million to

$23 million) becomes particularly ugly against the backdrop of the Tour's supposed financial distress.

Yet a situation this complex defies single-cause analysis. Money aside, why did the tour capitulate? Many point to fear over the antitrust battle with LIV. At first glance, this seems implausible: The Tour and DP World Tour had prevailed in nearly every early court skirmish against LIV and PIF. Moreover, PIF and Al-Rumayyan's continued refusal to comply with discovery requests had practically guaranteed the Tour's ultimate victory. But sources suggest the tour harbored its own discovery concerns, and even seemingly ironclad cases can unravel in the unpredictable theater of trial. Lost amid the shock of the announcement—and overshadowed by splashier headlines—was perhaps the deal's most crucial provision: within 10 days, all pending litigation between the tour and PIF would vanish, with both parties filing motions to dismiss. No discovery, no mounting legal fees. A clean slate.

A conspiracy theory emerged in the wake of the framework agreement, one worth addressing: Some golf insiders speculated that Augusta National made the deal through Dunne and Herlihy, both club members. The conjecture wasn't entirely baseless. Augusta National had been named in LIV Golf's August 2022 antitrust lawsuit against the PGA Tour, with serious allegations against the club. The lawsuit claimed that chairman Fred Ridley had threatened to withhold Masters invitations from players who joined LIV Golf, and that club officials had collaborated with the tour to "address" the LIV situation. Perhaps most explosively, it alleged that Ridley had directly pressured 2022 Masters participants to avoid the LIV Golf Invitational Series. The club's entanglement deepened with the Department of Justice's antitrust investigation, which expanded beyond Ridley: LIV's January 2023 filings accused Augusta members Condoleezza Rice and Warren Stephens of lobbying the Department of Justice to exclude the club from its probe. Given these circumstances, some theorized that Dunne and Herlihy were Augusta National's covert operatives, deployed to negotiate a deal that would bury these controversies.

But this theory belongs in the realm of social media speculation. Having spent two years investigating Augusta National's inner workings for another story, I can say this with certainty: the club's power, while considerable, operates with far more subtlety and sophistication than such a traceable intervention would suggest. The very transparency of Dunne and Herlihy's involvement argues against Augusta National's hand in the matter.

As of writing this book in late 2024—a full 18 months after the framework agreement—the secretive nature of the negotiations remains unexplained. When pressed repeatedly by Congress, Dunne offered only that the discussions were "fragile," prompting Senator Blumenthal's pointed observation: "Most executives and CEOs are legally and morally obligated to keep board[s] of directors informed." The Tour's subsequent messaging only deepened the mystery. Monahan's CNBC interview claim about "taking a competitor off the board" backfired in a Department of Justice antitrust investigation, while Dunne's varying accounts to multiple media outlets—the Associated Press, *USA Today*, Golf Channel, and *Sports Illustrated*—produced a contradictory narrative. Even basic terminology became contentious: Tour officials chastised media outlets for describing the deal as a "merger," despite using that very word in their own announcement.

The question of leadership proved equally murky. Tour officials, including Dunne and Monahan, insisted they retained control through board votes and organizational structure, while PIF and LIV circles portrayed Al-Rumayyan as the new power broker. Players were hurt; they had been enlisted not just to reject LIV but to secure the Tour's very existence, only to discover they'd been fighting for an institution that would ultimately embrace their supposed enemy. The deal's structural flaws, which legal experts predicted would doom it in its original form, forced the tour to later seek private equity partners—further evidence of its hasty conception. Yet these governance and planning failures pale in comparison to the Tour's most egregious misstep: its treatment of September 11 victims' families.

After Monahan's defiant response– "Have you ever had to apologize for being a member of the PGA Tour?"—to comments that

9/11 advocacy groups made in condemning LIV players, the tour quietly began channeling resources to a coalition called "9/11 Justice," a grassroots movement made up of the survivors, first responders, family members of those lost, and all volunteers and lower Manhattan residents, students and workers who are now suffering fatal illnesses due to their exposure to Ground Zero. Clout—a public affairs firm that the Tour had been working during golf's civil war—also started assisting 9/11 Justice. "We didn't pay anything" except for some incidentals, 9/11 Justice president Brett Eagleson told Politico in a September 2024 interview. In a related note, 9/11 Justice protested several of LIV's first events in the summer of 2022, the demonstrations taking place outside the tournaments' gates.

Then came June 6, 2023. The same families who had stood outside LIV's gates watched in disbelief as Monahan appeared on CNBC alongside Al-Rumayyan. More stunning was the revelation that Dunne—who had lost dozens of colleagues and friends on 9/11 when the south tower of the World Trade Center fell—had orchestrated the deal. The betrayal cut deeper than any business arrangement; it was a moral collapse that left wounds far rawer than those it sought to heal.

"It's a gut punch to wake up and read the headlines today that the PGA has turned its back on the 9/11 community and decided to get in bed with the kingdom," said Terry Strada, national chair of 9/11 Families United, in a statement. Eagleson said the tour proceeded to "ghost" him. In a twist, Clout publicly disavowed itself from the tour and stayed with 9/11 Justice. As for why the announcement took place on CNBC, documents released during the Congressional hearing revealed the Tour was seeking a "softball" interview to control the deal's narrative. "They are also taking all of the recent lessons from the Boeing Saudi announcements, which went extremely well in D.C., nationally, and internationally," an internal tour document read. "The worst thing we can do is have naysayers lead the chorus."

The callousness of using victims as political pawns belied a new reality for the Tour. The thing about engaging with a regime involved with, well, all the entanglements that can be found in a three-second Google search of that regime is that those issues are not in the past. That was made clear early in 2024, when Al-Rumayyan was accused of carrying out instructions from Saudi Arabia Crown Prince Mohammed bin Salman with "malicious intent" in a lawsuit filed in Canada. The lawsuit alleges that a former Saudi intelligence officer's children have been unlawfully detained by the Saudi government. It is a mere allegation, but it's also not the first of its kind, and it's worth noting that the accuser is Dr. Saad Aljabri, who has been praised by American, English, and Canadian intelligence agencies for his work in helping combat violent threats against citizens.

The outcry over sportswashing transcended concerns about human rights violations or Khashoggi's murder—it was about the specter of future atrocities, and golf's complicity in them. Each new headline would demand an answer from a sport that had surrendered its autonomy. To call PIF merely a "partner" obscures the reality, because with PIF possibly investing billions in the tour, you better believe they are going to have a significant voice in how the tour is run and where it's going.

Once the framework agreement was signed, the PGA Tour found itself trapped. PIF demonstrated its willingness to reignite hostilities by signing Rahm months after the supposed peace deal (though the Tour's courtship of private equity could be seen as the first shot across the bow). Anyone who believes PIF or the Saudi Kingdom would gracefully accept defeat fundamentally misunderstands their nature. The notion that LIV's backers would simply retreat if the Tour aligned exclusively with private equity isn't just naïve—it's potentially catastrophic.

Beyond the immediate strategic blunder, the June 6th deal did something far more damaging: it legitimized dealing with the adversary. The Tour's moral authority evaporated the moment it embraced the very money it had condemned its players for considering, and the agreement's secretive nature alienated many of the Tour's staunchest defenders. With Monahan already admitting to an unsustainable business model, and sponsors beginning their exodus, whatever moral high ground the tour once claimed has crumbled beneath its feet.

The Al-Rumayyan allegations shattered any illusion that ethical concerns could be neatly compartmentalized. They proved that moral questions in golf's civil war never truly fade—they merely lurk beneath the surface, waiting to erupt. June 6th and the subsequent revelations delivered body blows to the sport's integrity, and the punches came from all directions: from those who claimed to be guardians of the game, from those who promised to protect it, from those we trusted to steward it. This crisis was forged in the furnace of naked ambition, and not just by the headline-grabbing defectors like Rahm, Mickelson, Johnson, Koepka, and DeChambeau who gave LIV its initial legitimacy. Tour players who saw the schism as a chance to leverage better paydays share in the culpability. While some stood firm, risking careers and reputations to guard principles larger than themselves, others among golf's most influential figures chose personal enrichment over the sport's well-being.

Professional golf surrendered to exhaustion. Its fans, media, and leaders were so weary of war they accepted peace at any price. The moral outrage that erupted on June 6th dissipated into summer's haze, replaced by fatigue. Golf's audience had no stomach to revisit a conflict that had consumed 18 months of discourse, especially when confronted with the murky complexities of global economics and the endless chorus of whataboutism. This is sportswashing's true power: it doesn't defeat resistance—it wears you down until you're numb.

The PGA Tour escaped extinction; job accomplished, I suppose. But I go back to the 2024 Players, as Monahan took the stage to address the media for his annual "State of the Tour" address. "Can you believe he's still standing, that he survived this?" a fellow writer whispered. Survived? *Survived?* Technically, yes. Despite calls for his resignation from policy board members weeks earlier, Monahan emerged as head of the for-profit Enterprises division, ascending to become America's second-highest-paid sports executive. He preserved his power, his position, his control.

But *standing*, I'm not so sure. When you abandon your principles and betray those who preserved them, you may remain upright, but you've lost the right to stand tall. There's no point in surviving a crisis if we lose everything that matters along the way. It's surrender, disguised as victory.

•   •   •

Stewart and Brora had once viewed a projected £400,000 in visitor fees for 2020 as a windfall. By the end of 2024, they had nearly doubled that sum over the summer. "For a wee golf course from the Highlands, it's definitely doing well," Stewart says with a characteristic mix of pride and humility. Having peered into the abyss and pulled back from its edge, Brora now has room to breathe. The club's 2021 purchase of its land secured greater autonomy over its future. Staff has grown to 25 workers in 2024, with plans to add five more positions in 2025. Yet while they're eager to move forward, Stewart and the members remain acutely aware of how their salvation came about.

"The love that the world showed Brora at the time, it was quite a humbling thing to be a part of," Stewart reflects. "I know I love my course, but it seems like a lot of people love it too. Or saw that we loved it, and did what they could to make sure that love wasn't lost."

Looking ahead, the club is considering practical improvements: a new irrigation system for the greens, replacement sheds for the maintenance crew, expanded merchandise offerings in the pro shop. The board is still exploring ways to enhance visitor experiences while preserving the club's essence. For Brora, this prosperity represents uncharted territory, but its heart remains unchanged.

"What brings people here is the connection they feel with the place, so whatever we do we have to make sure that remains, more money or not," Murray says. "We made it through and survived and are wiser, stronger for it. But you can't lose your identity."

CHAPTER 5

Noise

Carradale • *"Golf, but Louder"* • *Bots* •
Machrihanish and Dunaverty • *War of words*

He gingerly steps out of a utility cart to say hello, his gait hobbled by injuries and time but functional through stubborn will, and the calluses felt from his extended handshake reveal a physicality and strength earned by honest labor. His broad shoulders and shaved head cast an imposing figure, although a smile can be discerned underneath his white mustache. "I hope you're enjoying Carradale," Robert Strang says. "It's a wee course, but it's ours, and we're proud of it." He speaks in the collective first-person, nodding to the three members I'm with at Carradale, a whimsically unrestrained links on the east coast of the Kintyre Peninsula. In truth, we are playing on his work.

Originally a fisherman, Robert has been caretaker of Carradale for the last 39 years after he came ashore to spend more time with his family. He has been the head man on staff since he took the job; for most of that stretch he's been the only man on staff, and the club's lone employee. His son Gareth lends a hand when he's off duty as a fire department watch commander, and several members will help with the various odd jobs that come with golf course conservation. But mostly what you see at Carradale—which has been called "the most sporting nine in Scotland"—is fulfillment of Robert's doing. If he's not mowing Robert can be found cutting back shrubs and gorse that lie at the heart of the property, or in his shed fixing maintenance equipment. He's also the public-facing representative of the club, the one who collects fees if he's around the clubhouse. If he's not there to take your cash there's an honesty box by the 1st tee, and he'll make sure to track you down at some point during your trek to bestow an official welcome.

Robert is a bit of a local legend. Aside from his duties at the course, he's been a volunteer firefighter at Carradale Community Fire Station since 1987 and became its captain in 1996. This area of the country belongs to the Argyll and Bute local government; out of the 32 councils in Scotland, Argyll and Bute is the second largest at 6,907 square kilometers (the state size equivalent of Delaware), but it is 27th in population at 88,000 and those residents are scattered throughout the region. The lack of population density puts the utmost importance on volunteer departments to carry out civil service. An advocate of improving processes, Robert was instrumental in engineering a program that changed the way on-call firefighters are deployed to emergencies across Argyll that's saved countless lives. For his efforts, Robert was awarded the King's Fire Service Medal by Charles III in early 2024, becoming one of the first Scottish natives to win the award since His Majesty took the throne in 2022.

If that wasn't enough, he is an elected representative as the area's councilor, organizing and executing projects to better the Carradale community; the Carradale paper of record estimates he's raised over £50,000 for national and local charities. In most parts of the world Robert would be called a renaissance man, polymath, a real mensch. Here, he is known simply as a Scotsman.

"Robert is a true pillar of the community," says club secretary Gordon Abernathy. "Little seems to happen in Carradale without his involvement."

The reach of a single person like Robert is remarkable, yet it also reflects the intimate nature of life in this corner of Scotland. Even by Argyll standards, the village of Carradale is small, less than 600 people. The club's clubhouse serves as the social fulcrum of town, its main room furnished simply with a scattering of tables and chairs. Here, locals gather for tea and biscuits, or to greet the occasional golfer drawn to these links. Two locker rooms and a diminutive kitchen with sparse storage complete the humble interior. The building's modesty is intentional; there's no reason to be inside, not with what's outside the club's doors.

The club was founded in 1906 and laid out by its founding members. The opening ceremony was consecrated by a local pastor who remarked, "This was a course for which beauty and scenery and bracing air was not to be surpassed in all Scotland and which for riskiness and hazard in losing balls it would command all their skill." The opening hole makes the reverend's words seem like hyperbole. It's a 165-yard par three that goes straight up hill—a nasty, good hole, albeit far from extraordinary. It's not until reaching the green at the crest of the hill that the minister's blessing rings out. Before you is a vista of headland and pasture that disappears into the Kilbrannan Sound, its waters greeted on the other side by the green meadows of the scared Isle of Arran, a beautiful piece of rock with a number of courses that's accessible only by ferry. I'm hesitant to call it one of the best views in golf, except I can't think of any better.

If Carradale was this panorama and nothing else it would be worth the trip (£20 for nine, £30 for the day). Instead what follows is a links that's riotously original and inimitably fun.

The 2nd, with its tee box next to the 1st green on top of the world, is a 340-yard par four that unfurls to the sea, requiring an approach that goes slightly back uphill over a stone wall. The 3rd, a 230-yard par three, is a blind tee shot played through the ruins of a castle. The 4th has a wonderful little tee situated above the water that requires a

40-yard walk through gorse; depending on the wind, the 270-yard par four is reachable or a pain to reach in two. The 5th is another par four under 300 yards. But the green—I kid you not—is roughly the size of a living room couch and can only be hit by tossing your approach on the hill past the green and letting it roll down the backstop. The 6th is listed at 310 yards yet requires a drive over a rocky bay and plenty of gorse with an elevated punch-bowl green with the peninsula's mountains in the background. A long par three (185 yards) heads back to the sound, and anything chunked will be lost to the gorse. The front nine ends with a 210-yard uphill par three that plays like a four, and a 290-yard par four that plays like a three. You walk off thankful that a place like Carradale exists and furious it is so far from home.

"You can't master Carradale. You know where to go and what to do. The ground is too firm and unforgiving to oblige," says Paul Davis, a former amateur standout in the Scottish ranks who lives half the year in town. "It's a shorty, yes, by distance. It requires every club in your bag, and rarely do you play a hole the same way."

The £30 daily pass might be the best deal in golf, given the tee sheet never has more than 10 or so groups on the day. Annual membership for an adult is £210 (with 50 percent off reciprocals at local clubs like Machrihanish, Dunaverty, and Tarbert), and the club provides free golf to children. The only downside we can surmise is the lack of a bar, yet there are usually several communal bottles of Glen Scotia single malt in the cabinets for those needing a taste.

"Hidden gem" has become a cliché, and in our interconnected age, true undiscovered treasures are increasingly rare. ... but if any club warrants the distinction, it's Carradale. While almost wholly positive, the title carries a bittersweet undertone. It's impossible to overstate Carradale's remoteness; though it's just a 15-minute helicopter ride from the west mainland of Scotland, by car it's a four-hour drive. Most visitors are merely passing through to Campbeltown or the celebrated Machrihanish links 40 minutes south, and the lack of amenities and humble numbers on the score card (par 32, 2,293 yards) don't make it appealing to visitors. Robert's position as sole salaried employee reflects a deeper challenge: finding staff in an aging community growing smaller with each passing season.

Yet the very elements that make Carradale seemingly inhospitable transform it into a sanctuary. Its isolation and expansive views truly give the visitor a chance to unplug, while the course itself seems to have emerged organically from the landscape, though maintained to perfection.

After my round, I sought out Robert, eager to express my gratitude and enthusiasm, and admittedly curious to learn more about him. I'd been cautioned to tread carefully; he was wrestling with personal difficulties, and members were protective of his well-being. I found him by the fence between the 1st tee and car park, and as I effused about my newfound passion for his course, he nodded with the quiet acknowledgment of one who has long known what others are just discovering.

"We are lucky, aren't we?," Robert says. "This place means very much to me. I'm here every day, and I don't take it for granted. Sometimes I will stop and look to see how beautiful it is. There is peace here. Where everything can fade away."

•   •   •

In its first two years, LIV Golf fell short of most of its grand predictions and promises, yet it delivered emphatically on one slogan: "Golf, but louder." Because the ensuing noise was deafening.

While the civil war in golf played out across multiple theaters— courtrooms, boardrooms, locker rooms—LIV's most significant impact came through its disruption of golf's discourse. Though LIV supporters might claim victory in shaping the narrative of this schism (a term itself grown tiresome through overuse), the reality is that chaos—not control—has defined these past three years. The emergence of LIV—its present form, its potential future, and the rippling consequences of its existence—created a gravitational force so powerful that the sport found itself unable to escape its pull. It wasn't merely a topic of conversation; it became the conversation. In this light, the destabilization of golf's ecosystem, precisely what LIV promised to achieve, must be acknowledged as a victory for the insurgent force and a significant setback for the established order.

Part of this was by design, and we know this because LIV has told as much. One of the companies enlisted by LIV for promotion of its launch was End Product, a social-first sports content studio in England. Incredibly, End Product published its strategy in the lead-up to the Saudi circuit's first events, which remains publicly available on its website under the related work tab:

"The most controversial launch of a tournament in sports history"? Probably. New shotgun starts, team leaderboards, no cuts and huge prize money. There was a lot for golf fans to wrap their heads around. That's why our social strategy was all about bringing the noise. Create so much coverage that people couldn't help but find out what the fuss was all about.

This context illuminates Norman's brazen proclamations about a league that—mere weeks before its launch—had yet to publicly reveal its roster. It explains why defector after defector undermined their credibility with transparent propaganda masquerading as conviction. Critics dismissed them as snake oil salesmen, but skilled manipulators know their true task isn't to convince you of a miracle cure—it's to instill doubt that your current situation needs remedying. The whole charade was transparently absurd, yet as philosopher George Costanza sagely observed, "It's not a lie if you believe it."

Speaking of manufactured *noise*, the phenomenon of "LIV bots" demands attention. This umbrella term emerged to describe social media accounts whose devotion to the fledgling league transcended mere fandom into the realm of parody. In the wake of LIV's debut, these accounts gained notoriety for their combination of rumor-mongering, zealous cheerleading, deliberate misinformation, and targeted harassment of PGA Tour players and media perceived as Tour loyalists. The artifice became comically apparent when LIV's initial broadcasts highlighted supportive tweets from accounts that—upon cursory investigation—had been created simultaneously with the league's June 2022 launch. Yet beneath this veneer of absurdity lies a more troubling reality about these accounts' true nature and purpose.

A bot is an automated software application that operates without human intervention, and when deployed en masse, these programs constitute a bot farm. While such farms serve legitimate purposes—search engines use them for web indexing, and websites employ them to monitor performance metrics—they also present significant cybersecurity risks, enabling fraud and system manipulation. Over the past decade and a half, these digital armies have increasingly been weaponized to distort social media discourse and propagate misinformation. Their operators create countless fake accounts across platforms like Facebook, Twitter, and Reddit, programming them to like posts, share content, and follow other users in coordinated campaigns. While political actors frequently deploy these tools, unethical marketing firms also harness them to undermine competitors or artificially boost their clients' visibility. A parallel industry has emerged in the form of click farms, where human workers are paid to manually interact with online content—clicking ads, posting comments, and engaging with social media. When these human networks focus on swaying political opinion, they become known as "troll farms," representing a troubling convergence of technological automation and human manipulation in our digital discourse.

The impact of digital manipulation ranges from seemingly trivial to profoundly serious. Consider the 2018 fan campaign demanding Warner Bros. release Zack Snyder's version of *Justice League* after the director's departure from the project. While this pressure ultimately led to a four-hour recut of the film in 2021, a subsequent *Rolling Stone* investigation revealed that the movement had been amplified by bots and inauthentic accounts. More than 20 individuals involved with both versions of the film came forward, most suggesting that Snyder himself had orchestrated the manipulation campaign. Yet such entertainment industry machinations pale in comparison to state-sponsored digital warfare. A 2017 Freedom House study revealed that nearly half of the 65 countries examined employed digital armies to disseminate propaganda and silence critics. The threat continues to evolve:

in 2024, the U.S. Department of Justice dismantled a sophisticated Russian operation that used artificial intelligence to generate convincing American personas on social media, leveraging these false identities to promote Kremlin objectives—from justifying the Ukraine invasion to inflaming domestic political tensions. China's approach is equally calculated but more overt: their "50 Cent Party" (unrelated to the hip-hop artist) comprises government employees paid to promote Communist Party messaging and derail critical online discussions.

An alleged past abuser of bot farm practice? Saudia Arabia.

Online attackers have been part of a broad effort dictated by Crown Prince Mohammed bin Salman and his close advisers to silence critics both inside Saudi Arabia and abroad. Before his death, Jamal Khashoggi was a common victim of this harassment. Another high-profile target was actress Amber Heard when she was locked in a contentious defamation trial with actor Johnny Depp. During the trial, Heard was made out to be an abusive and manipulative liar by mainstream news and social media. Following the trial, investigative journalist Alexi Mostrous obtained over one million tweets from Depp "fan" accounts, and discovered that, according to one data scientist, around half of those tweets were from inauthentic sources with Saudi ties. Why go after Heard? Several Depp movies were financed by Saudi money, Depp was an advocate at a Saudi film festival, and Depp is reportedly friends with MBS.

As our own exercise, I reached out to several social media data analysts and web security platforms that protect against bot farms to get an idea of the LIV bot scope, granting them anonymity given the sensitivity of the subject. Using the four-month timeframe of May 31, 2022 (when LIV announced its initial field) to October 30, 2022 (the date of the inaugural season finale), the answers ranged anywhere from 16 percent to 71 percent of Facebook and Twitter accounts and posts with LIV, LIV Golf, or a LIV Golf team name were artificial or manipulated, with the average hovering around 34 percent. One-third of all that noise, fake. "Factor in the engagement against what we can see versus what has been reported," one analyst said, referencing LIV's poor viewership and YouTube ratings, "it may be higher."

It's unclear what, or who, was behind the campaign, only that there was no doubt it was a coordinated effort.

These digital operatives serve multiple, insidious purposes beyond merely promoting LIV Golf. They work systematically to undermine the PGA Tour's credibility, tarnish its players' reputations, and degrade its product. Their tactics range from straightforward criticism to manufacturing chaos through calculated deception. In one notable instance, several players were forced to address "rumors" of their imminent departure to LIV—rumors that originated from a dormant account that had suddenly awakened after nine years of silence to develop an inexplicable passion for professional golf. Bot farms also engage in targeted harassment campaigns; according to DataDome, a cybersecurity firm specializing in bot protection, most users remain oblivious when they're engaging with these artificial antagonists. Perhaps most disturbing is their strategy of recruiting disaffected individuals who feel alienated from mainstream society, particularly those in incel communities. This manipulation creates a volatile dynamic: while the initial spark may be artificial, the resulting community of aggrieved, confrontational followers poses a very real threat to civil discourse. While it's possible that LIV Golf does not have direct influence over the affair, what's undeniable is that the bot operations occurred and continue to various degrees into 2025.

Not all LIV's digital warriors were synthetic constructs. The golf schism presented an irresistible opportunity for anonymous figures to reinvent themselves as industry "insiders," and with LIV desperate for legitimacy, these self-proclaimed experts found themselves suddenly elevated to authority figures. Their price for occasional genuine scoops was unwavering advocacy that bordered on indoctrination. Consider this gem from "LIV Golf Insider": "Pat Perez is a top 10 golfer in the world right now. Nobody can deny that. Glad he's playing at #LIVGolf so everyone can see his talent. The whole world watches LIV Golf." This about a player who had languished at 132nd in his PGA Tour swan song.

The chorus was amplified by those harboring deep-seated resentment toward mainstream media and celebrity culture, who seized upon the professional game's civil war as a proxy battle against their perceived oppressors. Add to this volatile mix the internet's natural population of contrarians and trolls, eternally eager for keyboard combat, and LIV achieved its goal of flooding the zone with noise. The digital cacophony wasn't merely background static—it corroded golf's foundations, transforming reasonable disagreement into tribal warfare and nuanced discussion into absolutist declarations. What LIV hadn't anticipated was the players themselves igniting an inferno, as defectors and tour loyalists alike abandoned their customary restraint to trade salvos in an increasingly bitter war of words. What began as controlled propaganda mutated into an acid rain of accusations and counter accusations, turning a business and ideological dispute into a scorched-earth campaign.

• • •

I've offended the bartender. His craft, his sensibilities, his faith in his fellow man. Despite five weeks immersed in Scotland's pub culture and growing confidence in navigating drink orders, I've clearly transgressed some unwritten rule; when he asks, "Excuse me?," in a voice an octave below his natural register, it's not because he's misheard—it's an opportunity for my redemption. On any other day, I would have yielded. I'm pathologically agreeable, the type who stays silent when served the wrong meal, who apologizes when someone else mangles my name. But tonight, I plant my flag: "A shot of 15-year single malt Glen Scotia, mixed with a shot of amaretto, cherries if you have them, on the rocks." The bartender complies, making no effort to mask—perhaps deliberately showcasing—his anguish.

Context is crucial here. Campbeltown, population 4,600, once crowned itself the whisky capital of the world, home to 30 proud distilleries. The town's proximity to the sea imparts a salty, briny element to the drink, and master distillers grasped this "maritime" character would pair well with robust and smoky hints of flavor. This combination of organic influence and human imagination created something wholly distinct among whiskey across the world. The deep natural harbor made distribution effortless, transforming the spirit into both economic cornerstone and cultural touchstone. Which makes my order roughly equivalent to showing up at a Green Bay Packers tailgate with a tofu burger and quinoa salad.

Still, I refuse to wear the shame the bartender has sentenced on me. The golf that day had been too good: a double helping of Scottish links perfection, beginning at Machrihanish and closing at Dunaverty, leaving me too elated to repent.

Machrihanish demands more than just a casual commitment—it requires the kind of planning usually reserved for expeditions. The course lies at the terminus of the Kintyre Peninsula, splendidly isolated at Scotland's southwestern edge, where nothing stands between you and the Atlantic save for Northern Ireland, its coastline shimmering like a mirage across the North Channel on clear mornings. The gulf stream's influence here works quiet magic, wrapping the peninsula in a microclimate that defies Scottish stereotype—winters stay mild, and even in the depths of January, the ancient marram grass rarely freezes. The land itself is pure, fertile soil supporting hardy vegetation and pristine dunes sculpted by centuries of Atlantic winds. But the journey tests your resolve: three and a half hours from Glasgow, a drive that winds through highlands and along lochs and hugs the coast, which, while beautiful, demands your full attention on narrow, winding tarmac. With golf meccas in St Andrews and East Lothian calling from easier locations, you do question whether Machrihanish truly warrants such a pilgrimage. Scotland's golfing riches are so abundant that driving to this remote outpost might seem like gilding the lily.

And then you make the drive in, pull into the car park, step into the salt-laden air and see the first hole, and you understand why Old Tom Morris proclaimed, "The Almighty must have had golf in his eye when he made this place."

Machrihanish was founded in 1876 and called Kintyre Golf Club. Three years later, Morris was brought in to extend the links to 18 holes and redesign the layout. There were slight modifications done during World War I and again when the Royal Air Force built a runway next door, but Morris' layout is largely what you play today. For most of its existence, Machrihanish was a secret unto the Scottish, and the links' remoteness made it a mystery to even most of its countrymen. But the course gained global attention thanks to Michael Bamberger's *To The Linksland* (1992), a book that has a rightful claim to the best golf work ever produced. Bamberger fell in love with this place; in the new clubhouse, which was built after a fire consumed the original building in 2018, one of Bamberger's quotes hangs above the new bar-restaurant: "If I were allowed to play only one course the rest of my life, Machrihanish would be the place." Golf's writer laureate does not waste words and only writes what he means; you don't have to look hard to see what he found.

Jack Nicklaus crowned the opening hole at Machrihanish as golf's finest first act, a pronouncement eternalized on a weathered plaque near the tee box where the Golden Bear's words still catch the Atlantic light. The hole demands an opening shot across a sweep of beach, its fairway tracing a diagonal line along the coastline from right to left like a rapier slash across the landscape. While there's generous room to play conservatively to the right, that supposed bailout is guarded by four hungry bunkers, and even a safe drive could leave you facing an approach of 220 yards or more to a green that offers little forgiveness. The coastline-hugging design presents a temptation to cut the corner, but the beach claims countless balls from those whose ambition exceeded execution, or those who simply caught the dreaded hook. The second shot provides no relief; while most links courses reward a running approach short of the green, two bunkers stand ready to swallow anything slightly off-line or lacking conviction. If the Almighty did design this land for golf, He clearly wasn't interested in padding the scorecard with easy pars. This is Machrihanish's handshake: firm, uncompromising, unforgettable.

While the opening hole tends to dominate conversations, the subsequent eight holes weave a spell every bit as enchanting. Like its northeastern cousin Cruden Bay, Machrihanish winds through the dunes in a tango with the natural landscape. Beyond the closely cropped fairways and greens, the land remains as untamed. There is no standard green design; some are sunk in punchbowls, while others are on raised plateaus or flattened dune tops. It's an upshot of Morris using the ground at his reach. The 3rd hole is a superb par four, a blind tee shot to a green guarded by four bunkers and the contours of the beach dunes, with mountains on the western side of the island of Jura waving in the distance. This is followed by a short par three with cavernous bunkers and a tabletop green, with the 5th a mean dogleg to a punchbowl putting surface. The next three holes form Machrihanish's gauntlet: two par fours under 350 yards bracketing a muscular 430-yarder at the 7th, each one proof that length alone doesn't define difficulty. The 9th offers a moment of mercy—but only if you find the fairway—before you walk to the 10th tee with the dawning realization that you've just experienced what might be the finest opening nine holes in golf.

If Machrihanish has an Achilles' heel, it's that the inward nine lives in the shadow of its predecessor. To call it a "letdown" would be uncharitable—"comedown" better captures the transition, like the gentle descent from a soaring high. The back nine still holds several good holes, and it remains unmistakably cut from the same Scottish cloth as the front. In fact, its more subdued character offers something the dramatic opening stretch cannot: a clearer window into how the environment shaped this game. Here, Morris's genius reveals itself in subtle but straightforward ways, letting the land speak for itself. The club's pro, Jennie Dunn, mentions they maintain the links with fewer than five on its grounds crew—partly a function of their remote location, but more significantly a philosophical choice. While modern four-wheeled mowers now traverse the fairways, the links remains mostly unchanged from what players would have experienced a century ago, its contours and character preserved like a living museum to the golden age.

I played Machrihanish alone that morning. My only interactions came from two foursomes who waved me through, their silhouettes briefly breaking the horizon before disappearing into dunes. Initially, this solitude seemed at odds with my mission to understand what these places and this game mean to their people. But as the round unfolded beneath the vast Scottish sky, the isolation revealed itself as a gift—a chance to decompress after the intensity of Open week with its 14-hour workdays, to fully absorb the privilege of walking this ancient links, to take inventory of my journey so far and appreciate that I had the chance to do it.

To suggest that golf can serve as a thruway to inner peace risks sounding mawkish, except to those who have experienced this truth. The spectrum ranges widely: from profound spiritual awakening to a few precious hours of mental clarity, unburdened by professional pressures and life's complications, to simply those fleeting moments when our phones stay silent in our pockets, their endless notifications temporarily muted. This pursuit can manifest anywhere—at your local Thursday men's league, on the driving range, during those minutes of anticipation on the 1st tee, in the simple act of taking practice swings in your backyard. Yet certain places seem specifically designed forces greater than us to facilitate these flashes of transcendence. Machrihanish, with its wild beauty and detachment, its sublime links and connection to the earth, its ability to suspend time itself, reveals itself as something more than a golf course to be played—Machrihanish is not a course to be played but a presence to be felt, as primitive as the tide crashing against the sands below.

And yet, as remarkable as it is—one that wholly justifies the journey to it—what grabbed me like Machrihanish grabbed Bamberger was 15 minutes down the road.

•　　•　　•

I had been warned about Dunaverty. I had met with one of my editors, Jay Coffin, and his family in St Andrews a few weeks back, and when I relayed my itinerary, his face lit up like the Rockefeller Christmas tree when he heard Dunaverty. "It's the damndest thing. You see these mobile homes and camp site on the 2nd and 3rd holes, on this cliffside land that, if it were in America, would be worth millions of millions of dollars. So you think, *Wow, great view,*" Jay told me.

"Except the view gets better and better over the next 12 holes, and the course is a blast."

Even by Scottish standards, the welcome is unassuming. The clubhouse is spartan and fitted with an honesty box for times when the register is unmanned. That day, a woman behind the counter, deep in her novel, barely lifted her eyes as she gestured toward the 1st tee, assuring me the course was mine alone. The opening stretch seemed pleasant enough—a gentle 320-yard par four climbing uphill, followed by a stout par three and a tempting drivable par four framed by Jay's promised mobile park and coastal panorama. The 4th, a 177-yard par three, dips to a green tucked mysteriously behind a hillock, invisible from the tee. In totality, holes that ranged from very cool to very good to very neat.

But then you ascend from the 4th green to the 5th tee, perched above a burn that tumbles into the sea, and suddenly you're transported to a realm so sublime that it feels less discovered than revealed, less played than experienced, and you know with certainty that while you'll eventually have to leave, a piece of your heart will forever reside in this corner of Scotland.

From the 5th tee to the 10th green you embark on a trek from sea level to a hill called Mount Zion, with the shore and its beaches serving as both backdrop and hazard. The 5th is a 257-yard par four, slightly uphill but drivable albeit with rough on the left and beach on the right. The 6th is a 245-yard par three, guarded by mounds that are meaner than Catholic school nuns. The joke at Dunaverty is that the 6th is a harder par four as a three than the previous hole's par four. The 7th is a charming mid-iron par three to an elongated saucer green that seems to float between sea and sky. The 8th demands precision, your drive threading between dunes to a fairway that bends left toward the ocean like a final embrace. The 9th tumbles downhill, another drivable par four culminating in a punchbowl green that cradles a well-struck tee shot. Behind the 10th—a short but demanding par three to a green split by nature's own design—sits a simple wooden bench. It might be placed there to contemplate the magnificent panorama: ocean to your left, golf course unfurling before and right, the Kintyre

Peninsula tapering into infinity, and Northern Ireland's coastline sketched against the horizon. Or perhaps it's merely to catch your breath after scaling what feels like a Scottish Everest.

After the 11th—yet another drivable par four that plunges back to earth like a roller coaster's final descent—the course veers inland, maintaining its links character through ever-present wind and distant sea views while acquiring a pastoral charm from the gentle bleating of sheep and lowing of cattle in neighboring fields. The 17th crosses the burn once more, a house's driveway bizarrely but perfectly bisecting the space between hazard and green. The closing hole feels almost apologetic, suggesting Dunaverty's architects (local members, as at Carradale) had exhausted their canvas after seventeen strokes of genius. No matter. The raw numbers tell little of this place: 4,800 yards, seven par threes, a modest par 66. Yet—and I write this with the weight of having experienced golf's most celebrated grounds—I struggle to recall any course that delivers such pure, unadulterated joy as Dunaverty.

"This was my second time playing Dunaverty. I took a day trip out there on my own, on a whim, one weekday in March," says Andy Lightbody, a veterinary surgeon that lives in the central belt of Scotland near Stirling. "I came off the course that day and immediately told the rest of my friends that it was the most fun I'd ever had on a golf course."

"When playing it again in July it was great to see the others enjoy it just as much. I feel it's a course that you can fully relax on and just try something a bit different with your shots-something I struggle to do when I'm playing on some of the 'bigger and better' courses. I'm a big fan of blind tee shots and that anticipation of what you're going to find as you step over the top of hill, so I'm well catered for at Dunaverty. It also helps that after five holes I was still under par for the first time in my life. That didn't last too much longer."

Yes, Dunaverty remains hidden, as secret as a confession whispered in church. Most Scottish visitors have never heard its name, and Campbeltown stands alone in offering anything beyond basic lodging and early-evening silence. That this place dwells in such obscurity represents a systematic failure of the game. You cannot truly call yourself a golf romantic until you've listened to what Dunaverty has to say.

So after Carradale's charms the day before, after Machrihanish's natural majesty, and now Dunaverty's spell ... you're damn right I ordered that 15-year Glen Scotia with amaretto and cherries on the rocks. This peculiar drink, like this forgotten bend of Scottish golf, belongs to the category of treasures that reward the curious and the brave—those willing to venture to discover something extraordinary, who understand they know what others don't.

• • •

The day after New Year's—on the windswept pineapple fields of Maui overlooking the Pacific—is not where you'd expect an admission of existential concerns. Reaching the Tour's season-opening event at Kapalua is the closest thing to a working vacation players get during the year. It's a limited field, historically reserved for those who have won in the previous season (albeit now expanded to include any non-winners who finished inside the top 50 in the Tour's season-long points list), a no-cut event with a guaranteed six-figure payday. There aren't many fans, and most of the players' families spend the week at the beach. If you've made it to Hawaii, you're at the top of your profession, and the system is working in your favor. That was especially true for Mackenzie Hughes. The Canadian came out on the bumpy side of hard math when he finished 51st in the FedEx Cup Playoffs last August in the first campaign where the top 50 earned a trip into the PGA Tour's signature events. It was a particularly cruel fate given the 33-year-old was inside the magic number every week of the 2023 season except the one where it mattered most, in Memphis, a T-58 finish dropping him from 47th to outside the fire. Yet Hughes was in Kapalua thanks to a rules provision that retroactively moved him in after Jon Rahm signed with LIV, proving that while some subjective version of meritocracy may reign in golf, bureaucracy isn't far behind. Now that Hughes was here, he had plenty to say.

A few weeks prior to Hawaii, Hughes went viral for a Twitter thread following Rahm's defection. "Men's professional golf is in a sad place. The direction it's headed right now isn't healthy or good for the sport," Hughes wrote. "And I know many of you are upset with the recent developments—I would be too." In Kapalua's media center—which was really an underground cart garage—my friend, *Golf* magazine writer Dylan Dethier, asked Hughes about that tweet. Hughes had a lot to say that day—about greed, selfishness, short-sightedness. At the crux of his opinion was that the advent of LIV and the Tour's response seemed to be solely about money, and that focus, he worried, made fans question if players "love playing golf anymore."

"They don't know where certain guys are playing, and there's spats between the LIV and the PGA Tour, and it's not unified in any way, shape or form," Hughes said. "There's negotiations going on that are unclear, they have been dragged on for a long time. The fan just wants to watch golf. I think you watch sports for an escape from other nonsense, but I think golf has brought a lot of nonsense onto its plate, and now you don't get just golf, you get a lot of other stuff going on. It's a circus."

The emergence of LIV Golf transformed professional golf into something akin to a reality show—those guilty pleasure programs that are simultaneously entertaining, mesmerizing, and appeal to our baser instincts. The resulting schism in professional golf played out like an episode of "The Real Housewives," complete with melodrama, self-sabotage, unintentional comedy, shady business deals, and larger-than-life personalities. There's a reason these series are called guilty pleasures; we know they are high-octane garbage, the emptiest of calories. Which, occasionally, is fine! However, when such conflict becomes the main course, it makes you sluggish and depressed, raises your blood pressure and clogs your heart. It becomes poison. Precisely what happened with the endless stream of complaints and accusations hurled between both sides.

While the war of words was exhausting, it paled in comparison to the fundamental issues at play: LIV golfers becoming representatives of an oppressive regime, and their subsequent legal battles with their former tour over contractual disputes. Most reasonable fans understood the problematic nature of these actions without requiring constant reminders. What truly alienated fans wasn't just the underlying ethical concerns, but the incessant sniping from both camps. While real life is often filled with such discord, sports traditionally offered an escape where performance, not rhetoric, determined outcomes. The existential nature of this conflict, however, overshadowed the actual competition, inverting what should have mattered most in professional golf.

LIV Golf's representatives generated a disproportionate share of the controversy. Their repetitive claims of being "not politicians," complaints about facing consequences for their choices, and deployment of bad faith arguments created an exhausting narrative. The situation was further complicated by players like Brooks Koepka and Jon Rahm, who publicly dismissed LIV Golf only to later join its ranks. The hypocrisy and contradictions speak for themselves.

1. Weeks after LIV Golf's launch, Ian Poulter was booed on the 1st tee at the Old Course on Thursday of the 150th Open and proceeded to duck-hook his drive almost out-of-bounds. Afterward, Poulter was adamant what we heard didn't happen: "I actually thought I had a great reception on the 1st tee, to be honest," Poulter insisted. "All I heard was clapping." When asked again about the boos, Poulter remarked, "Oh, my gosh, I have heard not one heckle. In three weeks, I've heard nothing." When again pressed on the matter, Poulter said he heard nothing negative. "You lot can write whatever you like about being heckled and booing. You've walked 18 holes. Did you hear one comment? You can write whatever you like."

2. Bryson comparing the PGA Tour-LIV battle to competing pizzerias in an interview with Tucker Carlson, which I needed to put in print in case the internet is ever wiped out to ensure this isn't lost to history: "It's so weird, because it's like—let's use this as a reference. I heard this earlier this week. You have a pizza shop that's been in existence for 50 years and all the customers go to it and it's a great product. All of a sudden, a new pizza shop opens up, right? And they start paying the customers to come eat at their place, and that pizza is

potentially a little bit better of a pizza, right? And then, all of a sudden, that original pizza house goes, if you go over there, we're banning you from ever coming back to our pizza shop. What's wrong with that economic model?" Honestly, no notes, perfect analogy.

3. Pat Perez sounding off on the Tour during his LIV introduction: "They didn't listen to the players. Somehow, the tour, they keep talking about 'Oh yea, we work for you, we work for the players.' But it's the opposite. Seems like we work for them. We don't have a say in anything." This from a guy who made nearly $30 million in his career over 20 years despite just one top 10 finish in a major and three wins, two of which came in the fall season.

A tempest of sound and fury, signifying nothing.

The PGA Tour players, however, were equally culpable in the complaint department. Davis Love III, serving as the American Presidents Cup captain, went as far as threatening a player boycott if LIV defectors were allowed to return. Billy Horschel took issue with LIV players competing in the European Tour's premier events, while Charley Hoffman weaponized a controversial ruling to suggest why players might "jump ship" to another tour. James Hahn's persistent criticism of the Tour was so severe it became surprising he hadn't departed himself.

When the Tour implemented rapid changes to retain its stars, a contingent of lower-ranked players voiced their displeasure at being overlooked. This culminated in a 2023 letter to the policy board from 21 current and former Tour players demanding transparency about ongoing PIF negotiations. The petition, however, carried limited weight—among its signatories, only two ranked within the Official World Golf Ranking's top 150, making it roughly equivalent to interns questioning the CEO's strategy.

Some criticisms did carry merit. Scottie Scheffler raised a valid point questioning why Tour players should bear responsibility for cleaning up LIV's mess. Rising stars Viktor Hovland and Xander Schauffele boldly challenged Tour leadership and Commissioner Monahan directly. Hovland criticized management's treatment of players as mere labor rather than members, emphasizing that "without the players, there is nothing." Schauffele pointedly noted after the June 6th bombshell that Monahan had "a long way to go to gain the trust of the membership." Meanwhile, Rory McIlroy found himself repeatedly defending the Tour's position against LIV in weekly press conferences. Yet the endless volleys of criticism from both sides ultimately became tiresome and drowned out the more substantial conversations that needed to occur. The focus shifted from golf itself to an exhausting war of words that served neither the sport nor its fans.

Worse, the only noise we needed to hear, we didn't.

Jay Monahan's silence from LIV's launch through the framework agreement left players fighting a battle that shouldn't have been theirs. His behind-the-scenes maneuvering generated its own kind of noise—questions about what exactly the Tour was doing, particularly in the months following the framework agreement. The Tour's opacity regarding negotiations left the sport in an uncomfortable limbo. (More troubling still was the suggestion that negotiations weren't actually taking place.) With concrete information scarce, the golf world could only rely on increasingly caustic rhetoric, creating a toxic atmosphere that Schauffele captured perfectly: "I haven't really put a whole lot of thought, honestly, into what would make me feel good about this whole thing."

The media's role deserves scrutiny as well. While we had an obligation to report on legitimate grievances and keep the public informed, questions remain about whether every complaint deserved amplification. Perhaps some of the drama would have been better left unreported, wrapped metaphorically in a diaper rather than broadcast to the masses.

As Hughes noted, people turn to sports as a refuge from the very things golf had come to embody—political maneuvering, power plays, and endless squabbling. The consequences became clear in 2024: PGA Tour viewership declined while LIV Golf failed to attract a meaningful audience, even as recreational golf enjoyed unprecedented popularity. Perhaps most galling was that neither organization seemed to acknowledge—much less care about—how their war of attrition was affecting their most important stakeholders: the fans.

Hughes' observations in Maui struck such a chord because they high-lighted a brutal irony: in their battle for golf's future, both tours were alienating the very audience they needed to survive.

●   ●   ●

My wife and I depart Campbeltown for Oban, before heading back to Inverness, with five hours of Scottish highway stretching before us. But the direct route—the A83 parkway hugging the west coast—won't do. Instead, we veer onto the B842, a serpentine whisper of a road that will add precious minutes to our journey. I explain this detour to my wife, knowing the timestamp it puts on our day, but also knowing its necessity.

Heading north, we retrace our steps from the past few days. Carradale's parking lot materializes before us, a humble patch of earth that could barely host a dinner party's worth of cars. We're alone here, our solitude extending to the clubhouse where I quietly deposit a bottle of Glen Scotia double-cask single malt. My wife insists on seeing what drew me here, despite the protest her knee will surely raise—a Division I athlete's career cut short by injury, then betrayed by a failed surgery. The first hill looms like a test, but she's determined. She's seen how this place transformed me, and love compels us to share the landmarks of our hearts. What we talked about and felt, that is for us.

What is for you is what I saw, which was Robert in the distance on the 6th green. He had equipment laying on one of the hills that comprised the punch bowl green, yet his gaze is to the east, to the waters and Arran. Shortly after my initial visit I discovered Robert had lost his wife, right before he received his accommodation from King Charles, and it doesn't take much of a Google search to discover his pain. Dumb as it sounds, I wanted to go over and somehow let him know that I knew, that I was hurting for this man I had just met. But I remained where I stood. He was a man at work, finding his own piece of peace in a world gone quiet.

CHAPTER 6

Power

Farmer vs. The Developer • Trump's courses •
A powerful ally • R&A and the Open

He is more than a farmer. Michael Forbes is also a part-time mechanic and has labored in quarries most of his adult life, and he's the last of a dying breed of salmon netters off the Aberdeenshire coast. Yet history will remember Forbes as a farmer who wouldn't sell his farmland.

It's not much, 23 acres of pasture that lay a stone's throw from where the sea meets the dunes of Balmedie. The property wears its age openly; there are half a dozen outbuildings covered in rusted iron, and weathered agriculture equipment scattered throughout the yard. Forbes grew up on this property, first as a teenager before purchasing the estate himself in the 1980s. When his father died, he moved his mother Molly back on the farm; Molly turned down his invitation, wanting some independence, and instead parked a mobile-home steps away from Michael's house. For more than five decades, this has been Forbes' anchor. For the past 20 years, it's been his battlefield.

The developer first came knocking around 2005. He was building a golf resort on the surrounding area—450-room hotel, 950 holiday apartments, 36 golf villas, and 500 houses, along with two championship link courses—and the developer wanted Forbes' grounds for the project. The initial offer was £350,000, in addition to a £50,000 yearly stipend for an unspecified job at the resort. Forbes met the developer on the Balmedie beach and shook his hand, yet Forbes was turned off by the encounter. "All he spoke about was money and [himself]," Forbes recounted to *People Magazine* in 2020. "I said to myself 'Who the hell is this?'"

The proposals from the developer grew, at one point reaching to £1 million with an additional £350,000 set aside for a new house. Forbes wouldn't budge. Part of it was principle, which only deepened as the conflict ensued, although over the years Forbes asserted his steadfastness is tied to the land itself. "To me, you can't put a price on it. I just won't sell, and he knows that," Forbes said in 2007, according to the *Guardian*. "All my family came from here. My grandfather fished down here, my father fished down here and my uncles fished down here, and I'm last in line and will see it out. I'm right in the middle, you see. I wasn't against the golf course from the start. I was helping him out and repairing their roads and things, and then they just went mental because I wouldn't sell. They said they would make my life a misery, which they are."

The developer was used to getting his way, always, and took his argument to the media. In a press conference to raise support for his project, the developer went after Forbes. "The sad thing is that a gentleman who has a small area near the site ... the area is in total disrepair," the developer said in the fall of 2007. "Take a look at how badly maintained the piece of property is: it's disgusting. Rusty tractors, rusty oil cans. I actually asked him, 'Are you doing this on purpose to try and make it look bad, so I have to pay some more money?'"

In the coming years, the attacks would intensity. "[Forbes] has always been dirty, sloppy and unkempt in his personal appearance and demeanor [sic]. He is a loser who is seriously damaging the image of both Aberdeenshire and his great country," the developer said in a 2009 statement. "His property is a disgusting blight on the community and an environmental hazard, with leaking oil containers, rusted shacks and abandoned vehicles dumped everywhere. It is a very poor image and representation for the world to see of Scotland."

The pressure campaign began quietly at first. After Forbes stood his ground, mysterious complaints started appearing. Health inspectors showed up unannounced at his gate, demanding to investigate reports of environmental violations. Animal welfare officers came to probe allegations of cruelty—allegations that evaporated upon inspection. Even the police arrived one day, questioning him about an unlicensed shotgun he'd never owned. Then came the lawyers' letters, each envelope landing like a stone on his doorstep. They accused Forbes of vandalism against the developer's property—charges he vehemently denied. The hostilities escalated when Forbes discovered his water supply cut off, the pipe leading to his home mysteriously severed during the developer's excavation work. Though the company denied any wrongdoing, Forbes saw it as another attempt to flush him out. The developer pushed for a compulsory purchase order to forcibly remove Forbes from the property.

For his part, Forbes protested the development. A campaign emerged where hundreds bought small interests in Forbes' land, making a title transfer harder should it ever come to pass. Forbes spray-painted "NO GOLF COURSE" on his barn. Forbes became a celebrity for not backing down.

The developer's plan was ultimately approved by the local council, and 18 holes of pristine links golf emerged from the Aberdeen coastline in 2012. The course is perennially listed as one of Scotland's best tracks—*Golf Digest* has it listed at No. 10 in the country—and its dunescapes are as dramatic as it gets in the sport. In October 2024, the developer's company announced the second links at the site would be open for play in 2025.

However, the Aberdeen project has been controversial. The promised paradise of luxury hotels, homes, and villas never materialized, save for a modest 21-room boutique hotel. More damaging was the 2018 assessment by Scottish Natural Heritage, which revealed the course's construction had severely damaged protected dunes—a site of special scientific interest sacrificed for sport. The project's reputation suffered another blow in 2024 when the developer was found liable for financial fraud, including false valuation of the Aberdeenshire property, resulting in a $354.8 million disgorgement order (currently under appeal). The disillusionment reached inside the project itself when Neil Hobday, the developer's former consultant project director, confessed to the BBC that he was "hoodwinked and ashamed that I fell for it and Scotland fell for it."

The battle between Forbes and the developer gained worldwide attention. The developer—known for his bombastic style, riches and fame—against the blue-collar, no-nonsense Forbes. Their fight spurred protests, demonstrations, documentaries TV specials. Life imitated art as Forbes' story eerily paralleled the 1983 film *Local Hero*, where a Scottish beachcomber thwarts an American corporation's plans to buy out his coastal village.

As of writing, Forbes, now in his 70s, remains at his Balmedie property, and has become a folk hero, a symbol of resilience in the face of corporate power. A portrait of Forbes and his wife reenacting the famous "American Gothic" painting (the oft-parodied sketch of man in overalls and suit jacket carrying a pitchfork, evoking rural 20th-century Americana) is held in the National Galleries of Scotland collection. In 2012, Forbes was named "Top Scot" at the Glenfiddich Spirit of Scotland Awards, an honor voted by the public. In retaliation, the developer said he was banning Glenfiddich from his golf properties.

In 2024, the developer won the United States presidency for the second time.

•   •   •

Don't worry … we are not venturing into politics. That is our proverbial rough, where reasonable discourse has given way to tribal shouting matches and reflexive dismissals. Yet Donald Trump is among the central characters in golf's civil war. His role, his influence, is as unavoidable as it is complex. To write Trump out of this story would be to leave an essential chapter untold. So when we talk about Trump, it's how his actions and ambitions have shaped the sport's landscape, including the schism and Scottish golf.

Trump's emergence as a golf power broker grew from an unlikely intersection: celebrity and soil. His prominence on pro-am circuits, fueled by the mainstream success of "The Apprentice," granted him access to the sport's elite players and decision-makers. But it was his real estate empire that secured his place in golf's hierarchy.

The story began in 1999 with a single course in West Palm Beach, Florida. Over the next 25 years, Trump would assemble a portfolio of 18 properties, each acquisition expanding his influence in the game. Until his 2016 presidential bid, Trump was widely regarded as golf's white knight in America—a businessman willing to invest in the sport while others retreated. During a period when thousands of courses were closing their doors and participation numbers were dropping, Trump was doubling down on golf's future.

His impact was measurable. His courses became showcases of championship golf, with a few ranking among the finest in their area codes. The Trump portfolio hosted prestigious events like the LPGA Tour Championship (2001-2008), which made history when it offered women's golf's first million-dollar winner's purse in 2006, and the PGA Tour brought its WGC-Cadillac Championship and Puerto Rico Open to Trump venues. The USGA entrusted his courses with testing the next generation through its junior championships. This wasn't just collecting golf courses, it was amassing influence in a sport that prides itself on tradition and exclusivity. Trump's courses became more than just places to play; they were statements of ambition, luxury, and power.

For all his golf properties and events, Trump hungered for the sport's ultimate crown jewels: major championships. They are more than just tournaments; they are coronations, of the venues and those associated with them. It's the sport's equivalent of becoming a "made man." His quest to host a major seemed improbable, yet the gates to golf's inner sanctum began to open. The first win came in 2012 when the USGA selected Trump National Bedminster to host the 2017 U.S. Women's Open. Two years later, an even grander victory: the PGA of America awarded its PGA Championship to the same New Jersey venue for 2022. Trump's grandest coup was still to come. In 2014, he acquired Scotland's Turnberry Resort, a mystical links that had already hosted four Open Championships with a fifth Open visiting in 2020 considered a formality. Trump had transformed himself from a wealthy golf enthusiast into one of the sport's most potent forces.

The unraveling began a year later, with a golden escalator ride.

On June 16, 2015, Trump's presidential announcement speech shattered the delicate balance between his golf empire and the professional game. His inflammatory remarks about Mexican immigrants—characterizing them as criminals, drug dealers, and rapists, with the qualified afterthought that "some, I assume, are good people"—sent shockwaves through corporate America. NBC, Macy's, and Univision swiftly severed their relationships with Trump's business empire. Pro golf's leadership and key players—true to their cautious, reserved natures—initially responded with silence. The sport had perfected the art of avoiding controversy, treating political storms like weather delays, something to wait out in the clubhouse. But Trump forced the issue. In a late June interview with Tim Rosaforte on Golf Channel, Trump attempted to draft the entire golf world as his allies. "I've had tremendous support from the golf world, because they all know I'm right," Trump declared, adding, "I've been great to golf. I've been investing while everybody else was fleeing."

This presumption of solidarity forced golf's governing bodies out of their traditional reticence. In an unprecedented move, they issued a joint statement distancing themselves from Trump's claims:

> "In response to Mr. Trump's comments about the golf industry 'knowing he is right' in regards to his recent statements about Mexican immigrants, we feel compelled to clarify that those remarks do not reflect the views of our organizations.

> "While the LPGA, PGA of America, PGA Tour and USGA do not usually comment on presidential politics,

Mr. Trump's comments are inconsistent with our strong
commitment to an inclusive and welcoming environment
in the game of golf."

The first to pull the plug was the PGA of America, relocating
(before canceling) its Grand Slam of Golf exhibition mere weeks after
Trump's campaign launch. Yet the organization maintained a tenta-
tive embrace, keeping its 2017 Senior PGA and 2022 PGA Championship at Trump venues—a hesitation that would later prove costly. The
following year, Cadillac did not renew its sponsorship of the WGC,
and the Tour moved the tournament from Trump Doral to Mexico
City. Then PGA Tour commissioner Tim Finchem said the move was
not a political exercise "in any way, shape or form," although given the
Tour had been at Doral for the past 55 years, the timing was suspect.
Trump responded in characteristically caustic fashion: "I hope they
have kidnapping insurance."

The Women's Open at Turnberry became golf's next flashpoint.
Six weeks after Trump's inflammatory remarks, the championship
proceeded as scheduled, with then-LPGA commissioner Mike Whan
caught in an impossible position. Trump, sensing vulnerability, publicly challenged Whan to move the event while trumpeting his contributions to women's golf, though neither Whan nor the LPGA actually
controlled the championship, which then fell under the Ladies Golf
Union's purview. Trump turned the championship into his personal
stage show. His helicopter descended during the first round like a
modern-day chariot, and he commandeered attention with a press
conference at the hotel. When questioned about the R&A potentially withdrawing future Opens from Turnberry, Trump's response
dripped with confidence: "Doesn't matter to me. I have to do what's
right."

Turns out it did matter. When reports surfaced that the R&A
would indeed bypass Turnberry for future Opens, the decision felt
inevitable. Trump had given golf's oldest governing body the justification they'd been seeking.

In Europe, particularly Britain, Trump's polarizing nature tilts decisively in one direction. A Statistica survey showed just 14 percent of Britons approved of Trump after his presidency, though this antipathy had deep roots predating both his political career and his battles with Forbes. The disconnect runs deeper than politics; it cuts to the heart of cultural identity. Trump's signature style—his bombast, his unrelenting self-promotion, his bigger-is-better worldview—stands in stark contrast to traditional Scottish sensibilities. Where Scots prize understatement and quiet dignity, Trump broadcasts his greatness from metaphorical mountaintops. The Scottish preference for modest competence over loud confidence isn't a weakness; it's a societal cornerstone. Think of it as two opposing philosophies: the Scots speak softly and carry a big stick; Trump insists his stick is the biggest in history, whether he's holding one or not.

This chasm found its perfect metaphor in the coat of arms controversy. In 2008, as Trump courted Scottish approval for his Aberdeen project, he adorned promotional materials with what he claimed was the Trump family crest: an ornate design featuring a gold floral pattern, a helmeted shield bearing three lions and two chevronels. It was meant to legitimize his Scottish connections through his mother's heritage. There was just one glaring problem: the Trump family had no official coat of arms. The design was revealed to be an almost exact copy of the Marjorie Merriweather Post family crest, the previous owner of Trump's Mar-a-Lago resort. The only significant alteration? The Latin word "Integritas" (meaning, *integrity*) had been replaced with "TRUMP." While he successfully trademarked this appropriated heraldry in America, he ran headlong into British law, where assuming another family's coat of arms is illegal, a protection of heritage that dates back centuries.

The coat of arms controversy proved a harbinger of Trump's Scottish misadventures. His battle against offshore wind turbines near his Aberdeen course escalated into a diplomatic incident. After threatening Scotland's prime minister that the country would become "a third world wasteland that global investors will avoid," Trump found himself before Parliament. His testimony became instant political theater.

Asked for evidence that wind farms would destroy tourism, Trump replied with characteristic bravado: "Well, first of all, I am the evidence. I'm more of an expert than the people you'd like me to hire... I am considered a world-class expert in tourism." The response drew derisive laughter from Parliament members. Trump's subsequent lawsuit against the government ended in defeat, with him bearing their legal costs.

The controversies multiplied. Environmentalists decried the Aberdeen course's impact on protected dunes. Critics pointed out the cognitive dissonance between Trump's public dismissal of climate change as a "hoax" and his Irish golf resort's application for a sea wall, which cited global warming as its justification. His prolonged battle with Forbes, the quintessential Scottish everyman, painted Trump as a bullying outsider unable to comprehend local values.

These episodes cast a long shadow over his Turnberry acquisition. To the R&A's old guard, Trump's purchase looked less like stewardship and more like an attempt to buy golf's most prestigious trophy, the claret jug itself. The R&A's membership, accurately stereotyped as traditional, dignified, and attention-averse, found themselves increasingly uncomfortable with their unwanted association. Their discomfort was compounded by a streak of old-world skepticism about an American hosting their championship, particularly one who seemed to embody every trait they disdained. Trump's presidential campaign rhetoric in 2015 finally gave the R&A their exit strategy. Reports quietly circulated that Turnberry would remain off the Open rota until the organization could be assured the focus would remain on golf rather than the course's controversial owner. It was a diplomatically worded exile that spoke volumes about the collision between Trump's grandiose style and golf's most traditional institution.

The R&A initially proved to be an aberration. After Trump's stunning 2016 election victory, professional golf largely fell into step with the new president. The parade to his properties began almost immediately: Tiger Woods, Rory McIlroy, Ernie Els, and Lexi Thompson all made trips to play rounds with the president-elect. This allegiance wasn't surprising; golf's American fanbase runs deeply conservative, with a 2023 Sportico.com poll revealing golf's Republican following exceeded even NASCAR and UFC, and only NCAA football and Major League Baseball claimed more right-leaning audiences. Jack Nicklaus, the sport's most decorated champion with 18 major titles, had supported Trump early in the campaign.

The USGA maintained its commitment to host the 2017 U.S. Women's Open at Trump Bedminster in northern New Jersey, where the president made a conspicuous appearance during championship week. Later that year, Trump celebrated with the victorious American team at the Presidents Cup at Liberty National, embodying golf's embrace of its most powerful patron. Though his frequent golf outings drew the same criticism Barack Obama had faced, and questions swirled about lobbyists and foreign interests buying access through Trump's golf properties, his relationship with the professional game remained largely stable throughout his first term.

That took a major turn following the attack on the United States Capitol by Trump supporters on January 6, 2021 after Trump's 2020 election defeat. Four days after the insurrection, the PGA of America announced it would no longer hold its 2022 PGA Championship at Bedminster. "The PGA of America Board of Directors voted tonight to exercise the right to terminate the agreement to play the 2022 PGA Championship at Trump Bedminster," said Jim Richerson, president of the PGA of America, in a statement. "It has become clear that conducting the PGA Championship at Trump Bedminster would be detrimental to the PGA of America brand and would put at risk the PGA's ability to deliver on many programs and sustain the longevity of our mission." In supreme irony, the day after the insurrection, Trump awarded the Medal of Freedom to two golfers: Gary Player and Annika Sorenstam.

Turnberry remained in exile. The major championships Trump had pursued with such determination, the crown jewels he thought were finally his, had slipped through his grasp. The very establishment he had worked decades to join, spending billions to build and buy his way into their ranks, had turned its back on him.

But in golf's civil war, alliances shift. While the sport's traditional powers had closed their doors, another faction saw opportunity in Trump's fall from grace. A group that didn't just welcome his polarizing presence—they were counting on it.

• • •

The relationship between Saudi Arabia and Trump is brazenly transactional. Even as Trump's reputation deteriorated, Saudi Arabia viewed him as a valuable political asset, calculating that his potential return to the presidency merited cultivation. For Trump, LIV Golf proved a fortuitous lifeline after golf's establishment institutions—the R&A, PGA of America, and PGA Tour—severed ties. The Saudi-backed venture not only brought its tournaments to his properties with ridiculous financial compensation, but also provided the legitimacy in professional golf he desperately craved.

LIV Golf secured Trump's backing before it had even announced its player roster, incorporating his Bedminster course as one of eight venues in its inaugural 2022 series. Within a month, Trump Doral was designated as the season finale host, and by the following year, a third Trump property near Washington, D.C. joined the rotation. This alliance was hardly unexpected, given Trump's history with Saudi Arabia. During his presidency, Trump maintained an extraordinarily close relationship with Crown Prince Mohammed bin Salman, taking actions that drew criticism even from within Republican ranks. His controversial decisions included:

- Endorsing a blockade of Qatar (*New York Times*, June 6, 2017),
- Resuming arms sales that Obama had suspended over civilian casualties in Yemen (*Washington Post*, March 8, 2017),
- Supporting MBS's power consolidation through the purge of Saudi officials (*New Yorker*, November 6, 2017),

- Vetoing congressional efforts to end U.S. involvement in the Saudi-led Yemen campaign (*New York Times*, April 16, 2019), and
- Excluding Saudi Arabia from a U.S. list of child soldier recruiters, despite State Department recommendations (Reuters, June 18, 2019).

In the aftermath of Jamal Khashoggi's murder, Trump stood firmly with Saudi Arabia, declaring them "a great ally in our very important fight against Iran." This relationship's durability extended beyond his presidency, exemplified by Trump's son-in-law and former senior aide, Jared Kushner, receiving a reported $2 billion investment from the Saudi sovereign wealth fund for his equity firm, according to the *New York Times*.

While the American golf establishment recoiled from LIV Golf's Saudi connections, the venture gained credibility through its association with a recent U.S. president whose influence remained substantial among his base. The catalyst for the partnership runs much deeper. Saudi Arabia did a math no one else wanted to calculate in a post-January 6th world.

The Trump-LIV Golf alliance is sportswashing in its purest form. While Trump's golf properties boast legitimate credentials for hosting big-time tournaments, their architectural and competitive merits are incidental to Saudi Arabia's goals. Instead, this partnership is soft power diplomacy at work—leveraging sports to forge bonds between state-aligned entities and, crucially for Saudi Arabia, securing de facto legitimacy among roughly half of America's electorate. "Trump is an idol to his supporters," explains one LIV insider. "Brandel Chamblee and Golf Channel can denounce Saudi Arabia relentlessly, but how can Trump loyalists view Saudi Arabia as problematic when Trump himself embraces them so openly?"

In researching the subject for the book, multiple sources involved in LIV Golf's 2022 launch revealed to me that Saudi backing for Trump hinged entirely on his continued political influence. This commitment faced an early stress test when Trump-endorsed candidates suffered widespread defeats in the 2022 midterms. Combined with mounting legal challenges to both his presidency and personal dealings, internal discussions questioned whether maintaining Trump ties best served the kingdom's strategic interests. Three key factors ultimately cemented the partnership's continuation. First was Trump's early advocacy when LIV faced widespread skepticism. Second was the Saudi sovereign wealth fund's astute reading of the Republican presidential field. While some GOP voices championed Florida Governor Ron DeSantis as the presumptive nominee—and thus a potentially valuable alliance—PIF's senior leadership maintained that Trump would dominate any primary contest. Their assessment proved prescient when DeSantis's campaign collapsed in the Republican primaries. Third was the declining public approval of President Joe Biden's administration. As one former consultant put it: "The directive from above never wavered: Stay the course with Trump."

While Trump's embrace of LIV Golf could be dismissed as opportunistic desperation, his understanding of the venture's potential proved more sophisticated than many realized. In an interview with journalist Michael Bamberger during what should have been Trump's 2022 PGA Championship at Southern Hills, Trump demonstrated a grasp of dynamics that LIV Golf's opponents fatally misread:

"Here's the thing," Trump said [about LIV]. "You could take a rich guy and start a tour and lose $100 million for a couple of years. Every rich guy I know, I don't care how rich, including me after a couple of years, will say, 'Well, that's enough of that stuff.'

"And you sort of saw that on the Nike Tour where you've had about 10 different sponsors over the years, because sponsors got tired of losing money. Right? But Saudi Arabia loves golf. The top guys there love golf. I know them very well and they're very good people, the people that are involved. Five years ago they didn't know anything about golf. They're incredibly wanting to do this and they're willing to spend, they have unlimited pockets, Michael. Unlimited pockets. Right?"

The bet paid off. In 2024, Trump won the United States presidency and, for the first time, captured the popular vote—a feat he hadn't achieved in his previous two campaigns. Following years of tension with the Biden administration, the Saudis now had an ally back in the White House, and—technically—a business partner. An absolute, unequivocal win, right?

•   •   •

Phil Mickelson walked the 18th fairway at LIV Golf's 2022 event at Trump Bedminster beneath a canopy of artificial noise—dance music thundering from towering speakers that loomed over the green. Despite his controversial Saudi comments made months prior, Mickelson remained one of golf's most magnetic personalities, particularly in the New York area where the galleries had long embraced him as their own despite his West Coast origins. Yet on this Saturday afternoon in 2022, the six-time major champion had become a mere supporting actor. Barely a wedge shot away, Trump held court on a veranda, drawing the day's largest crowd as he orchestrated chants of "Four more years!" The scene laid bare LIV Golf's true dynamics—a former U.S. president commandeering attention from one of golf's most celebrated figures. The only cheer louder came from the 18th green a short time later, when a hype-man began firing tee-shirts from a cannon.

The third LIV Golf event at Trump's Bedminster estate defied categorization as a sporting competition—it was, unmistakably, a political rally masquerading as a golf tournament. Trump's gravitational pull proved inescapable: after playing Thursday's pro-am with DeChambeau and Johnson, he transformed the grounds into his personal stage. His golf cart cavalcade crisscrossed the course Friday and Saturday, with an entourage orbiting his command post near the 16th tee. The tournament's façade cracked further when Trump interrupted active play to stride onto the tee box Friday. Saturday brought Georgia Congresswoman Marjorie Taylor Greene—known for indulging in conspiracy theories and who months before had spoken at a fringe conference with ties to white nationalists, according to CBS News—into his circle. The spectators abandoned any pretense of following golf, instead trailing Trump's procession and leaving the actual competitors to play in near solitude. The atmosphere crackled with political electricity: chants of Trump's name mingled with anti-Biden rhetoric. One of my lasting memories of that weekend was a woman wearing a white shirt that had "Stick to Sports" in blue lettering joining a chorus of "LOCK THEM UP!" as players approached the tee—the message's self-contradiction apparently lost in her fervor.

Yes, this was Trump's domain. He has his backers and his backers' enthusiasm was undeniable. But the transformation of a professional golf tournament into a political theatre bordered on the surreal. Imagine the absurdity of Biden commandeering an NBA timeout to lambast his opponents, or "Meet the Press" hijacking the Super Bowl halftime show to debate Middle Eastern politics. It's hard to imagine because it would never happen, because that is unserious conduct for a serious league. This was not golf; This was something else entirely—raw propaganda operating without restraint or self-awareness. Being there felt like stepping into an alternate reality—a dystopian mutation of sports where the familiar rhythms and rituals of golf had been replaced by something more disquieting, leaving behind a haunting sense that we had crossed a threshold of no return.

LIV Golf had promised to revolutionize the sport with spectacle. Even LIV's architects had to wonder if this scene represented what they wanted … or perdition.

•   •   •

The R&A's principled stance on Turnberry deserves recognition—a position that has remained unshakeable since the 2015 Women's Open, defying both pressure and time.

"Major championships should focus purely on the golf course and the competitors battling upon it," R&A CEO Martin Slumbers declared in a November 2024 Golf Channel interview. "We cannot allow external media noise to overshadow what remains the original and most historic championship in golf. The tournament's integrity demands that golf alone commands the spotlight."

This wasn't a new proclamation but rather a reaffirmation of the R&A's unwavering position, one Slumbers had articulated when pressed about Turnberry during his annual press conference at The Open. "Our stance remains clear," he continued. "Until we can be certain the conversation will center exclusively on golf, Turnberry will not host our events. While this situation persists, we maintain our position—though circumstances may evolve in the years ahead."

Trump's public stance on Turnberry's Open prospects has oscillated wildly—from reluctant acceptance to claiming at LIV's 2022 finale that the R&A was eager to return. The R&A's response was swift: "There is no change to our position on this." Behind the scenes, Trump's maneuvering has been more calculated. The *New York Times* revealed his 2018 attempt to leverage diplomatic channels, pressing Ambassador Woody Johnson to influence British officials in steering the Open back to Turnberry. While Trump denied the report, Johnson—the heir to the Johnson & Johnson fortune—offered a carefully parsed response, stating only that he "followed the ethical rules and requirements of my office at all times."

Beyond Trump's presence, multiple sources indicate the R&A harbors deeper concerns about the financial underpinnings of his Scottish golf empire. Trump's unprecedented refusal to release tax returns as president has left lingering questions about the source of the nearly $400 million invested in his Aberdeen and Turnberry courses. The properties' financial performance raises additional red flags: Aberdeen has hemorrhaged money for 11 consecutive years, accumulating losses around $20 million, according to 2024 filings with Companies House (an executive agency of the UK government). Turnberry's ledgers remained in the red until 2022, finally achieving profitability after years of losses. While these financial complexities don't necessarily suggest impropriety, they add another layer of uncertainty to Trump's campaign to recapture golf's oldest championship.

What's obscured by the political tumult is Turnberry's breathtaking magnificence. The course commands a dramatic headland above the Firth of Clyde, where the ancient granite monolith of Ailsa Craig rises from the sea, while the misty silhouettes of Kintyre and the Isle of Arran paint the horizon. Though prestigious before Trump's acquisition, both course and resort had faded—its routing compromised by years of piecemeal changes, several holes falling short of their potential.

Trump's investment and architect Martin Ebert's vision transformed the links into something extraordinary. The redesign's hallmark is a legendary three-hole stretch along the churning sea: the 9th through 11th holes now rival the most spectacular sequences in golf, standing shoulder-to-shoulder with Pebble Beach's coastal run and Cypress Point's famed ocean holes. The 9th, a heart-stopping par-three across the cliffs, plays beside a lighthouse that doubles as perhaps golf's most dramatic halfway house. The 10th unfurls as a magnificent par five, its tee perched on the precipice, its green flirting dangerously with the water's edge. The 11th completes the trilogy—another par-three that seems fastened to the sea.

The course isn't without critique. Touches of American-style architecture occasionally jar against the raw Scottish landscape, and the closing stretch, while solid, can't quite maintain the seaside drama. Yet Ebert's renovation has elevated Turnberry far beyond its former self. In pure aesthetic terms, it may be unmatched in golf—a photographer's dream where every hole could grace a magazine cover. During Open week, our group of first-time visitors—hardened golf journalists and industry veterans—found ourselves struck speechless by Turnberry's raw beauty. Our collective verdict, stripped of pretense or qualification: *"Damn, this place rocks."*

But the ability to separate art from artist has its limits. Turnberry's announcement of a £1,000 green fee—the steepest in the United Kingdom (save for Ardfin's effectively higher barrier, requiring a two-night stay at £1,600 per night alongside its £500 round)—represents more than mere price inflation. It marks a philosophical departure from Scottish golf's democratic traditions of being open to all. This should not be a shock. In a 2014 interview with *Golf Digest*, Trump spoke of his belief that the sport's grow-the-game efforts are flawed: "I would make golf aspirational, instead of trying to bring everybody into golf, people that are never going to be able to be there anyway.

You know, they're working so hard to make golf, as they say, a game of the people. And I think golf should be a game that people want to aspire to through success."

Few moments crystallize Trump's worldview as perfectly as this transformation of Turnberry. In turning Scotland's communal golfing heritage into a marker of exclusivity, he demonstrated his core philosophy more clearly than any campaign speech or policy decision. Here was the essence of Trump distilled: the conversion of a golf touchstone into a fortress of privilege, wrapped in the veneer of luxury, but fueled by division.

•   •   •

My lone interaction with Trump came during the 2022 LIV Bedminster pro-am, as he played alongside DeChambeau and Johnson. While he regaled us with animated tales about Gary Player, one statement cut through the casual banter with unexpected prescience. "They need to take the money," he declared about PGA Tour holdouts, predicting an eventual merger. "You don't want nothing." The words seemed like typical Trump bluster at the time—until June 6's framework agreement shocked the golf world. There it was, impossible to ignore: Trump was right.

As 2024 draws to a close, the PGA Tour and Public Investment Fund have reportedly finalized their deal, yet the announcement remains strategically dormant. Both parties await Trump's inauguration, calculating that his Justice Department will prove more amenable to clearing the antitrust hurdles that previously stalled golf's realignment. The irony runs deep: the same Justice Department under Biden that investigated the Tour, Augusta National, and others for potential antitrust violations now serves as justification for this calculated pause. Perhaps more striking is the deafening silence from politicians who, during golf's Congressional hearings, painted Saudi Arabia as a national security threat. Their previous concerns have evaporated in the face of Trump's deepening Saudi ties. Industry whispers suggest a tacit agreement: Trump's blessing comes with the promise of a PGA Tour event at one of his properties.

The choreography of power became visible in the days following the election: PGA Tour commissioner Monahan sharing a round with Trump at Trump International in West Palm Beach. The very next day, Trump appeared ringside at a UFC fight, seated beside PIF governor and LIV Golf chief Yasir Al-Rumayyan. In February 2025, the PGA Tour announced it had asked Trump to join the negotiations with PIF, with Monahan and Tiger Woods meeting Al-Rumayyan at the White House. The symbolism was unmistakable—golf's one-time pariah had transformed into its ultimate powerbroker.

The game's traditional power structure didn't just bend—it broke, reformed, and repositioned itself around him. Unlike Scottish farmer Michael Forbes, golf's establishment ultimately couldn't withstand Trump's inexorable force of will.

CHAPTER 7

Worlds Apart

*North Berwick • The European Tour and the PIF •
The golf coast*

Golf's best players are in town for work. What matters is where they go for play.

The Renaissance Club is one of the anomalies of the Scottish golf landscape, a modern creation snuggling up to the classics. The course emerged from the vision of Jerry Sarvadi, an American aviation fuel magnate whose ambitions centered on creating a championship-caliber venue in golf's homeland. In 2005, Sarvadi secured a 99-year lease on a stretch of coastline from the Duke of Hamilton's family estate near North Berwick. To transform his vision into reality, Sarvadi enlisted Tom Doak, widely regarded as golf architecture's most influential voice of the past half-century. Doak, known for his minimalist philosophy and ability to work with natural landscapes, approached the project with candor, acknowledging the site's relatively modest natural drama and that meeting Sarvadi's requirements for professional-level difficulty would likely polarize opinions. The course opened in 2008 and by 2019 was the host of the Genesis Scottish Open, one of the premier events on the DP World Tour. Renaissance Club has hosted six Scottish Opens since its debut, and in 2022 the event was co-sanctioned by the PGA Tour. Played the week before the Open, it serves as a primer of sorts for links golf and has one of the best fields of any European event.

The course has evolved since its inception, with modifications tempering its severity for amateur players while maintaining its championship test. Like most Doak designs, it's a strategic, thinking-man's course, one that rewards precision and artistry, and there's a beautiful four-hole stretch that brings stunning views across the Firth of Forth. Against other DP World Tour and PGA Tour venues, Renaissance offers more architectural intrigue than most.

The problem for Renaissance Club has nothing to do with the course itself, but its address.

Renaissance finds itself in the shadow of titans, sharing a boundary with Muirfield, home to the Honourable Company of Edinburgh Golfers. Muirfield has hosted 16 Open Championships, with many considering it the finest expression of links golf in the country. Beyond Muirfield's grounds lies Gullane, where three distinct courses unfold across the region's dunescape. Each offers its own examination of a golfer's skill, with Gullane No. 1's elevated tees providing panoramic views of what feels like a quarter of Scotland. A short journey east reveals Dunbar, whose ingenious routing presents a masterclass in design. Here, each hole flows organically from the coastline, creating an 18-hole chess match (if chess was actually entertaining). The region's embarrassment of riches continues with Kilspindie, whose modest length dances along the shoreline, its charm lying in subtle contours and clever green sites. Archerfield's pine-framed fairways offer a distinct aesthetic from traditional links, while Luffness New and The Glen remain hidden gems, their relative obscurity a testament to the area's extraordinary depth of world-class golf rather than any shortcoming.

This concentration of excellence makes East Lothian revered among golf addicts. Against such company—and in an environment where age and maturity bring further distinction and character—Renaissance struggles to command reverence. For those visiting during the Scottish Open, Renaissance certainly delivers the presentation expected of a professional tournament—ample parking, viewing areas, and modern amenities ensure a comfortable spectator experience. However, for those seeking something more tribal, ethereal, visceral, who want to see the game at its most natural and unguarded, an experience beckons just two miles down the road.

In my discussions of Scottish links golf, I've exercised restraint with superlatives, dispensing them like a master sommelier shares rare vintages—sparingly and only when the moment demands their truth. The absolutes I've held onto I'm emptying here, for they are not exaggerations, because the West Links at North Berwick cannot be overblown. It's been called unique—ironic, given that its 15th hole, the Redan, is perhaps the most replicated hole in golf architecture. But unique feels inadequate, too pedestrian. While its features can be copied its essence remains inimitable and beyond comparison. It is one of one.

Any course ranking focused on pure enjoyment that doesn't place North Berwick among its highest echelon betrays a fundamental misunderstanding of the game. Yes, its welcoming fairways and merciful rough contribute to its playability, but North Berwick's genius lies in how it presents puzzles you never knew golf could pose. Stone walls become central characters—obstacles to play over, around, and at the famous 13th, directly through. There are hallows and mounds and burns, and what Phil Mickelson has called the craziest green in golf, the 16th, which is narrow and raised and cut in half by a gully. Each element feels both eccentric and essential, creating a round where every shot becomes indelible. The routing builds like great literature—an engaging opening, rising action that keeps you spellbound, a climax that fills you up while wanting more. While there's not a weak hole in the collection, the inward nine might represent the best stretch of golf holes anywhere on earth.

Perched above the Firth of Forth, which provides a backdrop to nearly every shot, the land undulates with the evidence of nature's patient artistry of wind, water, and time, conspiring to create perfect golf ground. Some first-time visitors are turned off by several blind shots or dismiss its unconventional nature as quirky. These critics reveal only their own limitations, for no place captures golf's soul better than North Berwick. There are golf courses, and then there is this, a place that transcends the very category it defines.

The game's elite players have turned North Berwick into their hangout during Scottish Open week. Jordan Spieth, Justin Thomas, and Rickie Fowler transform into one of us, their tour bags placed on modest pull carts for their early-week ritual. The tradition has spread—Sahith Theegala has become a regular, Justin Rose the same. Before this year's tournament I spotted recent PGA Tour winners Chris Gotterup and Austin Eckroat playing in the pissing rain.

"It's great. I try to go play on Monday or Tuesday when I get here. I mean, it's awesome," said Thomas this summer after taking the first-round Scottish Open lead. "It's such a cool golf course. I'd like to play some of the other ones around here, but I love North Berwick so much. It's hard to not go there."

Max Homa wrote his own chapter in North Berwick's growing legend when, after making the Scottish Open cut on Friday, he couldn't resist playing an emergency 18 at North Berwick despite an early tee time the next morning. Homa wasn't just a tour pro; he was a golfer succumbing to North Berwick's call.

"Living in Arizona, it's not so easy to get a tee time and make it out to North Berwick," Homa said at the 2023 Scottish Open. "So when I was there I had to take advantage. It was on my bucket list for a long time. I'd always wanted to play, and so I had to make the most of it.

"Last year, I was obviously trying to play and win a golf tournament. But I'm also human. I want to have some human golf dork experiences. And it worked out. I played great the next day after playing North Berwick. Sometimes when you get that joy of doing something you wanted to do since you were a kid, that can make you find that love for golf, the invigoration that it gives you. So last year was a blast. It was a really, really great golf course. And just a really fun day."

Professional golfers follow a meticulous script during tournament weeks: practice, play, recovery, repeat. When not at the course they retreat to rental homes for food or rest. That North Berwick compels these creatures of habit to break protocol, to squeeze in another round between championship preparations, stands as its most compelling testimony.

North Berwick's only flaw stems from its inevitable discovery. What was once golf's best-kept secret has become, in the past 20 years, a bucket-list destination, a transformation accelerated by tour players sharing their rounds across social media. The days of spontaneous visits, when one could stroll up to the starter's hut and be playing minutes later, have vanished. Tee times are now commodities, requiring advance planning or local connections to secure. But this is hardly a criticism, merely the tax levied on perfection.

I find myself struggling for the right description to capture North Berwick, only that there's a release of bliss this links can conjure that others cannot. So, instead, I share a chance encounter with Rose near the clubhouse on a Saturday afternoon in 2023. I kept my distance— he was there with his children, and there are sacred lines even us crooked journalists won't cross. But as I made my way toward the 1st tee, a cluster of members had drawn Rose into conversation. Though their query was lost to the wind, his response rang clear.

"Yeah, we're lucky, right, where we play," Rose said. "But this? This is real golf."

•　　•　　•

For all the discussion of where golf's going and who's behind the wheel, there's no question the DP World Tour's been relegated to the backseat. The circuit's fate was a bargaining chip in professional golf's schism; Saudi Arabia viewed it as an avenue into the sport's ecosystem, the PGA Tour deemed its European counterpart as means to keep an emerging threat at bay. The DP World Tour product itself, however, was an afterthought, and actions (and inactions) by both the PGA Tour and LIV Golf manifested the long-held fears of the Old World pundits: The league had become a second-class citizen.

The European Tour's decline bears witness to more than just shifting market forces, telling a story of loss, transformation and gradual unraveling of tradition. In the fading echoes of the "Fab 5"—Ballesteros, Faldo, Langer, Lyle, and Woosnam—lies a reminder of what European golf once represented. It wasn't just victory they chased, but a shared dream of proving European golf could stand shoulder-to-shoulder with their American counterparts. Yet the steady exodus of homegrown talent to the United States underlines the tug of war between ambition and cultural loyalty. Today's European stars—McIlroy, Rahm, Fitzpatrick, Lowry, Hovland, Åberg—all live or play full-time in the U.S.

McIlroy's departure still cuts deep. The initial hope that he would stay, nurtured by early signals from his camp, spoke to a desperate desire to retain at least one transcendent talent who could serve as a bridge between Europe's storied past and its uncertain future. Instead, McIlroy ultimately chose to play elsewhere.

"I just feel that I will become a better golfer if I also play in America," McIlroy said in 2009. "I will be playing in world-class fields with more world ranking points on offer, and the only way for me to get better is to play alongside better players."

The purses are richer on the PGA Tour, although money alone didn't drive Europe's talent across the Atlantic. It was the promise of a life less fragmented, less exhausting. On the PGA Tour, tournaments flow naturally from one region to another, creating a rhythm that allows players to breathe, to build relationships, to feel something close to stability. The European Tour offers no such grace, scattering its 42 events across 26 countries, with more than half the stops outside of Europe. PGA Tour events often have better world ranking point allotments, the keys that unlock golf's major stages. America also has the year-round warmth of Florida, Texas, and Arizona, where players find more than practice grounds. They discover the ability to plant roots, to build routines, to create something resembling home.

Staying in Europe becomes an act of defiance, a choice that speaks to values beyond career advancement even as the professional tide pulls in the other direction.

In the 2010s and early 2020s, the European Tour was caught in a destructive spiral. First came the exodus of stars, leaving behind not just empty galleries but wounded communities. Lower attendance led to corporate partners turning away. The reduced purses sent the remaining good players seeking greener pastures. The Ryder Cup requirement (to be on the European team, a player must play in a handful of events to retain membership) offered a bittersweet consolation—a glimpse of what European golf could be. These fleeting resurrections only threw the everyday reality into sharper relief. Nothing captured this quiet descent more than the five-month absence in 2024 of any top 20 player in an event after the Desert Swing in January.

The financial truth told an even bleaker story. The European Tour operated in the red nearly every year in the 2010s, finding temporary relief only when hosting a home Ryder Cup every fourth season. The numbers painted a stark picture—a $10 million loss in 2017 alone—revealing an institution walking an increasingly precarious tightrope. Then came the pandemic; while other tours found ways to adapt, Europe's stricter health protocols forced a devastating three-month shutdown and slashed purses. The Ryder Cup decision crystallized the Tour's desperation—some officials pushed to play without fans in 2020 just to secure TV revenue, while others insisted on waiting until 2021 to preserve the event's soul. As empty courses stretched into empty months, whispers grew into open concern: Would the European Tour survive?

The European Tour's courtship with Saudi money revealed more than financial desperation—it marked a moral crossroads masked as opportunity. The relationship wasn't new so much as deepening, and Keith Pelley had been its quiet architect. The European Tour CEO made history by welcoming Saudi Arabia into golf's mainstream, sanctioning the Saudi International as an official event in January 2019. The timing spoke volumes, just months after Jamal Khashoggi's death forced the world to confront the darker realities of the Saudi regime. Pelley's initial response to the inevitable backlash betrayed a telling ambivalence. He first tried to create distance, quietly omitting the Saudi International from the Tour's season-opening announcements—a subtle acknowledgment of the storm to come. Yet when criticism arrived, his puzzlement seemed almost practiced, as if he couldn't quite understand why golf should wrestle with questions that the broader business world seemed content to ignore.

"After the incident [murder], many blue-chip businesses and many governments continued to do business in Saudi, [and the] entertainment business is still flourishing," Pelley said. "There was Italian Super Cup with AC Milan and Juventus [in January], and Ronaldo scored the winning goal and celebrated, and we tried to find any kind of criticism for Ronaldo, yet our players were criticized. Why was golf singled out? I was perplexed why we were."

"I went over there first and listened to his Excellency (Crown Prince Mohammed bin Salman) at a sports conference, talk about how ... the country wanted to change, needed to change, wanted to use sports as a catalyst, was committed to golf."

The courtship between the European Tour and Saudi interests in 2020 revealed a dance of desperation and calculated risk. When the pandemic threatened the Tour's survival, Pelley and his team first turned to their natural allies, the PGA Tour, seeking a lifeline. But those calls went unanswered, as the PGA Tour was absorbed in its own pandemic survival. The silence pushed European golf's leadership toward more controversial suitors—the Saudis and Premier Golf League, with the sophisticated Raine Group whispering possibilities in their ears. The PGA Tour's power brokers read these flirtations as they were intended, a leverage play to force American golf's hand. The gambit proved effective: by November, the tours announced their "strategic alliance," with the PGA Tour claiming a 15 percent stake in European Tour Productions for $85 million. A deal that looked less like partnership and more like a premium paid to keep European golf from landing too far from the fold.

"Raine Capital presented a very compelling offer to take the European Tour to another level, but in a different direction," Pelley said during the announcement. "Ultimately, we felt partnering with the PGA Tour was the best option for our members and for global golf, a decision that was made unanimously by the board of directors."

The European Tour's apparent salvation came wrapped in compromise, first through the PGA Tour alliance, then through a naming rights deal with DP World that promised to double purses for 2022. But stability proved fleeting. As LIV Golf ignited civil war across the professional game, the European Tour found itself caught between powerful suitors. Its value to the Saudis was clear: a pathway for banned LIV players to earn world ranking points, in exchange for PIF's considerable resources. These overtures produced an unexpected result—not a Saudi deal, but a tightened American grip. The PGA Tour nearly tripled its stake in European Tour Productions to 40 percent, while offering the top 10 European Tour players PGA Tour cards each year. (For what it's worth, in its antitrust lawsuit against the PGA Tour, LIV asserted that Keith Pelley was interested in LIV's fit with the Euro Tour but rejected the offer after pressure from the PGA Tour.)

The deal painted a deceptive portrait of mutual benefit: The PGA Tour neutralized a potential LIV ally while the European Tour secured its future. Yet the 2023 financials told a different story. Despite the Ryder Cup's traditional role as financial savior, soaring costs in Rome in 2023 slashed profits by 40 percent compared to Paris five years earlier. The PGA Tour's $20 million bailout merely kept the lights on. A leaked internal memo from PGA Tour executives, revealed through a Florida lawsuit, delivered the coldest assessment: the European Tour was "an underinvested and borderline distressed asset" whose "event model may be unsustainable."

The renewed alliance, with its carefully worded "guaranteed underpin" safety net stretching to 2027, revealed both salvation and submission. While the PGA Tour's support offered financial breathing room, it came at the cost of independence, a gilded cage that would preserve the European Tour's existence while quietly stripping away its autonomy. The shifting power dynamics became clear in the months that followed. The 2023 framework agreement with PIF listed the European Tour as a partner in golf's new for-profit future, yet when PGA Tour Enterprises emerged in 2024, a European voice was notably absent from the boardroom. The irony wasn't lost on European Tour members, who watched in bitter disbelief as the PGA Tour secured the very Saudi partnership their own leadership had rejected. Meanwhile, the Tour's competitive integrity continued to bleed. The exodus of its top 10 players each year to America wasn't just a drain. It was a systematic dismantling of European golf's ability to nurture and retain its own stars.

"Yeah, I'm getting quite depressed now, as I speak on behalf of my old tour, the European Tour," Colin Montgomerie said in a 2024 interview with the website GolfMagic.com. "Yes, it's weakened; there's no denying it. You can paint it up as much as you want. You could paint it rose-tinted, whatever you want to do, but come on. [In] any business [if] you give away your top 10? Top 10 in your business every year is going to be weaker, isn't it? So [it's] great for the PGA Tour; I can't believe they accepted it, to be honest, because they're taking spots away from Americans, but good on them to get them. Unfortunately, Europe has suffered, and the European Tour will suffer because of it."

As 2024 draws to a close, history threatens to repeat itself with whispers of yet another Saudi courtship, this time seeking a separate deal with PIF independent of its PGA Tour partnership. Pelley's 2024 departure for Maple Leaf Sports and Entertainment feels symbolic, leaving behind a league caught in the undertow of forces it hoped to navigate.

The European Tour's tragedy runs deeper than mere circumstance. It's easy to cast the tour as a victim of powerful outside forces. The truth carries more force. Leadership's refusal to reimagine a more focused, distinctly European identity, one that embraces its continental roots rather than chasing global mirages, has left the tour unmoored from its cultural anchors. In trying to be everywhere, it risks becoming nowhere.

The sharpest irony lies in Pelley's role. His team first welcomed Saudi influence into golf's ecosystem, then wielded that relationship as leverage against the PGA Tour—only to watch both potential partners strike their own deal, leaving European golf on the outside looking in. The European Tour emerges not so much as victim but as architect of its own isolation, having played kingmaker to forces that would ultimately sideline it. Pelley's unrepentant stance, his refusal to acknowledge the missteps even as he departed, underscores the Tour's failure to reckon with its choices.

"I don't look backwards, I look forwards. That was part of our tour. The Saudis put on a great event for our members," Pelley told Golf Channel in a 2023 interview. "So I don't look back at that in any such way. The Saudis wanted to get involved in the game and if they hadn't got involved with us in the DP World Tour I believe they would have found another avenue. So I don't regret that."

Even with modest resources, the ingredients for renaissance remain: emerging players hungry to write their stories, in cosmopolitan stops like Paris, London, Rome, Munich. For all its inner complaints about being relegated, the DP World Tour still has the chance to control its own future. There is hope in the courage to reimagine itself as something authentically, unapologetically European, a return to roots that could paradoxically open the path to renewal.

• • •

Along Scotland's East Lothian coast lie 22 courses from 19 clubs across 30 miles of linksland. It is an ideal canvas for the game—rumpled dunes, firm fairways, seaside views, windswept pastures, all in a microclimate locals swear keeps their temperatures and turf more playable than courses just an hour away. The placement of each course speaks to something beyond chance, suggesting the touch of a higher power who understands not just the geometry of the game, but its ability to light a divine spark.

"This is our 14th trip to Scotland. For the last five we've come back here," says Johnny Brown, a contractor originally from Gainesville, Florida. "You need to see [everything in Scotland] at some point.

Once you have, you narrow the choices down to the courses you want to play over and over. For us, that's here."

Brown and his five companions have shared this ritual for years, two weeks in Scotland's golfing heart each June, though life's interventions pushed them to July this season to honor a wedding. Their anchor has always been Gullane, a village of 3,000 where warm restaurants light the evening hours and the Golf Coast unfolds in every direction. This year they've chosen Edinburgh as their base, facing anywhere from 15 minutes to an hour by car or train to tee it up. When I suggest this might be a worthy evolution—the commute a small price for Edinburgh's cobbled poetry, vibrant culture, and natural beauty, the type of town where every corner you turn into feels like walking back into history—Brown's quiet smile shows that my assessment is wrong.

"No, that's not it," he says. "Our wives are coming over in Week 2, which was the compromise. It was their call."

Brown tries to mix it up every year, but there are staples: North Berwick, Dunbar, Kilspindie, Gullane Nos. 1 and 2. "If it was up to me, we could make the two weeks out of those places," Brown says. "There are probably better courses. At this point in my life [Brown is 49], you know what you like. North Berwick and Dunbar, if I wasn't married I would move my entire life here just to be by [them].

"My friends can be serious. If you don't know them you'd think they're cold. The reason I like [the set of North Berwick, Dunbar, et cetera] is I get to see grins and horseplay from them. I'm not trying to gush, but how many places you know can do that?"

I find myself nodding along while trying to thread my own list in my head. So let's pause to honor three among the 22 that speak with compelling voices:

—The Glen isn't just forgotten, it's practically invisible to most visitors, despite sitting less than a mile from North Berwick West Links. The initial climb up the first hole serves as a price of admission to something sweet: 16 holes perched on cliffs that deliver views surpassing even its celebrated neighbor. The panorama sweeps from Bass Rock to Fidra, with the sea commanding your attention at every turn.

While not a pure links (there's parkland character in its wispy rough), the Glen delivers pure fun. The course isn't particularly long or punishing, most holes under 400 yards, but that's exactly what makes it brilliant. It's golf as it should be: playable, walkable, and endlessly entertaining. The 13th "Sea Hole" stands as one of the coast's most dramatic holes. This blind par-three demands a leap of faith, sending your ball over a hill to a green perched 80 feet below on the cliffs. Anything less than good and the sea claims another victim. Local knowledge reveals its true character; depending on the wind, players might need anything from a wedge to a 5-wood to find the green. For visitors plotting their excursion, the Glen serves as the perfect afternoon complement to morning battles with the region's giants.

—Dunbar emerges as a quiet revelation along Scotland's eastern shore, its understated presence belying a spark that some maintain rivals, if not betters, North Berwick. The trek begins hesitantly, through fields where deer graze, a prelude that gives no hint of what's to come. At the par-three 3rd, the course begins its gradual awakening, drawing golfers toward their inevitable encounter with the sea. What follows is pure links golf in its most intimate form, where a narrow strip of land becomes a theatre for the dialogue between golfer and course and elements, demanding an array of shots and imagination. The course's heart, holes 10 through 14, can be a hurdle, especially into the prevailing wind. Yet Dunbar eases its pressure over the closing stretch, where the sea-hugging fairways frame the town of Dunbar that hovers in the distance. The greens lack North Berwick's dramatic contours and are often critiqued as dull, but they compensate with immaculate conditioning and true roll. By the time you make the turn you wonder why this course doesn't get more love; by the time you reach the closing holes, you're selfishly glad it doesn't, because all golfers like to have their secrets.

—To understand Muirfield is to embrace paradox. At first glance, it withholds what many expect from Scottish golf—there are no postcard views of the sea despite its near-coastal setting, no instantly memorable holes worthy of Instagramming, none of the mystique that envelops St Andrews or the charm that radiates from North Berwick.

In this restraint is its virtue. Muirfield offers what pundits consider the world's finest examination of skill and strategy. Its revolutionary design, two concentric rings of nine holes running in opposite directions, ensures each shot must be negotiated with a different wind angle. The course presents its challenge with clarity. The fairways, springy and true, offer paths forward; stray from the fairways and Muirfield bites with mean rough and nastier bunkers. Yet there's an honesty to this gauntlet. It's stern but never cruel, demanding but not sadistic. Unlike Carnoustie, which beats you down without purpose, Muirfield rewards good shots while punishing mediocrity, allowing survival through its orchestrated defenses. The par-three 13th is one of the best holes in major championship golf, 190 yards uphill to a green ringed by five sentries of sand, each ready to claim the slightest miscalculation. And the 18th provides a fitting denouement, its iconic doughnut bunker guarding a green that practically kisses the clubhouse behind.

Where I struggle with Muirfield is its exclusivity. The club's reluctant embrace of women members—prompted not by internal conviction but external pressure from the R&A—speaks to the ongoing evolution and ugly past of golf's relationship with equality. The green fees—£560 for a full day's golf—create another barrier, standing in stark contrast to Scotland golf's democratic roots. Perhaps the most telling aspect is the subtle but palpable atmosphere. While tales of extreme rudeness are overstated, there's an underlying current of reserve that feels at odds with the welcome found throughout the country. The club's twice-weekly opening to visitors stands as a commendable practice—especially when compared to America's exclusive venues—but this gesture somehow emphasizes rather than erases a sense of separation. The contrast with its neighbors makes these dynamics more pronounced. In a region where courses serve as community gathering places as much as sporting venues, Muirfield's guardedness feels like a note slightly out of tune with the surrounding symphony. To outsiders, it's a museum open to those with the means, and manners.

But Muirfield will always hold a warm spot in my golf memories. In 2009, I found myself at Muirfield's storied lunch between rounds, the type of spread that puts Thanksgiving to shame. Across from me sat a figure who seemed to embody every stereotype of privilege—his hair perfectly arranged, wearing a suit jacket that spoke of wealth far beyond my circles, carrying a smile that felt more like an assessment than a greeting. As another player mentioned the afternoon wind's gathering strength, this gentleman declared to the room with unflinching certainty, "No one will break 80, this I know." In his voice lay the weight of presumption, the comfortable authority of someone accustomed to having their predictions accepted as fact.

I'm not one who fits into the polished world of country clubs, and something about this man's curated superiority stirred a response that I channeled it into every swing that afternoon. It was an inauspicious start, a bogey suggesting perhaps his prediction held merit. But a week's worth of learning to speak the language of links golf, and a fierce draw that seemed to understand the wind's challenge, kept me going. Through conditions that demanded three, sometimes four extra clubs, I found an unexpected harmony with the elements and a higher calling to prove this S.O.B. wrong. Near the end I started coming off the tracks—a 15-footer for eagle at the 17th turning into a par, followed by a wayward drive at the last. From that lie came one final moment of clarity, my approach finishing to tap-in range sealing a 73 in the most challenging conditions I'd ever faced. I felt good for all of eight minutes.

In the locker room, reality arrived in the form of Vijay Singh—a figure who'd once shown kindness to me as a young autograph seeker. Singh was in town, getting acquainted with links golf before that year's Open at Turnberry. When Singh left, a visitor asked one of Singh's playing mates how he fared. "Oh, what could have been," an older gentleman said, as he dressed in a shirt and tie.

I still remember looking down, tying my shoes and thinking, *Holy cow, did I just beat Vijay Singh?* And then the gentlemen finished his sentence ...

"He played in 65, and didn't make a putt over eight feet."

• • •

Literally just over the fence from Muirfield's eastern edges, the Scottish Open at Renaissance Club stands as a poignant reflection of golf's evolving landscape—a testament to both tradition and transformation that mirrors the DP World Tour's deeper struggle for identity and relevance.

While DP World Tour stakeholders nurse wounds of perceived exploitation, their American counterparts grapple with their own complex matrix of decisions and responsibilities. Neither side emerges untarnished, yet healing remains possible. The PGA Tour could begin mending these bonds by embracing a month-long European swing centered around Scottish golf, acknowledging both the sport's roots and its shared future.

The framework is already in place on the front end. Historically, the Irish Open and Scottish Open have preceded the Open Championship, although recently the Irish has been pushed to the fall. In our proposal the Irish would return to its historical date before the Scottish. When played at the proper venues, the Irish and Scottish serve as a two-week links primer for the Open Championship to both players and fans. *Proper* is the operative word, however, and a word that does not always apply to either tournament. Issues with sponsorship, fields, the DP World Tour schedule, infrastructure and attendance have kept the Irish and Scottish Opens from consistently visiting the best links courses each country has to offer, instead defaulting to hosts that are seeking exposure or relevance. It's not that courses like Galgorm Castle, Mount Juliet, Loch Lomond, Gleneagles, and the K Club are bad; but in areas to which golfers routinely make pilgrimages these places are far from holy sites. The prevalence of parkland courses in these events strikes a particularly discordant note. These manicured landscapes stand in contrast to the links that define this region's golf identity. Links golf strips the game to its essence, probing not just a player's technical mastery but their emotional and spiritual resolve.

It's why links courses remain golf's ultimate crucible. A test that parkland golf—regardless of its merits—can never fully replicate.

The Renaissance Club's slight incongruity with Scotland's golfing spirit runs deeper than its modern design: its exclusive access and price tag feeling particularly misplaced for a national championship. Watching tournament golf here is akin to, well, maybe mixing fine Scotch whisky with amaretto—a treat for some, yet far from most people's preferred way to consume it.

The tournament organizers aren't blind to these contradictions; they're wrestling with the demands of modern professional golf. A successful venue requires proximity to urban centers for accommodations and transportation, a scarce commodity in Scotland and Ireland's geography. The course must not only test the world's elite players but also accommodate the infrastructure of professional tournaments: grandstands, hospitality areas, and space for thousands of spectators. The short lengths of classic links courses pose another challenge in an era where driving distance increasingly dominates professional golf.

Yet rather than seeing these constraints as insurmountable, they should inspire creative solutions that honor both tradition and progress. These venerable links have tested golfers' skills and souls for centuries—surely there's an avenue to challenge today's players in equally meaningful ways.

Above all else, there is the necessity of monetary backing. That's why the PGA Tour's involvement in a potential European swing is so crucial. With the Tour sanctioning the Scottish Open, the event's strength-of-field average doubled, most notably with more front-line firepower in 14 of the world's top 15 players teeing it up in 2024. The Tour's collaboration brought in Genesis as a sponsor, and Genesis increased the purse 28.5 percent over the previous year and a whopping 177 percent since 2016. A similar knighting of the Irish Open—which had a $6 million purse, lower than every PGA Tour full-field event—could produce dividends in the same ballpark, especially since the Irish has historically struggled with tournament sponsorship. With the PGA Tour serving as a benefactor in both players and dollars, the Irish can return to its normal spot on the schedule (it was moved to the fall in hopes of garnering a better field) and be freed from resorts like the K Club and Mount Juliet to explore more suitable playing venues. Lahinch, Ballyliffin, and Portmarnock are past Irish Open hosts that fans would like to see back in the rotation.

The Scottish Open deserves a bolder venue strategy, backed by the Tour's resources. While some dream sites remain out of reach—Royal Dornoch and Machrihanish are too remote, while Nairn, Crail, and Elie might not sufficiently test today's professionals—tour support could unlock other possibilities. Consider Cruden Bay. DP World Tour officials had originally scouted Cruden Bay as a potential Scottish host, although ultimately tournament officials wanted a site closer to Edinburgh. The upcoming equipment rollback by the R&A and USGA could bring North Berwick into play, and while scoring might be low, the course's distinctive personality would overshadow any concerns about red numbers. Gullane's proven track record and ample grounds make it a natural candidate to return to the rotation. Most intriguingly, the PGA Tour could pursue the ultimate prize: bringing the Old Course into the Scottish Open schedule. Such a move would elevate the tournament's prestige and strengthen its connection to the past.

The PGA Tour faces a lackluster stretch between the U.S. Open and FedEx Cup Playoffs, marked by weak fields and limited fan interest. Integrating the Irish and Scottish Opens would strengthen this period without disrupting existing events. The numbers tell the story: the 2024 John Deere Classic attracted just one top 25 player, while the 3M Open posted the Tour's second-weakest field of the season. This move would also help address the growing tensions with the DP World Tour. European players and officials have questioned the benefits of their strategic alliance with the PGA Tour, particularly after the PGA Tour pursued a Saudi deal it had previously advised the DP World Tour to reject. While strengthening these two prestigious European events won't completely heal these wounds, it represents a meaningful step toward rebuilding trust and demonstrating genuine commitment to the partnership.

The LIV era revealed an uncomfortable truth. The professional game had grown stagnant, resistant to innovation and fresh thinking. The key to progress is recognizing the DP World Tour not as leverage in broader negotiations but a force in golf's ecosystem. A robust European swing, backed by PGA Tour resources and commitment, would showcase the character and traditions that make European golf special. This isn't about absorption or subordination. It's about celebrating and elevating two distinct but complementary expressions of professional golf. The future of professional golf shouldn't be constrained by old hierarchies or rigid thinking. Innovation in golf doesn't have to come at the expense of what got it here in the first place.

• • •

The Summer Olympics play on the clubhouse TV, but the bar stands empty. Everyone has taken their drinks to the porch, where North Berwick's 18th hole dissolves into the town. It's a good hole, the 18th, a seductive temptress—277 yards, reachable with a 3-wood, with a forgiving acre of safety to the left. But a valley guards the green's approach, and the parking lot looms along the entire right side. It's the kind of risk-reward hole that transforms sensible golfers into gamblers, and everyone, invariably, gambles.

There's no grand veranda here. Just a handful of tables and chairs, now fully occupied while others stand about, yet no complaints rise from the crowd. After one of the wettest summers on record, Mother Nature has finally granted mercy, as if saying, "The poor bastards have had enough," and we've fled outdoors before she reconsiders her kindness.

As my summer in Scotland draws to a close, I'm spending my final week in North Berwick. They say a good story can never be long enough. That's how this week has felt, slipping away before I could properly savor it. I've found new friends, like Tim Gallant, who embodies who I hope to become. An American transplanted to Edinburgh who plays out of North Berwick, Tim is the kind of person you meet at the starter's hut and exchange numbers with before reaching the 1st green. I've reunited with old friends, like Craig Hardie, whom I met several Opens ago. Craig is everything you pray for in a playing partner: a hell of a golfer, brilliant conversationalist, and perfect host. His genuine warmth almost makes you suspicious; surely someone this nice must have bodies buried somewhere. Having grown up at the club, he's now introducing his daughter to the game. When he speaks of her improvement, his voice swells with a pride that tells me everything I need to know about his nature as a father.

But in this moment, as the fading sunlight stretches to gift us a few more precious rays, I find myself alone. I should be interviewing those around me—learning who they are, what drew them here, collecting their stories and secrets and feelings about North Berwick. That's why I came. The notebook remains in my back pocket. Instead, I'm trying to hold onto whatever time remains, to fully grasp the simple pleasure that this place exists.

Throughout the week, I've tried to capture what makes this place captivate my golf being. I've analyzed the architecture, studied the terrain, noted how each hole contributes to the course as a whole. I've documented its playability and how it elicits shots that exist nowhere else in golf. I've made observations about the people, the staff, how the club stands among golf's greatest venues yet carries itself with the humility of a neighborhood muni. Even the holes that leave others wanting—like the puzzling 200-yard tee shot at the 14th, followed by a blind approach with the sea lurking behind—fill me in ways few places can. Yet the connective tissue eludes me. Why do all these elements harmonize perfectly? As both a journalist and someone who loves North Berwick deeply, it gnaws at me that I can't articulate its spell. That after a week, a summer, years even, the answer remains just beyond my grasp.

But watching golfers finish their rounds on the 18th—all hugs, no handshakes—and linger afterward, lost in the moment ... I suspect they couldn't explain this place's hold on them either. Perhaps that's exactly as it should be. If magic could be explained, it wouldn't be magic.

CHAPTER 8

Character(s)

Classifying Phil • *Rory's near misses* • *Bob from Oban*

The pride of Scotland drags himself through the Caribbean heat, his weary frame moving with the deliberate pace of a man who senses the last drops of fuel are burning away. A dozen fans stand waiting in the coarse sand and ochre dirt, their enthusiasm undimmed by the oppressive humidity. "I will be back, I promise," Robert MacIntyre manages, his Scottish brogue warm despite his exhaustion, as he ascends a rickety set of makeshift stairs into the scoring tent. The scene around him is far from the postcard version of the Bahamas— no crystalline waters or swaying palms in sight. Instead, cracked sea beds stretch into the distance, their surfaces bleached by the relentless sun, while thick woodland looms on the horizon interrupted only by the skeletal frames of ongoing resort construction. The late-season fatigue is evident in every movement MacIntyre makes, and for a moment, I fear he might surrender to an air-conditioned sanctuary and vanish from sight.

He emerges from the tent, with marker in hand, and works his way down the rope line. Each "Great season, Bob!" is met with a gracious nod and genuine—if tired—smile. As he reaches the end of the line, he gives one final acknowledgment before breaking into a jog toward the clubhouse, desperate for hydration. As he turns, a voice cuts through the thick air from a nearby hospitality tent: "You've made it, Bob!"

The Hero World Challenge is golf's version of a Mardi Gras for its royalty—the carnival that comes only after the real encounters have been fought and won. It's an exclusive gathering of 20 players that somehow maintains the façade of competition with its peculiar dispensation of World Ranking points. The mathematics of entry are simple: 17 spots for the game's elite, plus 3 consolation invites for stars weathering temporary eclipses. All this unfolds at a pristine resort, where luxury villas await players—and more importantly, their families and entourages—exhausted from a calendar that can feel like an endless summer. Most treat it as what it is. The practice range transforms into an open-air lounge, where conversations about college football drown out the percussion of club meeting ball. Players drift in with their crews mid-Tuesday, perform cursory warm-ups, and split their attention between the nominal 72-hole tournament and call of beach and nightlife. The course offers little resistance, the galleries are sparse, and even last place pockets $150,000—more than many earn grinding through a year on the developmental tours. It's as relaxed as a Tour competition can get.

Nobody gave MacIntyre this head's up, or perhaps he refused to listen. He is fresh off a breakthrough season crowned with his first two PGA Tour victories. While his peers' courtesy golf carts remain conspicuously absent from the parking lot Monday morning, MacIntyre's already carved deep divot patterns into the practice tee. His solitary figure returns Tuesday and Wednesday, the intensity of his preparation creating an invisible barrier that warns, "Don't bother me, I'm at work." He's polite when interrupted, but his face carries the focus of a man who doesn't accept the concept of exhibition golf. The connection between this devotion and his recent success is impossible to miss. Yet watching him grind, there's an unspoken irony: if anyone has earned the right to ease off the throttle and savor the rewards of arrival, it's Bob MacIntyre.

His most prosperous season was also his most trying. For years, MacIntyre had shouldered a burden unique to Scottish golf—the expectations of an entire nation's dreams pressing down on young shoulders after his stunning T-6 finish at the 2019 Open Championship. He was just 22 then—a fresh-faced hope from Oban, a rural town on Scotland's west coast—who found himself cast as the heir to a kingdom that had waited a generation for its next golfing monarch. Those demands carry a responsibility that compounds with each passing season of unfulfilled promise. MacIntyre managed two victories on the European Tour, but they felt more like whispers than the roar his countrymen yearned to hear. He made the Ryder Cup team in 2023 off a runner-up finish at the Genesis Scottish Open, yet MacIntyre arrived at Marco Simone Golf Club in Rome in such poor form that the European press corps had already drafted his competitive obituary, wondering aloud if he'd be relegated to spectator until Sunday singles. Instead, he emerged as an unlikely hero, harvesting 2.5 points across three matches in Europe's win over the United States.

MacIntyre earned his PGA Tour card for 2024, and the opportunity prompted a transplant to Florida with his girlfriend, a move that promised proximity to his new competitive home but extracted a heavy personal toll. The transition stripped him bare. In a rare moment of vulnerability for a professional athlete, MacIntyre confessed to being lost in both game and spirit during those early American months. The loneliness of expatriate life weighed on him like a second shadow, his performance reflecting his interior struggle as he languished outside the Tour's top 100 well into the season. What followed was fantasy: a breakthrough victory at the RBC Canadian Open with his dad on the bag, then a triumph at the Genesis Scottish Open that transformed him into a national icon. The temptation was to view these victories as an eraser, wiping clean the struggles that preceded them.

But tales of simple redemption can be dangerous, particularly in a year when the golf world was forced to confront its relationship with mental health after the devastating loss of Grayson Murray to suicide at just 30 years old. So after the autographs are done, and we've drifted far enough from the circus of fans, cameras, and ambient chatter to find privacy, I ask MacIntyre, "Have you been able to appreciate not only being here, but having the type of season that bestows an opportunity like this?"

MacIntyre's response begins with a sound that defies simple categorization—a laugh that collapses into a sigh, or perhaps a sigh that tries to disguise itself as a laugh. His eyes drop to the ground; when they rise his words carry the ballast of unexcavated truth.

"To be honest, I've not done that yet, and I don't think I'll be able to do that until later on in my life," MacIntrye says. "That's just, it's work. I try to go week to week just try and improve every day, every week. I know myself, I never dreamed of having the two wins that I got. They were literally fairy tales, both of them. Having my dad on the bag, winning the Scottish Open, the one I always wanted. I get goosebumps just thinking about it, what I've done."

For the next few minutes, MacIntyre unspools the golden thread of his summer memories. As he speaks, I find myself reminded that joy resides not in the summit but in its climb. Yet there's wisdom too in allowing yourself moments to stand at the peak and survey the distance traveled, provided you don't gawk for too long. In real time, I watch as MacIntyre permits himself the briefest window to acknowledge what that voice from the hospitality tent had proclaimed: *Yeah, I have made it.* The boy from the little village on the outskirts of Scotland.

But I was not here to discuss how far MacIntyre had come from his wee days in Oban. I wanted to know why he went back.

•   •   •

I don't know how to classify Phil Mickelson. Protagonist? Antagonist? Arsonist? He was golf's smiling assassin, a man who fabricated conflict from peace with a dimpled grin and a calculated thumb's up. He held the sport hostage without care for collateral damage and became a casualty of his own avarice—a cautionary tale of what happens when the People's Champion decides the people aren't enough.

Two prevailing theories attempt to explain Mickelson's controversial actions as a founding father of LIV, but both miss the mark. The first portrays him as a maverick crusader, challenging the establishment in pursuit of players' rights and industry reform. While this narrative aligns with his carefully cultivated rebel persona, it crumbles under scrutiny. Throughout his three-decade PGA Tour career, Mickelson showed virtually no history of collaborative advocacy or meaningful effort to improve conditions for his fellow professionals. His track record reveals a pattern of self-interest rather than collective advancement. The second theory suggests desperation, particularly in light of the shocking revelations from his former associate Billy Walters in 2023. Walters alleged that Mickelson had wagered over $1 billion and lost approximately $100 million through gambling, even claiming Mickelson attempted to place a bet on the 2012 Ryder Cup while competing in it. (Mickelson denied betting on the Ryder Cup, though Walters maintained the bet was merely refused rather than never attempted.) Yet despite these staggering figures and the earlier sale of his private jet, financial distress didn't appear to be the primary driver. The golf community's consensus held that Mickelson remained financially secure. The true catalyst proves far more troubling.

Retaliation born of imagined victimhood consumes everything in its path. Each concession only sharpens its appetite and feeds on itself, like a wildfire turns everything it touches into kindling for further expansion. Fictional grievance is toxic because it burns without conscience or consequence—without purpose or limit—and when righteousness is conjured from delusion every destruction becomes permissible. It's the worst sort of "ends justify the means" mentality, because the ends weren't justified to begin with. Why Mickelson felt this entitlement after all the game had given to him is a shame, yet also not worth reflection. That is a matter of character, and sometimes the explanation for a character shortcoming is they have no character at all.

The most damaging aspect of Mickelson's transformation wasn't merely his defection, but the calculated façade of righteousness he constructed around it. His legacy crumbled not because he chose to lead a rival league bankrolled by a nation that he himself had characterized as murderous, nor because he deemed his worth greater than what golf's traditional institutions offered. These were his prerogatives, and the astronomical compensation he received made his motivations, if not admirable, at least comprehensible. What remains genuinely baffling and profoundly disappointing was his seeming compulsion to burn down the very institutions that had elevated him to prominence. Rather than departing with dignity, he launched a scorched-earth campaign against the PGA Tour—the organization that had provided him the platform, prestige, and prosperity that made him valuable to LIV in the first place. This vindictive impulse to destroy rather than simply depart reveals a troubling character flaw that retroactively casts shadows over decades of carefully cultivated public goodwill.

Shadows have long been his companion. Should there be any doubt, one only needs to remember Mickelson feuding with Detroit media and threatening never to return to the city following the revelation of Mickelson's ties to a mobster. Or the Saturday at Shinnecock in 2018, when he hit a moving ball in an act of petulance and defeat. Or the defiance after an insider-trading scandal. Or throwing two Ryder Cup captains under the bus. And any number of other gaffes, including a prescient 2019 moment when he told fans "You do you, I'm gonna do me" regarding his first dalliance with the Saudis when playing in the Saudi International. It's a thin line between self-assured and self-absorbed.

The traits that once made Mickelson the darling of golf have transformed him into its most divisive figure. His triumph at the 2021 PGA Championship at Kiawah Island stands as the perfect distillation of this duality. At age 50, he achieved what seemed impossible, marshaling not just raw power and delicate touch, but an unwavering self-belief that teetered on the edge of hubris. This was Mickelson in his purest form—the only version he's ever known how to be. The golf world had already consigned him to the role of decorated elder states-man, his achievements spoken of in reverent but distinctly past-tense terms. Yet when Mickelson sized up his competition—155 elite play-ers in their athletic prime—he saw only equals. His victory became a shared catharsis on those South Carolina shores, transforming him into something more than a golfer: he became proof that our past need not define our future, that time itself could be defied. For that, he earned a victory lap that should have lasted forever.

Now, that same willful stubbornness casts a darker silhouette.

During the final round at Kiawah's Ocean Course, Mickelson orchestrated a masterclass in psychological warfare against Brooks Koepka. He wielded silence and a deliberate pace as weapons, each calculated pause and measured step designed to unravel his oppo-nent's patience and composure. It worked. "I got trounced on that one," Koepka later admitted, adding with grudging admiration, "I thought it was pretty good what he was doing." The gamesmanship added to the mythos of Mickelson, showing that though this game is increasingly dominated by power, it can still be won with the mind. Yet two years later, when Mickelson accused the PGA of America, USGA, and Augusta National of conspiring with the PGA Tour to exclude LIV members from the PGA Championship, his strategic brilliance had curdled into something more cynical. He knew the PGA hadn't deviated from its standard qualification protocols, but truth had become subordinate to an agenda that he was desperately trying to sell.

The PGA Championship victory had cemented Mickelson's legacy as golf's ultimate warrior-poet. While others achieved more pristine records or scaled greater heights, few matched his childlike enthusi-asm for the battle itself, his pure joy in the competitive arena. Phil's journey was rarely elegant, often unsuccessful, but always marked by an infectious love for the fight. Which makes his current incarna-tion on what amounts to an exhibition circuit all the more jarring—a 45-time winner on the PGA Tour now struggling to contend in LIV's abbreviated fields. He had become the very person we'd swore he'd never be.

Before LIV, Phil's social persona charmed with its studied awkwardness—a master ironist playing the role of golf's endearingly out-of-touch elder. His performative obsession with his calves, his deployment of phrases like "hellacious seeds" and "bombs" weren't just dad jokes; they were calculated self-deprecation from a man comfortable enough in his legend status to play the fool. Yet now, his social media presence has devolved into something more desperate—the digital equivalent of a carnival barker, each post reading like a conspiracy theorist's manifesto, each attempted joke bearing the hollow ring of a fading showman grasping at relevance.

The irony is that when golf's great divide first erupted, Mickelson appeared ready to step away from the spotlight's glare. His return to competition in 2022—first at LIV's London debut, then at the U.S. Open—revealed a startlingly diminished presence. Gone was the swaggering showman who had made a career of bold declarations and bolder plays. In his place stood a chastened figure, speaking in careful measures, promising restraint. The game's greatest provocateur had, improbably, pledged temperance.

"I have had strong opinions and ideas regarding most of the governing bodies, and I've done a poor job of conveying that. I've made it public, and that's been a mistake," Mickelson said. Going forward, he added, he would be "a lot more thoughtful with my words and actions and try to keep a lot of those things behind closed doors."

Sports fans possess an almost limitless capacity for forgiveness, particularly when faced with genuine contrition. A humbled Mickelson, one who could acknowledge his missteps, might have found redemption in their eyes. The possibility, however remote, remained. Instead, he has chosen the path of amplification, seizing every opportunity to broadcast his grievances and justifications. His increased stridency seems to parallel LIV's declining fortunes—Rahm's celebrated defection failed to capture public imagination, and one of the circuit's supposed marquee moments: a 2023 playoff battle in Tulsa, proved so insignificant that the CW Network affiliates opted for syndicated reruns instead. As LIV's legal offensive against the PGA and DP World Tours crumbled, forcing its Saudi backers to pursue partnership rather than confrontation, Mickelson's position has become increasingly precarious. Should any future reconciliation between the tours materialize, he seems destined to remain on the outside—a cautionary tale rather than a conquering hero.

The financial windfall—allegedly hundreds of millions in Saudi money—might justify everything in Mickelson's mind. His American reception seems to validate this calculation. At the 2022 U.S. Open, an outsider would have struggled to identify him as the architect of golf's great schism. Save for a few scattered jeers, his rounds at Brookline played out like a pre-LIV highlight reel: the familiar cap tips, the trademark thumbs-up, his name still ringing through the galleries. But this apparent normalcy masked a crucial truth: major championship crowds in America are largely casual fans, viewing Mickelson's Saudi alliance as either refreshing candor or remaining blissfully unaware of his three-month exile. They saw only the carefully crafted persona—the aviator-wearing, button-down-dancing showman—that LIV had so eagerly bankrolled.

Yet beneath this veneer of business-as-usual lies a more complex reality, one that crystallized at the 2022 Open at St Andrews. He might have received a surprise at Brookline, but that was America and this was Scotland, where the game is more in tune with the havoc Mickelson has wrought and only gives forgiveness when it has been requested. The R&A's preemptive move to discourage Mickelson—a past champion—from attending both the Celebration of Champions and Champions' Dinner spoke volumes. His recounting of the exchange—"They said, 'Look, we don't think it's a great idea you go, but if you want to, you can'"—and subsequent acquiescence to their wishes revealed the true cost of his choices.

Following Mickelson through his Thursday and Friday rounds revealed a punishment far more devastating than the jeers that greeted other LIV defectors: calculated indifference. The man who had built his career on the electric current of audience connection found himself unplugged. Though polite applause still greeted well-struck shots, the quintessential Mickelson atmosphere—that crackling energy that filled even the quiet moments between swings—had vanished. His mediocre performance at St Andrews (72-77) barely registered as news; at 52, his game had begun fading long before his reputation dimmed. Yet the spiritual exile proved more telling than the scorecard. Without the intimacy and connection with the crowd, Mickelson floated like a ghost, knowing he was no longer of this world yet equally unable to leave it. The crowd's alienation, for him anyway, must have been worse than not showing up at all.

The depth of his isolation crystallized in stark contrast to Tiger Woods' reception that week. Woods, Mickelson's career-long nemesis, had commanded attention rather than affection since his "Hello, world" moment a quarter-century ago. He never achieved Arnold Palmer's beloved status or Jack Nicklaus's reverence; the "Tiger vs. Phil" narrative drew its power from Mickelson's ability to forge the very emotional connections that Woods seemed to disdain. Yet in his autumn years, Woods has undergone a remarkable transformation. His legendary guard has lowered, revealing a hard-won understanding that fans seek not to consume his greatness but to share in its twilight. This vulnerability, met by galleries who have grown to cherish rather than demand excellence, has created something profound: rounds that unfold as communal celebrations, marked by genuine warmth rather than mere spectacle. In his gradual opening to the public, Woods has discovered the very connection that Mickelson, in his pursuit of validation, had sacrificed.

Only a chosen few are awarded "The Stop." It is both earned and conferred, and it is always cashed in at the Swilcan Bridge. The legend makes his way over the crossing, pauses, perches his leg up on the stone ledge, turns away from the Old Course and toward the fans to his right and behind him, then back to the town of St Andrews and to the people craning their necks from pubs and hotel windows to say they saw it, and waves. The Stops of yesteryear are run annually on Open broadcasts, and pictures of The Stop are plastered in clubhouses across the world, because The Stop matters, a graceful transition of a golf legend from the pangs of now into the gloss of the past.

Tiger Woods was bestowed The Stop in 2022. It made sense; he was nine over through 35 holes, 20-something shots behind the leader and miles from the cut. He was just 46 years old, but his return from a savage car accident raised plenty of questions about an already tenuous future, and with the R&A likely deviating from its tradition of hosting the Open at St Andrews every five years it was unclear when the Auld Gray Toon would host again … and what type of shape Woods would be in when that time came. Woods is a student and historian. He is well aware of The Stop and hat it means, to himself and to others. Over the past decade, he had preached a cognizance of the finish line. And yet, knowing what was ahead, Woods glided over the most famous bridge in golf, stride unbroken. But he did raise his hat to the heavens, a concession made by his brain, even if his legs were taking direction from his heart. In classic Woodsian fashion, he made his own stamp on The Stop.

And then there was Mickelson. His credentials earned him his ceremonial moment. Had the Open been held a year earlier, Mickelson would have basked in adulation on the Swilcan Bridge, breaking records for most thumbs-up photos at the sacred crossing. But there was no pause for posterity, no final bow. Instead, he quietly putted out for a forgettable 77 and slipped away without ceremony.

There's a chance Mickelson will get one more shot at an Open at St Andrews. The game has shown that forgiveness can be earned, wounds can heal. But Mickelson has remained defiantly unchanging throughout golf's civil war, blazing his own path because that's the only way he knows. His greatest trait now his greatest liability. That's not just a problem; it's a tragedy of his own making.

•   •   •

For the better part of two years—in the void of true, public-facing leadership in the PGA Tour's battle against an existential threat—Rory McIlroy stepped into the role and battled for a sport he feared would be lost. Long before others grasped the gravity of the situation, he was sounding the alarm about rival leagues—first the PGL, then LIV—and their questionable financial backing. "I didn't really like where the money was coming from either. I wanted to be the first one to speak out against it," McIlroy said in March 2020. "I'm glad that I have. I'm glad that I've done that." As LIV Golf materialized from threat to reality, McIlroy transformed into golf's conscience and voice. Tournament after tournament, he faced the media with unflinching honesty, weaving personal reflection on his own game with insights about the state of professional golf. Where others offered platitudes or silence, he brought vulnerability, patience, thoughtfulness, and an undeniable charm that made his warnings impossible to ignore.

His most crucial work happened away from the cameras. Behind closed doors, McIlroy worked relentlessly to fortify the PGA Tour, championing reforms he believed would both stem the tide of defections and elevate the Tour's product. His commitment wasn't just professional, it was personal. "Every chance I get, I'm trying to defend what I feel is the best place to play elite professional golf in the world," McIlroy said in 2022 on why he was so vocal against the schism caused by LIV Golf. "If you believe in something, you have to speak up, and I believe very strongly about this. I really do. I hate what it's doing to the game of golf."

McIlroy became more than just a public entity. With Tiger's public appearances limited to a few weeks every spring and summer, McIlroy is the game's most compelling presence. He's on our television screens, because he's usually in contention, and when the broadcast goes to commercial breaks, he's there as well. The Ulsterman is talked about more than any current player because the most oxygen is saved for the things that matter the most. A top player for over 15 consecutive years now—significantly longer than almost all of his peers—McIlroy is considered by some to reside somewhere between celebrity and golf royalty. This can be a blessing, but also a curse, because the thing about being in the spotlight is, yes, it puts the highs and lows on display for all to see, but also anything you do. It can be innocuous, or it can have no connotation whatsoever. It is out there, part of the public domain to be consumed. The star's doings become content. You personally may abhor that this is the way things are, but it is also reality, and one that cannot be avoided. By putting himself on the line, he put his performances on the line, there's no questioning the gumption it takes to have conviction in both while displaying constant grace through the struggle that elevates McIlroy and his message.

The burden of being golf's moral compass exacted a toll on McIlroy, one whose weight didn't crystalize until the spring of 2023. The schism had devoured him, transforming from professional obligation into obsession. After a missed cut at the 2023 Masters, McIlroy faced an uncomfortable revelation: in his quest to save golf he was losing himself. "I've always thought I've had a good handle on the perspective on things and sort of where golf fits within my life, and trying to find purpose outside of golf in some way," McIlroy said in May 2023. "But I think over the last 12 months, I sort of lost sight of that. I'd lost sight of the fact that there's more to life than the golf world and this little silly squabble that's going on between tours, and all sorts of stuff." When he returned, the sport discovered McIlroy's grace is not infinite. Behind the polished public persona, he absorbed every arrow—the venomous online attacks from LIV's social media army, the gleeful mockery from LIV defectors that crescendoed with each near-miss at the majors, the talk around his RBC Heritage withdrawal. The golf world—in its rush to interpret his absence as petulance over the Masters disappointment—willfully ignored that he had sacrificed $3 million (in bonus money, by not showing up that week) to attend to personal matters. When a noticeably frost-bitten McIlroy emerged at the 2023 PGA Championship weeks later, those close to his camp offered a response that cut to the bone: *Why should he show respect to those who don't afford him the same?* It was a jarring reminder that even golf's most gracious ambassador could be pushed too far.

Elegance aside, it was easy to understand why McIlroy was pulling away. His position on LIV was well documented, and it appeared the civil war was entering a lull of sorts. The questions get redundant, and there's only so many philosophical and cerebral concessions Rory can make before he's a prisoner of his own version of *Groundhog Day*.

And then McIlroy realized he wasn't a prisoner, but a pawn. McIlroy, who took a stand for what he believed was right, was sold out by the very thing he was trying to defend.

"It's hard for me to not sit up here and feel somewhat like a sacrificial lamb and feeling like I've put myself out there and this is what happens." McIlroy said at the 2023 RBC Canadian Open, the day after the Tour's surprise agreement with Saudi Arabia's Public Investment Fund. Despite working to keep the Tour together, Tour leadership had failed to keep McIlroy in the loop. McIlroy did answer questions that day about the proposed deal, but pulled himself out of the following week's U.S. Open press conference, unwilling to entertain questions about a partnership he knew nothing about. When he did finally meet with the media at Los Angeles Country Club, USGA liaisons informed the press that McIlroy would walk away if one LIV/PIF question was asked. A month later, he pulled out of a scheduled presser at the 2023 Open, and ever since he's had a somewhat mercurial relationship with the press. This was punctuated by blowing out of the Pinehurst parking lot in 2024 after a heartbreaking one-shot loss to Bryson DeChambeau at the U.S. Open.

Let it be known that Woods understood he was the center of the golf universe and believed it was his duty to give time to those that gravitated toward him. Before the tournament, during the tournament, after good rounds and bad. If there's one criticism of McIlroy, he's been known to skip media requests if the day didn't go his way. The very people who had canonized him as golf's savior now turned to crucify him for daring to preserve his own humanity. The sport had grown so accustomed to his unwavering defense of tradition that his retreat—not a surrender, but a necessary act of self-preservation—was viewed as betrayal. This backlash revealed less about McIlroy's character than it did about a sports culture that demands martyrdom from its heroes, then condemns them for showing the scars of battle.

When fame reaches the heights that McIlroy occupies, it breeds a peculiar form of intimacy—what psychologists call "parasocial relationships." These one-sided bonds create an illusion of closeness, where millions feel they know a man they've never met, forging connections built on glimpses through television screens and press conference soundbites. It's the psychological engine that powers sports fandom, transforming athletes from distant figures into something approaching family. For McIlroy, this has benefits. It fuels the ovations that follow him from tee to green, why corporations pay millions to attach their brands to his name. Yet these phantom relationships exact their own price, encumbering their subject with expectations they never agreed to shoulder. The cruel twist is that Rory's reputation as "the good guy," the ethical center of professional golf, has become its own trap. The more he embodied these virtues, the more the public demanded that he remain frozen in this role—forgetting that even moral exemplars are human beings navigating their own complex truths.

It's fine to feel this way. What a dull way to go through life, without any emotional attachment. One of the beauties of sports is to develop these passions, to invest time and energy and support into a player or team. Yet 2024 revealed the limits of what we can rightfully demand from our heroes, as McIlroy's private struggles burst into public view with his brief divorce filing during the PGA Championship. Though the divorce papers were withdrawn a month later, McIlroy carried an air of exhaustion rather than competitive fire when he returned to work at the 2024 Open. His early exit seemed almost welcome, his face wearing the expression of a man ground down by the machine, burdened by fame, expectation, and obligation.

In many ways, McIlroy is the tragic figure of the internecine strife. That this time has coincided with multiple near-misses at majors— the 2022 Open, the 2023 and 2024 U.S. Opens—has made that a popular opinion. However, in an era where loyalty and principle were treated as commodities to be traded, McIlroy's integrity never wavered. And perhaps his finest moment came in apparent defeat at the 2022 Open.

It began that Tuesday, when McIlroy called the 150th Open his Holy Grail. On the surface the parallel was easy to grasp and followed the edict from Bobby Jones, who stated a golfer's career is not complete unless he has won at St Andrews, and far be it from us to debate this notion. On a deeper level, however, the grail quest resonated in a way that explains much of the love he engenders. For nearly a decade, McIlroy has been on a crusade, trying to hurdle the pressures of who he once was against the hope of what he could still be again. He proved those ambitions were not unfounded after an opening-round 66 and backed it up with a Friday 68. He went out in 33 on Saturday, then sent a shock through the grounds and to his competitors with a bunker hole-out for eagle at the 10th. McIlroy had turned the Home of Golf into a home game, and from that hole-out on, his opponents had to try and win the Claret Jug in front of a crowd that didn't want to see them do it. It's not that the reception to the rest of the field was cold, but the galleries were treating everyone else as minor annoyances, obstacles to a history they wanted to see achieved, and with their claps and yells and hearts, they were doing whatever they could to bring that history to life. When asked if it was clear who the rooting interest was, Scottie Scheffler politely pointed out the obvious. "They're chanting his name out there," Scheffler said on Saturday. "How can you not root for Rory?"

A Rory win seemed predestined. Every Open winner at St Andrews had been within four shots of the lead after 54 holes, meaning this rodeo was down to four: McIlroy, Viktor Hovland (his co-leader after 54 holes), and Cameron Young, and Cameron Smith. This would be Hovland's first time in the throes of a major, and the majors are notoriously unkind to the inexperienced. The Camerons were four shots back. Rory seemed in total command of his game and the crowds. All week, from his hotel room at the Rusacks that overlooked the Old Course's final hole, Rory would stare at the famous yellow leaderboard and he'd imagine the leaderboard nodding back. St Andrews hummed with a singular energy that weekend, every conversation converging on McIlroy's impending date with destiny. It wasn't discussed so much as revered—spoken of in hushed tones by those who couldn't quite believe their fortune to be present for what felt inevitable. Late into one night, the cobblestone streets echoed with an impromptu choir—a band of jubilant, whisky-warmed fans stumbling arm-in-arm, their voices rising in an off-key but heartfelt serenade: "Rorrrrr-y, Rory, Rory ... RORRRR-Y!" Heading into Sunday, the Open didn't feel like a competition as much as a coronation, and the people were

CHARACTER(S)

ready to greet their king. He was 18 holes away from his Holy Grail, and the only thing standing in his way was himself.

One issue: No one told Cam Smith. The Aussie didn't get word of Rory's coronation. Or maybe Smith thought the red carpet being rolled out on this brownish-yellow turf was for him. He made the turn in 34 and birdied the first five holes of the back to take the lead from McIlroy at the 14th. Smith followed with two no-nonsense pars. At the 17th, his approach coming up short of the Road Hole bunker, Smith putted through the bunker's edge—a decision that is both courageous and psychotic—and pulled it off, his ball coming to rest eight feet from the hole. It should have been the nerviest putt Smith faced in his life. Instead he cleaned up what remained with an ease that you're not supposed to have over such a length at such a moment.

Behind was McIlroy, who was having the damndest time getting his ball to drop. Let the record show that McIlroy hit all 18 greens in regulation. The putter ... well, the putter apparently missed its tee time. McIlroy birdied the par-five 5th thanks to a lag eagle putt, and he did the same at the drivable par-four 10th. But as he stood on the 17th tee those were the only red figures on his day, his four-shot lead now a one-shot deficit with Smith on the birdie-able closing hole. Rory's drive found the 17th fairway, and needing to get his approach close to keep his hopes and the hopes of so many alive, Rory answered with vigor: his second leaving 18 feet for birdie. McIlroy's ensuing putt looked like it was going right. It followed that route for the most part. But as it neared the hole, needing to go just a tad more right to *be* right, it stayed left. McIlroy had to look away, ostensibly toward the Jigger Inn but really looking off into nothing in particular. He looked betrayed. He looked indignant. He looked like a player who made a 4 when he needed 3. Smith birdied the final hole for a 64. McIlroy made par; he and Hovland were the only players in the top 14 who failed to shoot in the 60s on Sunday. He didn't one-putt a single green. This championship wasn't handed to Smith; he took it with a 30 on the closing nine. Still, the claret jug was in Rory's reach, and he didn't grab it.

Years from now, this Open will be told by its result, but the scores did not seem to encapsulate what had happened, what had been believed, what had been seen, and what had been felt.

When examining this Open, few of Rory's shots came to mind, at least not initially. What endured was the communion between McIlroy and the galleries. He entertained and galvanized those that followed, and they in turn returned the favor. That current of collective belief—even channeled through something as seemingly trivial as sport—is powerful, for there is something sacred in moments when thousands of strangers unite, their individual hopes dissolving into a single shared dream.

There are few transcendent athletes, yet even fewer who possess a gravitational pull. Ascribing why those who have it can be difficult, but not always. Tiger, for one. For years, Woods tried to keep the public at arm's length, but his performance emitted a greatness so bright that it was hypnotic through sheer coercion. McIlroy's play, even at his best, could never match that. Rory's magnetism is distilled to something simpler. Fans were pulled toward Rory because, unlike Tiger, he allowed us in. He wanted us in. And what we saw is not some god or legend, but a man who at times is so human that it hurts. On that Sunday night I wrote:

That's what McIlroy has done, over and over, but best encapsulated at the 2019 Open at Royal Portrush, when he came undone after a valiant Friday charge in front of his countrymen to make the cut came up short, and at the 2021 Ryder Cup, when he was brought to tears discussing his team's belief in him when he didn't have his best. Wins and defeats happen at every tournament, most of which are forgotten by history. Emotional concessions like Rory's resonate louder and longer than any result could, because, while the majority of us will never know what it's like to be that good at sport, pain, and heartache are universal truths.

There are cynics who dismiss the Rory faithful as soft, who see the adoration as mere participation-trophy sentiment. And yes, sometimes the devotion feels excessive, the forgiveness too readily granted. But focusing on wins and losses misses what matters. McIlroy understood this truth when he spoke of the Holy Grail—the magic isn't in claiming the prize. And in those moments of the chase, those flashes of brilliance and sincerity, no one of his era captivates quite like Rory McIlroy.

The truth is, the 2022 Open will be just a date forgotten by history, and future generations won't know or care what happened. But those who watched and felt the 150th Open know it was something that cannot be forgotten. Cam Smith won the claret jug that week, but he was not its champ.

•　　•　　•

A sidenote on characters. Golf's civil war has claimed an unexpected casualty: villains. The professional game's traditional circuit, already short on black hats, watched nearly all its provocateurs defect to the upstart tour, where they've largely faded from mainstream consciousness.

The thing is, sports thrive on antagonists. They create tension, deepen storylines, and generate emotional investment that transcends mere fandom. Max Homa captured this dynamic at the 2023 Players: "When I ask friends outside golf about their least favorite players, they light up. That enthusiasm, whether driven by controversy or not, is vital for golf's entertainment value and fan engagement." Or, as Harry Higgs put it to *Golfweek* in June 2023: "[LIV] took all the assholes... and that's a problem." His coarse assessment underscores a truth—effective sports villains require a particular brand of audacity.

Consider Patrick Cantlay. His villain status stems not from manufactured drama but from an authentic willingness to disrupt golf's genteel norms. At the 2023 Ryder Cup, when European fans mocked him over reports he'd complained about playing without compensation, Cantlay responded by draining the winning putt and tipping an imaginary hat to the crowd. His corporate-complaint-department demeanor made the moment even more deliciously antagonistic.

One might expect LIV defectors to assume enhanced villain roles during majors, but majors already possess inherent gravitas. It's the weekly tournaments that need compelling antagonists to break their monotony. Moreover, there's a fundamental difference between being a sports villain—often based on trivial grievances, and sometimes nothing at all—and serving as a proxy for a regime facing serious human rights accusations. The irony is striking. In the past, when certain players drew fan antipathy, it felt almost unsporting – golf traditionally eschews such personal animosity. Their presence in contention, however, undeniably energized tournaments. Now, with hindsight, those fan instincts appear prescient. They identified character traits that would later manifest in more consequential decisions. And those decisions don't deserve the emotional investment that makes sports villainy so compelling.

•   •   •

Sports journalism often falls into the predictable trap of the hometown pilgrimage—visiting an athlete's origins to craft a neat narrative about how place and people molded greatness. When planning my Scotland trip, I initially dismissed the idea of traveling to Oban. The remote coastal town seemed to offer little in terms of golf significance, and MacIntyre himself languished outside the world's top 75 players. Then MacIntyre rewrote my itinerary.

The first turn came at the Canadian Open, though it wasn't just MacIntyre's victory that commanded attention. It was the raw emotion of his father Dougie, who had flown from Scotland to caddie for his son that week. "I'm a grass-cutter," Dougie said, fighting back tears that he knew he couldn't stop. "Not a caddie. Honestly, it's unbelievable. Last Saturday I thought, 'Can I leave my job?' 8 o'clock the next morning I'm on a flight here. Wow." This wasn't mere sentimentality—Dougie's role as greenskeeper at Glencruitten— Oban's challenging hillside course where the MacIntyres live off the 12th hole—had been instrumental in his son's journey and where he taught Bob to play. The sight of father and son realizing their shared dream—the grass-cutter who had spent decades tending the earth so his boy could soar—delivered the kind of unscripted emotion that makes sports transcend competition.

His tale crested at the Scottish Open, where MacIntyre became the first Scotsman this century to claim his national championship. His 22-foot birdie putt on the final hole didn't just win a tournament, it unleashed a collective roar across Scotland—a nation's dreams channeled through one perfect stroke. Yet amid this professional triumph, MacIntyre was wrestling with a deeply personal decision. Despite establishing a practice base at prestigious Isleworth in America, loneliness had taken its toll. His announcement about his future revealed golf's eternal tension between global ambition and the pull of home:

"My rent is up I think about the end of August, and I don't think I'll be getting it renewed to be honest," Macintyre said. "Scotland is my home, and yeah, I've joined Isleworth. That will always be a place I go and practice in the wintertime but there's nothing like home. Scotland, this is where I want to be."

So yes, I charted a route to Oban, a seaside hamlet nestled in the northwest highlands that seems plucked from a Hallmark Christmas movie, where inevitably some world-weary urbanite rediscovers love with her childhood sweetheart. Ten days after MacIntyre's historic Scottish Open victory, the town of 8,000 had transformed into a celebration of their native son. Outside the weathered stone train station, a poster of Bob's beaming face declared "Brilliant, Bob!"—a testament to how deeply his triumph had resonated with his community. The locals, with their characteristic Scottish warmth, eagerly shared stories about both MacIntyre and their beloved town. They took pride in explaining Oban's true sporting heritage lies in "shanty"—a variant of hockey played with such ferocity that it makes its ice-bound cousin seem whimpy by comparison. Yet these conversations felt peripheral to the central mystery I had come to unravel.

The question becomes even more puzzling when you consider the professional golf landscape. Florida serves as a hub for tour professionals, offering year-round practice conditions, state-of-the-art facilities, and convenient access to tournaments across the American southeast. The concentration of elite players creates an environment of constant competition and improvement—iron sharpening iron, as the saying goes. Add in Florida's infamous state income tax advantage, and the decision to base there becomes reflexive for successful players. Yet here was MacIntyre, a rising star in his prime, choosing to navigate punishing transcontinental commutes to return to a rural Scottish town where the weather is mercurial even by Scottish standards. What was it about Oban that brought MacIntyre back?

"I'm not a golfer there," MacIntyre says in the Bahamas. "Everywhere else, that's what I am. In Oban, I am one of the boys. I'm Bob." The spotlight can make you play a role, can turn you into a character, if you're not careful.

MacIntyre's choice came after careful deliberation and counsel from fellow Europeans who had navigated the same waters, including Shane Lowry. The equation was clear: Florida's pristine facilities and optimal conditions should translate to better golf. But MacIntyre had discovered a more profound calculus: all the manicured practice grounds in the Sunshine State couldn't fill the void that absence from home had carved. If his soul wasn't settled, his swing wouldn't be either. What resonated most deeply was MacIntyre's clear-eyed acceptance of the potential consequences. "I don't know how it's all going to work," he says. "But I know what makes me happy, and I'll take that bet." The more he talks, the more joy I hear in his voice when discussing Oban, I realize this not as an admission of doubt but as a declaration of faith.

At first glance, mentioning MacIntyre in the same breath as McIlroy and Mickelson might seem premature—even with his recent ascent, they remain titans of the game, occupying their own stratosphere. Yet in an era where golf's narrative has been dominated by division and discord, MacIntyre authored two transcendent moments with Scotland as his ink and family as his muse. When the rest of the sport was looking forward for answers, MacIntyre found his by looking back.

I experienced the second of these moments not at the Renaissance Club in North Berwick but in a Prestwick pub, preparing for the Open Championship. When MacIntyre's winning putt went in, the scene in the tavern mirrored what played out on the television screen and across the nation—arms thrust skyward, passion erupting in primal shouts of "BOB!" I ask MacIntyre about this outpouring of national pride, and his response reveals the evolution of perspective. The initial euphoria and disbelief, he explains, had given way to something deeper—a sense of gratitude. "What we do as golfers, you don't get to share it very often," MacIntyre reflects. "After the win we had a big celebration, and pretty quickly I recognized I was only a small part of it. It was a win for home."

CHAPTER 9

Brother vs. Brother

Buddies • Fraternal order • Sellouts

The giant surveys his predicament on the beach. Two hours earlier John's drive would be lost at sea, but the tide has retreated, and his ball has escaped the dunes and skittered past a tidal trench. He is lucky—he has a shot and he knows it, but gratitude alludes him. All golfers know the walk of shame, journeying to a part of a golf course where their ball has no business being and attempting to defuse the situation with nervous laughter and a tired joke while onlookers do their best to look away. In John's case, his transgression has left the property, and the only consolation is that enough golfers have strayed here at the 17th at North Berwick to warrant a flight of steps leading from the hole's edge to the shore. There is an older couple on the beach, but they are walking in the other direction. He is alone.

John is one of my best friends and more like a brother. He and his fiancée have carved out time from wedding preparations to visit:

a gesture that means everything to me. He's also playing as good this day as I've ever seen him play. That it's coming at North Berwick— what I think is the best that Scotland has to offer—makes it transcendent. I am proud of him. But I'm also in a match with him, giving 12 strokes, and though he's playing brilliantly, so am I, just down 1 and very much in it. We are competing for a North Berwick flag, hat, and flask, and as much as I want to see him reach the finish line, there's a part of me of which I'm not proud of that would like to see him spin and out crash. Competition brings out the best of us, and also the worst.

Still, I like my chances. John is a colossus—6'5", 245 pounds of corded muscle—and he has an old-school move of pumping his left heel on the backswing that produces 290-yard power fades with ease. But here at the 17th, his fade morphed into a hard pull that betrayed him further by drawing hard. Like most amateurs, sand is the bane of his existence, and now he faces 140 yards to an elevated, fortified green he's never laid eyes on. *I have him*, I think.

Unlike my peers, I resist the urge to document everything. Our generation lives too much through screens already. I prefer to let moments breathe—to store them in memory rather than online— especially on sacred ground like this. But something compels me to break my rule. I retrieve my phone and capture John: studying his line, taking a final assessment, and then unleashing his swing.

The sequence in my camera roll jumps to Craig Hardie, our host and buddy, positioned front right of the green as I film from behind. John has made a marvelous out from the sand, leaving his approach 50 yards away from the green, and then puts his third to six feet. Craig's right hand floats upward, signaling the quality of the shot. John buries what remains for a par-net-birdie. The match is over. I'm happy for him, and I also hate his guts.

•   •   •

Professional athletes typically maintain a collegial detachment that borders on diplomatic immunity. The modern sports landscape—with its constant player movement, shared developmental pathways, and astronomical financial stakes—breeds pragmatic cordiality rather than lasting antagonism. These athletes recognize their stronger kinship with opponents on the field rather than with the masses in the stands who view them through tribal loyalties. As Jerry Seinfeld famously observed, fans are essentially rooting for laundry. But nowhere was this professional fraternity more evident than in golf, where the atmosphere passed beyond mere civility into something approaching genuine fellowship. Save for the tribal passion of Ryder Cup week, the sport's culture could feel almost too chummy: a dynamic cleverly captured in the Tour's old, double-edged marketing slogan: "These Guys Are Good." While rivalries occasionally emerged—think Woods vs. Mickelson or Norman vs. Faldo—they were exceptions that proved the rule. Professional golf operated as a traveling brotherhood of independent contractors, united by shared experiences and mutual respect. At times, critics argued the sport could benefit from more genuine antagonism, more natural villains to create compelling narratives. Be careful what you wish for.

The civil war shattered this fraternal order, creating rifts that extend far beyond tour allegiances. Even within the separate tours, factions have emerged over governance models, player obligations, and compensation structures. The sport has never felt more atomized, with individual players retreating into camps defined by lawyers and term sheets rather than shared competitive spirit. This internecine warfare has not only fractured golf's professional fellowship but has inflicted lasting damage on the game's carefully cultivated image of genteel sportsmanship and mutual respect.

The LIV defectors' response to professional consequences remains one of the most revealing and baffling chapters of the schism. Their performative outrage—oscillating between righteous outrage and wounded innocence when faced with criticism—laid bare both their naïveté and sense of entitlement. Despite their professional accomplishments, many proved stunningly unprepared for the backlash, having been cocooned for years in golf's culture of reflexive collegiality. No story better illustrates this dynamic than Hudson Swafford's exile from the "Sea Island Mafia"—a moniker despised by the group's patriarch, Davis Love III. The tight-knit enclave of tour players in St. Simons Island, Georgia, operated like a southern golf frat, complete with shared practice rounds, frequent dinners, and an unspoken code of loyalty. When Swafford, a three-time PGA Tour winner, became one of the first to accept LIV's lucrative offers, he discovered that the group's bonds had limits. Former friends began declining his calls, his regular foursome evaporated, and his standing invitation to Sea Island's elite practice facility quietly disappeared. In a community where golf relationships were the currency, Swafford found himself socially bankrupt, a cautionary tale for others contemplating similar moves.

"There's definitely some push back. I think it's crazy how some guys have made it personal. I don't know if it's jealousy, they didn't want to take a leap of faith or they didn't trust [LIV Golf]. I don't know what their thinking is. I basically switched jobs. I took a different job somewhere at a start-up," Swafford said at LIV Golf's finale at Doral in October 2022. "I don't get the personal vendettas that I've come across towards me. It's been quite interesting."

"There are definitely some friend dynamics that have changed on the PGA Tour. It's sad. It definitely hit home," Swafford continued. "I think everything will shake out in the end. There was definitely some animosity in the process, but at the end of the day it's just golf and everybody's doing what's best for them." Later that year, DL3 told his side of the story to Golf Channel: "Some of them don't understand why it's awkward or uncomfortable—why we are mad. They are getting paid a lot of money and they swallowed the Kool-Aid."

Then there's Sergio Garcia, the mercurial Spaniard whose brilliant shot-making has long been eclipsed by his volcanic temperament and endless grievances. When the DP World Tour banned LIV defectors from the Genesis Scottish Open and levied £100,000 fines for playing without releases, Garcia's response proved characteristically explosive. During the BMW International Open in Munich, according to reporting from the *Daily Mail*, Garcia unleashed a profanity-laden tirade in the locker room that left fellow players stunned. "Sergio flew off the handle, shouting 'this Tour is s***, you're all f****d, should have taken the Saudi money.'" Bob MacIntyre was there and was "disgusted," a player told the paper. "Sergio's reputation had taken quite a hammering anyway before this but this has sealed it for many of us." For what it's worth, MacIntyre took to Twitter, and without naming Sergio wrote "'Amazing how fast you can lose respect for someone that you've looked up to all your life" with hashtags of "10SecondRant" and "WeCanHearYou." This tantrum came just weeks after Sergio sounded off on a rules official at a PGA Tour event—"I can't wait to leave this tour, I can't wait to get out of here, a couple of more weeks and I won't have to deal with you anymore"—and after telling Rory McIlroy to stop talking about LIV following McIlroy's comments at the U.S. Open that LIV players were taking the easy way out. The DP World Tour certainly didn't forget about the outburst. "Sergio Garcia has not paid his £100,000 fine, nor has he given any indication that he intends to," the tour said in a May 2023 statement. "We will therefore take appropriate action if he continues not to respect the Sport Resolutions panel's decision." According to the *Telegraph*, Garcia made a last-minute effort to become eligible for the 2023 Ryder Cup by offering to pay his fine; the DP World Tour allegedly denied the plea. The outburst—from a player who had earned over €30 million on the European Tour alone and whose Ryder Cup heroics had made him a continental icon—epitomized the burning of bridges that characterized LIV's early days.

While McIlroy emerged as the PGA Tour's most vocal defender, routinely needling LIV and its defectors with calculated precision, even his crusade produced moments of high farce. None more theatrical than "Tee-Gate," a bizarre confrontation at the 2023 Hero Dubai Desert Classic that perfectly encapsulated golf's descent into petty melodrama. The incident unfolded on the practice range, where Patrick Reed—competing thanks to a temporary court injunction— attempted to greet McIlroy. The Northern Irishman, usually the epitome of professional courtesy, pointedly ignored Reed's approach. In response, Reed, a former Masters champion, tossed a LIV-branded tee in McIlroy's direction before walking away. McIlroy's rationale for the snub carried its own absurdist weight: Reed's attorney had served McIlroy with a subpoena on Christmas Eve, disrupting the McIlroy family holiday at his home.

"I was trying to have a nice time with my family," McIlroy explained with characteristic directness. "If someone shows up on your doorstep and delivers that, you're not going to take that well. I'm living in reality. I don't know where he [Reed] is living. If I were in his shoes, I wouldn't expect a hello or a handshake." The fact that Reed wasn't personally involved in the subpoena—a detail lost in the ensuing media circus—only added another layer of tragicomedy to the spectacle. The entire episode, captured by cameras and endlessly dissected on social media, crystallized how golf's civil war had reduced former champions to playground-level squabbles. It was simultaneously the most memorable and least consequential moment in the sport's ongoing schism.

But McIlroy aside, most PGA Tour players initially maintained a studied silence regarding LIV Golf. While they harbored strong opinions behind closed doors —many viewing the defections as abandoning golf's merit-based ethos—they refused to engage in what they viewed as beneath their professional dignity and (mostly) respected LIV's wish for autonomy. But the watershed moment arrived six weeks after LIV's London debut, when Phil Mickelson, Bryson DeChambeau, and nine other LIV players filed an antitrust lawsuit against the PGA Tour in the Northern District of California. The 105-page antitrust complaint, which challenged their suspensions and sought the freedom to play both LIV and PGA Tour events, crossed a line that united virtually every remaining tour player in opposition. The lawsuit's revelations—including Mickelson's supposed "sabbatical" following his "scary motherfuckers" was actually a Tour-imposed suspension, and that DeChambeau had signed with LIV in February while publicly denying any involvement—generated headlines, yet Tour players saw past the salacious details and dense legal language, focusing instead on what they viewed as both a professional betrayal and existential threat. To them, the lawsuit revealed LIV's true endgame: not peaceful coexistence, but the systematic decon-struction of their way of life.

"What they're doing by going over there is detrimental to our tour. You can't have it both ways," said Will Zalatoris the week after the lawsuit was filed at the 2022 FedEx St. Jude. "A lot of guys will be pretty frustrated if they're allowed to do both."

"It was really emotional for a lot of people. For me it was the law-suit. That's when it really got personal for me," Brian Harman told Golf Channel at the end of the year. "I can't fault anybody for any financial decision they've made. That's theirs to make, not mine, but it [the antitrust lawsuit] felt like an attack on the way I provide for my family and the way that I do it. That I took very personally."

Even Joel Dahmen, a man universally beloved for his laid-back demeanor, got into the mix. "It sounds like some people want their cake and eat it too. Please stay away in your fantasy land," Dahmen said. "I don't have an issue with anyone going to LIV. I have an issue with them wanting to come back and play. If the grass is so green, why do you want to come back?"

A week after its filing, the lawsuit produced a surreal two-hour hearing over LIV players' temporary restraining order to compete in the FedEx Cup playoffs—a legal spectacle where both sides' attor-neys seemed determined to undermine their own arguments. LIV's legal team, in particular, delivered a masterclass in self-sabotage. They elevated the FedEx Cup—a postseason format that even dedicated golf fans struggle to explain—to "the Super Bowl of golf." They acci-dentally confirmed critics' biggest suspicion by admitting LIV's prize money was "recouped against contracts," contradicting the circuit's repeated claims about purse independence. In perhaps the hearing's most tone-deaf moment, they characterized Swafford, Matt Jones, and Talor Gooch as "these three poor kids"—never mind that Jones was 42 and the trio had collectively earned $36 million on the very tour they were suing. The geographical gaffes proved equally stun-ning: they relocated the Arnold Palmer Invitational from Orlando to Ohio, and couldn't correctly identify the host city of their own Saudi

International, placing it in "Riyadh or Jeddah" rather than its actual location in King Abdullah Economic City.

The Tour's defense had its own stumbles, most notably when its lawyers claimed the LIV event at Trump Bedminster boasted more "elite" players than the PGA Tour's Rocket Mortgage Classic field. Judge Beth Freeman cut through both sides' hyperbole, pointedly observing that the "remarkable" number of defections suggested deeper issues at play. The proceedings, while rich in unintentional comedy, revealed something broken in professional golf's ecosystem. Here were players who had shared courtesy cars and locker rooms for decades, now allowing a foreign kingdom to pay their legal fees to wage war against their former colleagues through proxy attorneys. As the lawyers traded barbs about tournament prestige and player worth, the sport seemed to be eating itself alive, destroying the very foundations of professional fellowship that had distinguished golf from other sports. Watching these accomplished athletes reduce their legacy to courthouse theater, I found myself wondering if professional golf—at least in its traditional form—was worth preserving at all.

The temperature was turned down after those following months, and by the 2023 Masters you'd be hard-pressed to know the game was in war. Many LIV players played practice rounds with their former tour counterparts, and while tour players weren't jazzed about getting sued and the ramifications that could have, most of the individual relationships remained intact. Yet beneath this veneer of normalcy, the sport's fractures continued to deepen. While individual friendships largely survived—tour players could separate their personal relationships from their fury at being sued by former colleagues—the institutional warfare ground on through press releases and pointed comments. As both circuits struggled to articulate compelling visions for their futures, the vacuum of leadership bred internal strife. The PGA Tour's board room became its own battlefield: Jimmy Dunne, one of the framework agreement's principal architects, stormed out after players who felt betrayed by the Saudi deal effectively sidelined him from subsequent negotiations. Days later, Mark Flaherty's resignation further destabilized the Tour's governance. The crisis of confidence spread: veterans who had once passionately defended their respective tours now retreated into cynicism or turned their competitive fire toward their own colleagues. What had begun as a clear ideological divide between tours had devolved into a maze of competing interests, with no clear path forward and diminishing trust in those charting the course.

McIlroy, naturally, found himself at the center of the Tour's power struggle. His November 2023 resignation from the Tour's policy board initially seemed amicable enough; he cited the familiar chorus of personal and professional commitments while suggesting the framework agreement had fulfilled his mission. But when the deal's momentum stalled through 2024, McIlroy attempted a return to the board's inner circle, with Webb Simpson offering to surrender his seat. The response was swift and stunning: a power bloc consisting of Tiger Woods, Patrick Cantlay, and Jordan Spieth shot down his reinstatement. The opposition stemmed from multiple fracture points: Cantlay and McIlroy had long clashed over the Tour's strategic direction, while Spieth and McIlroy's relationship imploded earlier in 2024 after McIlroy dramatically quit a player group chat following Spieth's declaration that the Tour could thrive without PIF investment. Sources close to the board cited deeper concerns: lingering resentment over McIlroy's initial departure and suspicions that his attempted return was influenced by his business ties to Strategic Sports Group through his Boston Common team in the nascent tech-focused golf league that he co-founded with Woods. While these reservations carried some merit, the optics were staggering—golf's most influential voice, the man who had effectively served as the Tour's wartime consigliere through its darkest hours, was now being told by his peers to watch from the sidelines.

The civil war spawned a cascade of internal rebellions that threatened to tear both tours apart from within. On the PGA Tour, rank-and-file players seethed as superstars leveraged the crisis to create a two-tiered system, essentially pulling up the ladder behind them with elevated events and concentrated purses. LIV's paradise of unlimited largesse crumbled in Year 2 as budget constraints set in, creating friction between the Saudi circuit's highly paid captains and their increasingly restless foot soldiers. Tournament directors waged their own battles as the designation of "elevated" status transformed the Tour's calendar into a caste system of haves and have-nots. The relationship between players and tour leadership deteriorated into open hostility. While these feuds generated endless content for golf media's outrage machine, they revealed something damning: the sport's façade of gentlemanly comportment had been a mirage. These weren't the dignified stewards of a noble game—they were actors in an increasingly cynical production, their previously lauded professionalism proving as hollow as their proclamations of loyalty. The Tour's old marketing slogan "These Guys Are Good" had acquired an unintended irony; they weren't good, not in any way that truly mattered. They were merely better at pretending than most.

·   ·   ·

In what would prove to be a catastrophically expensive moment of inspiration, I fired off a casual social media post before departing: *"If you're making a buddies trip to golf's Holy Land, I'd like to interview you and your group for one of the chapters. Pints on me."* I drastically overrated the public's aversion to media—or more likely, underestimated just how many pilgrims would eagerly trade their stories for free booze. While the exercise introduced me to a wonderful cast of characters, my credit card statement remains scarred from Belhaven Best taps and Famous Grouse bottles.

Yet those pub sessions—financial devastation aside—became the heartbeat of my journey. Each interview felt like dropping into a celebration already in progress, catching people at their most alive, most present. Whether I caught them preparing for the 1st tee or coming off a rain-soaked foray, their eyes and voices danced with the same spirit. The conversations proved therapeutic for me, too. During those moments when the grind of travel wore me down—when I'd gone too many days with nothing but tepid trickles from primitive Scottish showerheads (how has a country this cold not mastered the art of hot water pressure?)—witnessing such pure, unfiltered happiness from my fellow golfers restored my psyche. The conversations tend to blur together now: countless phantom practice swings demonstrated against pub walls, animated recreations of bounces off the linksland terrain, and an infinite stream of inside jokes that prompted my polite, uncomprehending laughter. But what remains crystallized is the universal sincerity that radiated from these golfers—their reverence for where they were, and for each other.

"You don't get to see your friends often anymore after a certain age," says Al Martinez, a New Yorker now living abroad whose buddies and cousins from the States have met in St Andrews. We're at the Keys, the traditional stomping grounds of caddies in St Andrews, and Al motions to me to come closer as if he's about to tell a secret. "They were asking if I get homesick. Listen to them last night; they don't even see each other, and they all live within 30 minutes of each other. That's life. It's hard to get things coordinated. Getting everyone to go here is something we all rally around. Do you know how hard it is to get a bunch of 40-year-olds excited about the same thing?"

Buddies trips aren't just part of the Scottish golf experience— they're its lifeblood. According to the Scottish government's latest economic impact studies, golf tourism pumps approximately £300 million annually into the country's economy, with an overwhelming 60 percent of visitors arriving in groups of six or more. Their motivations vary: some come seeking golf's equivalent of a religious awakening, to worship where it all started while getting a chance to experience the shrines they've read or heard about; others are chasing the alchemy that happens when longtime friends step away from their daily lives and into an adventure together—the kind of bond-strengthening journey where stories are born in seaside pubs and forged between shots. There are the skeptical converts, initially resistant but drawn in by tales of Scotland's distinctive golden light streaming across the links during summer evenings that makes even the worst scorecards seem beautiful. They've watched the drama unfold on TV during countless Opens, seen the world's best humbled by pot bunkers and mercurial weather, and finally decided they need to see it for themselves.

While you could argue that places such as Pebble Beach, Bandon Dunes, or Ireland's southwest coast offer similarly compelling golf destinations for Americans, Scotland seems uniquely engineered to facilitate these middle-aged odysseys. The practical advantages are compelling: green fees and accommodations run reasonable compared to premium U.S. resorts, and East Coast travelers can reach Edinburgh or Glasgow in roughly the same time—sometimes even faster—than it takes to reach California or Oregon. For the purists, the logistics are merely perks. For them, the links are akin to finding the source of the Nile. These wind-swept, rumpled fairways, where the game and daily life are one and the same, offer an authenticity that simply can't be replicated elsewhere.

"Spiritual," says Scott Ford, a Tennessean who has made his way to St Andrews with his friends, trying to help me solve the question. "Lot of guys are golf guys, but how much they subscribed to the Scottish mystique varied. We get here, and everyone gets it. They coalesce around this pull they didn't know existed. In your head you're thinking, *Okay, is this going to live up to what everyone says it is?* You realize quickly words don't do it justice. What's been cemented for me is how much more all of this means when you're with others. It would be intense and heartfelt solo, I don't doubt, but getting to share that feeling with people close to you is what's taken it over the top."

Ford talks about golf like a sublime poet may talk about a mountain top, and when I spot him later that afternoon at Crail with his friends—suspecting, with quiet gratitude, that he had quietly arranged for my green fee—I realize his earlier eloquence wasn't schmaltz. Thanks to Crail's intimate layout, our paths cross repeatedly throughout the day, and each time I find him in a state of wonderment—pointing out subtle contours in the links that others might miss, gesturing at the architectural brilliance of each hole, throwing his head back in laughter as the North Sea wind transforms the flagstick into a thrashing metronome. He's experiencing the course with the wide-eyed joy of a child discovering something spectral for the first time.

Ford was just one of roughly 150 people who responded to my social media beacon, and throughout that summer I encountered countless other groups deep in their own Scottish journeys. I'll admit that many of their stories shared common threads, and on the surface, few offered earth-shattering revelations. Yet in this very uniformity lay something meditative —a shared experience that transcended individual portraits. These golfers, from different corners of the world, kept stumbling into the same ineffable spell. When trying to explain their connection to these courses and towns and people, they'd start with concrete details—the history, the challenge, the beauty—but inevitably drift into the mystical, as if describing a catharsis or enchantment. They couldn't quite capture the essence of what made it so special, only that they had been irrevocably changed by encountering it.

From Jack Selati, an investment banking analyst, who did a North Berwick-Kingsbarns-Muirfield-Castle Course-Jubilee tour with his buddies after their graduation from Colgate University: "We were already close friends. Traveling to another country to see some of these places, as your 'getting started' with adult life, you hope it's going to be special because you don't know how many trips like this you're going to take. We got lucky with weather, and I think the courses themselves, the land they were on, all surprised us. But mostly I think how the trip brought us closer together, that this love of golf and the uniqueness of Scotland brought out the best in us."

From Louis Jefferies, a physical therapist who came over with his old high school golf teammates from Sacramento, California to bounce around St Andrews and the Highlands before heading to Prestwick to watch the Open: "There's eight of us and most live by the Pacific, so we had a few talks about, would this be easier for everybody to just [do the vacation] in the U.S.? Half the boys have families. But one of the guys said, 'No. Trust me, it will be different in Scotland.' I thought he was full of shit [laughs]. This place does take you back to the roots of why you fell for golf in the first place. It makes me more appreciative for golf, you know? I don't think a U.S. trip would have done that."

From Bill Katt, a retired salesman from Arizona: "I came over with several men from my club. This is the sixth year for most of us. We were just talking this morning in the car, it is funny you can play golf with someone every week for 10 years, and learn more about them once you get over here. You don't make this flight and spend the money unless you really get the game, and I'm sure that is part of it, a self-fulling prophecy. But I've seen it, there's something about golf here that makes everyone equals. For all the terrific golf, I've come to enjoy how golf is really what is bringing us together."

Most of these are guy trips, though the configurations tell stories of their own: coworkers who've shared windowless offices, former teammates who once chased championships together, neighbors who graduated from driveway conversations to transatlantic expeditions, club members whose weekly Nassau bets have evolved into taking over a quaint Scottish bed and breakfast. Perhaps none captures the beauty of these trips than a group from Missouri, arising from a desperate hearts classified ad in the newspaper back when newspapers mattered. Before the Covid-19 pandemic rewrote everyone's travel plans, they crossed the Atlantic like clockwork every other year; this summer marks their first return since 2018.

"We've been through all of it," reflects Joe Pearson, running a hand through his wind-tousled hair as he recounts their shared history over a Guinness at The Criterion, which for my money is the best bar in St Andrews. The owner of an audiologist supply company speaks with the warmth of someone thumbing through a family album: "Marriages, divorces, career changes, kids being born and heading off to college. We peaked at 30 people one year, including four women who could outplay most of us." This year's group has contracted to a lean dozen, with many original members now scattered across different time zones and state lines. The bonds remain, tethered by an ever-active email chain that pings day and night. "The ones who couldn't make it have been blowing up our phones," Pearson says. "They're trying to place bets on matches we haven't even arranged to play! But you know what? It's great. I think seeing us back here, it gives them hope. They'll find their way back to Scotland too, sooner rather than later."

Among the groups I encountered, one story emerged like a whispered legend. It began with an email from Miles, a tour guide who casually mentioned shepherding a group of religious sisters across Scottish links for the past decade. Intrigued by this holy pilgrimage of a different sort, I pressed for details, only to learn that client confidentiality (since when did the golf guides adopt the professional discretion of physicians and lawyers?) prevented him from revealing their identities. But like all good legends, this one had multiple witnesses. While waiting by the Old Course's 1st tee to see a couple of my colleagues from rival *Golf* magazine off, I heard it again from a weather-beaten local: eight nuns who make an annual visit to town. The mind immediately spins fantastic scenes: habits fluttering in the sea breeze during backswings, theological debates over the morality of breakfast balls, whispered "Father forgive me" prayers after slicing drives into the gorse. My pursuit of these golf mothers became something of an obsession. At Fortrose & Rosemarkie, I nearly sprinted across the parking lot after spotting a group of older women disembarking from a tour bus, only to discover they were headed for a seaside stroll rather than the course. One final desperate email to Miles was not returned, but weeks later, while nursing a pint at the Auld Hoose in North Berwick, I mentioned the story to a stranger who claimed previous employment in the golf booking industry. His eyes lit up with recognition, and I leaned forward, hoping to confirm this ecclesiastical mystery.

"I don't think they were nuns," he tells me. "My understanding was they were part of a rosary group, and they came every year for a conference in Edinburgh and would venture out to play golf the weekend before. They would do prayer groups afterward and answer questions about faith. I hear they could play. Never held up a group once."

The truth was a bit of a bummer, not helped by his somewhat sexist remark about slow play. (That said, as one who grew up Catholic, pace isn't our forté.) Yet there was something oddly comforting in knowing that somewhere, amid the hooks and shanks and four-letter outbursts that plague golf's secular masses, there is a group of devout golfers quietly mixing their birdies with blessings, offering a counterweight to golf's constant stream of divine invocations that are decidedly not prayers.

Serendipity sometimes launches the best traditions, as proven by a group of women from Denver and Boulder, whose love affair with Scottish golf began with airline chaos two decades ago. Stranded in Edinburgh by a series of flight cancellations, they decided to leave the airport, rent clubs, and discover the charms of the city's parkland layouts. What started as a travel mishap bloomed into a ritual—this marks their twelfth trip to Scotland, and this year they're staying for two weeks weaving through Edinburgh to the Golf Coast. Their partners have joined for the second time in the trip's history and will share some tee times, although the women have protected three rounds just for themselves, preserving the spirit of that first exploration.

Staying on that front, I've never witnessed—or perhaps had failed to notice—so many mixed groups on Scottish trips, a heartening signal that golf's historically male-dominated culture is finally evolving. I also saw a number of high school and college teams of men and women, and a group called Youth on Course, which brought kids over to Scotland who otherwise wouldn't have the means.

I kept waiting for some grand revelation to emerge from all these encounters, but as time and distance provide perspective, I've come to realize that the lesson lay in the ordinary. No one captures this truth better than Michael Roth, whom I met in a Dornoch coffee shop on a misty morning. His Scioto Country Club polo—one of my favorite courses from my Ohio roots—sparks a conversation while we wait for our java to brew. He walks me through the itinerary he was on with a friend and the friend's brother with the precision of someone who had rehearsed it countless times in his mind: 10 links, what they had played and what was still to come, about how he and one of his buddies had been trying to do this for 15-plus years ... and then, mid-sentence, emotion grabs him.

"I don't know why I'm crying," he says softly, dabbing at his eyes with a paper napkin. My journalist's instincts immediately tensed, anticipating some dramatic confession. Perhaps he'd recently faced mortality, and this was a second chance at life? Maybe there was an empty seat in their foursome, reserved for someone who never made it to see these shores? Instead, when he finally steadied his voice, Michael simply offers, "I guess I just always wanted to do this Scotland thing, and it's finally happening."

It wasn't until months later that I finally realized how the moment captured the pulse of the Scottish experience. These links have a way of transforming the ordinary into the sacred, not through grand revelations or divine intervention, but by turning dreams into footprints in the sand. Sometimes, that's miracle enough.

• • •

Among the many rifts and fractured relationships spawned by LIV Golf's emergence, two stand out as particularly poignant—not for their broader impact on the golf community, but for how they transformed what were once beautiful aspects of the sport into something more complicated and bitter.

Jon Rahm's defection to LIV, while jarring, didn't shock those who closely followed the undercurrents. His connections to the Saudi-backed venture ran deep through his Phil Mickelson ties—Phil's brother Tim had shaped Rahm's early career as both his college coach and first agent, and they shared management representation. LIV's strategic pursuit of international stars made Rahm an obvious target, and the whispers only intensified after the 2023 Ryder Cup. Behind the scenes, multiple sources revealed to me Rahm's mounting frustration with the PGA Tour's hierarchy. He harbored a deep-seated belief that the Tour had failed to properly showcase his talents, while players he considered his inferiors wielded disproportionate influence over the organization's future. Following his victory at Augusta in 2023, Rahm's stature elevated him to a realm where only major championships could truly define his legacy. He had a lifetime qualification to the Masters, U.S. Open exemption through 2031, and extended entries into both the PGA Championship and Open Championship.

That's a lot of runway for a 29-year-old, with plenty of room to add to it.

But the sharpest sting came from Rahm's own words, which now echo with acidity. Looking back through the archives feels like excavating artifacts of a different era. For the sake of historical record, here are three of his most definitive statements:

In February 2022: "This is my official, my one and only time I'll talk about this, where I am officially declaring my fealty to the PGA Tour."

At the 2022 U.S. Open: "I've never really played the game of golf for monetary reasons. I play for the love of the game, and I want to play against the best in the world … I have always been interested in history and legacy, and right now the PGA Tour has that … That's all I can say. It's not my business or my character to judge anybody who thinks otherwise. And for a lot of people, I'm not gonna lie, those next three, four years are worth, basically, their retirement plan. It's a very nice compensation until they retire and sail off into the sunset."

In August 2023, worth noting given the surprise framework agreement happened in June: "I laugh when people rumor me with LIV Golf. I never liked the format. And I always have a good time with Phil Mickelson and Sergio Garcia in the practice rounds of majors. Phil respects my decision, and I respect his [choice]. Mickelson has told me that I have no reason to go play for LIV, and he has told me that multiple times."

The frequency of his emphatic denials about joining LIV became almost a running commentary in itself. In short, a tough look.

The word "narrative" feels reductive, but the reality is stark: LIV Golf's roster had become synonymous with controversial figures, its bankroll tied to a regime with a troubling human rights record. Rahm's arrival shattered this paradigm. Here was a universally respected figure, one of golf's most principled voices, whose mere presence offered LIV a chance to rewrite its public image. Beyond just adding one of the sport's two premier talents—a direct counter to criticisms that LIV merely attracted declining veterans and unfulfilled prospects—they gained something far more valuable: legitimacy. Yet this realignment came with a price. By accepting their offer, Rahm transformed from independent star to standard-bearer for a problematic regime. His 2024 BBC interview, where he framed his defection as a potential catalyst for reconciliation between golf's warring factions, rang hollow. What appeared dressed as martyrdom for the sport's greater good instead revealed itself as an opportunistic move that exploited—and ultimately damaged—the fragile peace between tours.

The betrayal cuts deeper because Rahm represented something rare in professional golf: an intellectual force whose reverence for the game's traditions matched his playing prowess. In a landscape populated too often by what can only be described as out-of-touch, petulant children masquerading as professional athletes, Rahm stood apart through his thoughtfulness and perspective. His understanding of golf's rich history and cultural significance made him special. That's what makes his choice so difficult to reconcile: he possessed the wisdom to understand the full weight of his decision, yet proceeded anyway. Whatever resolution eventually emerges from professional golf's civil war, this chapter will remain an indelible stain on Rahm's legacy.

Which brings us to Henrik Stenson, who in March 2022 was introduced as the European captain for the 2023 Ryder Cup. The announcement had languished in limbo, delayed by swirling rumors of Stenson's flirtation with LIV Golf—whispers he notably failed to quash during that February's Saudi International. The DP World Tour's stance had been unequivocal: any association with LIV meant exile from the Ryder Cup's storied tradition. Yet the landscape shifted when Mickelson's inflammatory comments seemingly torpedoed LIV's momentum. Even amid this apparent reprieve, the DP World Tour remained vigilant. They understood the stakes: if LIV rose from the ashes and Stenson defected, it would deal a blow not just to the Ryder Cup but to the foundation of European golf.

At his coronation press conference, Stenson's words rang with apparent conviction. "There's been a lot of speculation back and forth," he acknowledged, before drawing his line in the sand. "I am fully committed to the captaincy and to Ryder Cup Europe and the job at hand. We're going to keep busy with that, and I'm going to do everything in my power to deliver a winning team in Rome." When pressed specifically about potential LIV overtures, Stenson emphasized the unique gravity of his position: "The captain does sign a contract. He's the only one that does that. Players and vice captains don't. But the captain has an agreement, and those agreements are between Ryder Cup Europe and the captain, so I'm fully committed to my role as a captain and working hard towards the result we want in Rome."

Months later, when the final putt dropped at LIV Golf's Bedminster event in July, Stenson's legendary composure finally cracked. The sunglasses came off, arms spread wide, and an uncharacteristic smile broke across his face. For a man whose emotional restraint had earned him the moniker "The Iceman," this display spoke volumes. It wasn't just his first victory in years—it was vindication, celebration, and perhaps a touch of defiance. The financial calculus was staggering. The tournament win itself brought $4 million, supplemented by a $1.5 million team bonus split with Ian Poulter, Lee Westwood, and Sam Horsfield. Add to this his reported $50 million signing bonus, and Stenson had secured his family's future for generations. Yet as he celebrated on that manicured New Jersey grass, an invisible ledger balanced these material gains against a different kind of cost.

While his fellow LIV defectors that week near Manhattan faced complex questions about ethics and golf's future, Stenson's moral equation was brutally simple. His transgression cut straight to the heart of golf's most sacred team competition. After pledging himself to Europe's Ryder Cup cause, after accepting the mantle of leadership that only two dozen others had worn before him, he sold that honor for Saudi millions.

Like other players that week outside of New York City, Stenson faced a line of inquiry about morality and ethics and tearing the system down. But his burden was less layered and complex than those aforementioned entanglements, and its simplicity makes it all the more problematic. After selling himself to LIV, Stenson was stripped of his Ryder Cup captaincy. In a game that pounds its chest on integrity, Stenson cheapened his by breaking his word.

Stenson is not the only LIV player to say one thing and do the opposite. But Stenson's betrayal transcended individual opportunism. His wasn't merely a personal choice; it was the abandonment of a collective trust. He had been chosen to lead Europe's greatest sporting tradition, to carry the hopes of a continent. Instead of owning this breach of faith, Stenson compounded his transgression. Through social media posts and statements at Trump Bedminster, he attempted to shift blame to Team Europe itself—as if they, not he, had broken their covenant.

"I don't feel like I've given it up. I made every arrangement possible here to be able to fulfill my captain's duties, and I've had great help here from LIV to be able to do that. And still, the decision was made that I was to be removed," Stenson said. "I'm obviously disappointed over the situation. But it is what it is, and yeah, we move on from there now." When asked if he knew he would lose his captaincy with his move to LIV, Stenson deflected blame again, saying the decision was made for him. "We had ... we had discussions, and I informed them of the decision to go and play in LIV tournaments. [Team Europe] had a short period of time where they were kind of discussing or debating what was going to happen, and I was informed of their decision shortly after," Stenson explained.

Except it wasn't their decision, it was his. This attempt at reputation laundering only served to illuminate the depth of his ethical failure.

What makes this particularly sad is that Stenson asserted how much his captaincy meant. "It's a huge honor as you know, and just looking back at, you know, being a junior back in Sweden, back in the day, watching Seve [Ballesteros] and [Jose Maria] Olazabal play in the Ryder Cup; and then having that dream of one day playing in the Ryder Cup and I managed to achieve that dream and do it multiple times, and then getting the question of leading Team Europe, it's beyond the dreams, really," Stenson said at that press conference. Once a man breaks his word, all his future truths ring hollow. Even if Stenson meant what he said after, that's the devil's bargain he chose—and those are always harder to stomach than imagined.

One would think those with LIV Golf would do their damndest to distance Stenson from the fallout. The message didn't make its way to the broadcast booth. Analyst Jerry Foltz's attempt to equate the atmosphere at Trump Bedminster with the Ryder Cup revealed either willful delusion or profound ignorance. Having walked those grounds that week, I can attest the event resembled the Ryder Cup as much as your Thanksgiving family football game resembles the Super Bowl. Yet this is the alternate reality Stenson chose to inhabit, a funhouse-mirror version of professional golf that stands as the Ryder Cup's philosophical opposite. At LIV Golf, there are millions to be made playing golf that doesn't seem to matter. At the Ryder Cup, there is no money involved, although that's the point: What is on the line can't be bought.

•　　•　　•

Scotland has blessed me with several unforgettable visits alongside close friends. My first companion was John, who joined me for an ambitious loop before the 150th Open Championship. We carved a memorable path through Scotland's east coast, tackling the modern marvel of Dumbarnie and the rugged beauty of Murcar Links, along with Cruden Bay and Brora. Between rounds, we wandered the Old Course as St Andrews prepared for its momentous celebration. The following year brought a different adventure, as I united with my neighbor Dan and friend Justin near Edinburgh before heading south to Royal Liverpool. We weaved through a string of classics in Elie, Crail, Gullane, and North Berwick. Having shared my perspectives, I'm eager to let their experiences take center stage.

Dan's story deserves special mention, though tinged with what I consider betrayal. He was primed for another Scottish odyssey this summer until life intervened with what he claims was a legitimate excuse: impending fatherhood. I can't stay frustrated with Dan—he's both a genuine soul and a golf obsessive of the highest order. One of my most treasured memories remains watching Dan encounter

Scottish links for the first time, the courses he watched endlessly on YouTube now under his feet.

"The scenery exceeded my expectations. Man, every course we played had absolutely breathtaking views," says Dan. "I look back at the pictures from that trip regularly, and I've thought of getting a few framed, but even the best pictures don't do it justice. I'll never forget the view from the 2nd green at Elie, the 1st tee at Crail, the 17th at Gullane No. 1, the 18th at North Berwick … all of North Berwick, to be honest."

"The trip had a lasting impact on making all golf more enjoyable for me, because it gave me a better appreciation for the quirky and random aspects of golf. I used to complain, even if only to myself, about some of the odd holes at my local courses, but after playing in Scotland I've come to appreciate the weirdness. I'm still probably too focused on score—that will be a lifelong battle—but the experience in Scotland definitely helped, as there seems to be less of an emphasis on score."

Dan wanted me to remind you that, should you go to Scotland, "Leave some time for non-golf sightseeing. Edinburgh is a very cool city, give yourself at least a day to explore." Also, "Practice bump-and-runs and putting from everywhere."

My good friend John—who made a pointed fashion statement when I saw him over the holidays by sporting the North Berwick cap he'd won from me in our summer match—echoed Dan's wisdom about building breathing room into a Scottish golf itinerary, but when pressed about his most vivid memory from our adventure, he bypassed the spectacular golf moments entirely. Instead, his thoughts drifted to an unexpected incident, a travel misfortune that could have derailed our carefully planned journey but instead revealed the bonds that golf pilgrims form on the road.

"The only international flight I could find departed the U.S. at night and got into Scotland around dawn, where we had our first tee time around 9:00 a.m.—admittedly, objectively stupid and ambitious," he says. "While I was waiting on your delayed flight from JFK, a local noticed my golf travel bag, struck up a conversation, and we had an impromptu discussion about the game for the next 30 minutes or so—ranging from what courses we were going to play, suggestions on where to go before/after the round, who I thought was going to win that year's Open and a variety of other topics. Looking back, it serves as a reminder for how welcoming the Scots are and how much they value the game of golf—and how much they want to share that love with the people that visit."

John embodies that rare and wonderful balance in golf—fiercely competitive when the chips are down, yet never losing sight of the game's deeper joys. This quality shines through in his essential advice for Scotland first-timers. Even as someone who has carved out a successful business career through his competitive drive—who carefully marks his ball and grinds over four-footers in casual rounds—John grasped what the Scottish golf experience is about.

"If you're playing golf in Scotland, you've been given the opportunity few can afford nor will ever get to experience," John says. "Nobody likes to play poorly or in adverse conditions, but if you let either determine the trip's success, you're missing the point. A true golf junky should get butterflies walking Swilcan Bridge, regardless if you're 2 over or 20."

Few gifts in life compare to friends who share your deepest passions. With John, Dan, and Justin, I've discovered that Scottish links golf isn't just about the courses—it's about strengthening what we already have with every round and battle and pint. The groups I met this summer, that tell about the friendship and synergy and spiritual ties, I know it sounds corny but I know it's true because I've felt those things coursing through my veins. That's the power of Scotland, where we chase legends of the game, only to forge legends through brotherhood.

CHAPTER 10

Open and Closed

*The Open Championship • Closed shop •
Tiger, Xander, a Cinderella • The gift*

He was not the type of player that's supposed to be in a position like this at this point of an Open Championship. Dan Brown didn't look like a Champion Golfer of the Year, not as he huddled under an umbrella, his back to the relentless rain and wind, in a desperate attempt to light the cigarette dangling from his mouth. That's not a common sight nowadays; professional golf is dominated by athleticism and power, and here was Brown, taking on them and this course by ripping heaters like the service worker he contemplated becoming not long ago.

"That's just a bit of a bad habit that I've got into," Brown admitted afterward. "Do you know what, I only really do it when I'm golfing, to be honest, so I suppose it could be a coping mechanism. I was trying to sneak from my mom and dad ... They do know, but I don't do it in front of them, or I don't want to do it in front of them, so I try and hide it."

That ember at the smoking end of his dart was not the only fire that burned. You know the weather's bad when the animals say, "The hell with this"; the farm to the right of Royal Troon's inward nine was devoid of any creatures in its field. The Open's elements are often romanticized, for they call on a creativity and vision rarely seen, but the rain was so hard and cold and consistent during the third round that romanticism felt washed away long ago. The golf on display had little to do with skill; it was a test of the mind and heart. Only the baddest of men—in this case, the baddest of Cinderellas—were left standing. For the first time in a long time, golf had a true underdog in contention for one of its most coveted prizes.

"Yeah, we're still there," Brown said after his 2-over 73 on Saturday left him in a tie for second with 18 holes to go. "It was difficult. I'm a little bit disappointed with how the last two holes went because I did so well to get to where I got to, and yeah, it's a bit nasty to finish like that."

Brown should be proud. He played in the teeth of a storm, the afternoon wave facing a challenge nearly two shots harder than those that went off in the morning. There were par fours that couldn't be reached in two, with the par-three 17th requiring many to hit drivers that still came up short. As he alluded to, it wasn't a pretty finish, a bogey on 17 followed by a double at the last, yet Brown—ranked outside the top 250 in the world—would be playing in one of the final groups Sunday afternoon.

Sports fans gravitate toward the little guys, because their stories mirror our own struggles and aspirations, and Brown's journey cuts straight to the heart. His roots trace back to a small town where dreams often yield to necessity, where talent alone isn't always enough to bridge the gap between ambition and reality. When his initial pursuit of professional golf collapsed—first dropping out of college, then being cast adrift from the minor tours—Brown found himself broken and staring into a future he had not desired, filling out job applications at the local supermarket, his dreams seemingly sidelined to desperate pragmatism. The game that had once defined his identity slipped away, not from lack of passion but from that crushing mumble of self-doubt that told him his good would never be good enough. He gave up the game and retreated into depression, coming out only when the world itself paused. It was during the stillness of the pandemic that Brown found his way back to golf, if only because the empty hours demanded to be filled with something meaningful.

Brown has career stability now, earning his DP World Tour card for 2023 and winning the ISPS Handa Invitational that August, but he hasn't done much in 2024 and entered the Open missing six of his last eight cuts. However, it's what Brown represents—and what he doesn't—that makes what he's trying to do so intriguing.

On a surface level, it's been some time since a longshot had a chance at a major. Just once over the last 50 major championships has the winner been ranked outside the Official World Golf Ranking's top 35 … and that was Phil Mickelson, arguably the biggest name in golf outside of Tiger Woods, at the 2021 PGA Championship. Much is made of the fine lines in professional golf between the doers and dreamers, yet Brooks Koepka once called the majors easy to win, believing only 20 to 30 players had the capability to contend on the biggest stage when the lights shined brightest, and time has proven Koepka right. Brown could be a very large exception to Koepka's rule, though.

"Obviously it's not a normal week, but I feel like mentally I've been in a place where I've treated it like a normal week on the DP World Tour," Brown said. "I've not made it feel any bigger than what it is, and it is a lot bigger, obviously."

Yet there's a deeper, existential importance to Brown's Sunday. If there's a throughline from the last three summers of golf's civil war, it's that the top ranks have become increasingly closed off. It's no secret that the PGA Tour's signature events series has received mixed reviews from its own membership, specifically those in the rank-and-file. Some don't see these elevated tournaments as a chance to gather the game's best, instead viewing them as a way for the blue bloods to stay where they're at—and get paid handsomely in the process—while curbing upward movement for up-and-comers. One of the reasons LIV Golf was denied ranking points was limited relegation and promotion into the league. The sport's biggest names, on both sides of the debate, often seem more invested in their personal narratives than in their role as stewards of the game. Their actions reveal a deeper struggle between individual ambition and collective responsibility.

Professional golf has long been powered by and revolved around a finite number of planets, yet there still should be room for the little stars to shine bright. That it doesn't matter who you are or what you've done, where you play or where you're from, that everything on the line is ultimately up for grabs. Brown was the avatar for that promise.

Brown had never been in this position before, and major championships are notoriously unkind to novices. Out of the dozen with a viable shot at the claret jug, oddsmakers had Brown at 20-to-1, the worst figure of the bunch. That's miles better than the 1,000-to-1 odds he had at the start of the week.

"I suppose a lot of people probably thought I was going to be shaking this morning and really nervous, but I've been absolutely fine," Brown said. "Yeah, I didn't know. I didn't know last night if I was going to wake up this morning, be nervous, sweaty, whatever it might be, but I think I felt all right, and I think I'll feel all right tomorrow."

He didn't pull off the upset, imploding on Sunday to a 74 to finish nine back of the winner. That's immaterial. Even a lifetime of devotion doesn't guarantee these opportunities. If they do come, they're fleeting at best. But that's the point, because those moments, those dreams, are the things that keep you warm when life gets cold. Dan Brown kept the fire going for him and everyone else who dares for those moments, and unlike a cigarette, that is a flame that will remain lit for a long time.

•　　•　　•

The Open Championship holds a singular romance in professional golf, one that proves impossible to resist.

Professional golfers rarely betray emotion. Though their profession centers on a game, they approach it with the discipline of any vocation. Yet the British Open awakens something extraordinary in these competitors—a joy typically concealed beneath their professional veneer. In a sport increasingly governed by statistical precision, this championship demands artistic liberation. The emphasis on technical perfection yields to a more nuanced craft, where vision and feel supersede raw power and mechanical accuracy.

The players find themselves captivated by elements often peripheral to their competitive calculus. Their attention turns skyward, toward the source of the flagstick-straining winds. Though golf over here fundamentally remains a ground game, the atmospheric conditions become an integral strategic consideration. Success requires discerning when the wind might serve as an ally or emerge as an adversary, often acknowledging it can manifest as both within a single shot.

The playing surface itself commands attention in unexpected ways. The term *greens* takes on literal significance here, as these carefully maintained putting surfaces provide the sole verdant contrast to the course's predominant palette. The fairways, rough, and heather present in varying shades of brownish-yellow, creating a striking visual counterpoint to the royal-blue grandstands that punctuate the landscape. These sun-baked surfaces not only appear but perform with the firmness of pavement.

The course presents a series of tactical decisions. Players must navigate treacherous bunkers and undulations that can redirect their ball toward either salvation or peril. From 40 yards out, they deliberate between putter and wedge, inevitably discovering the putter prevails. They attempt to formulate strategic approaches on courses renowned for rendering such careful planning obsolete as their strategies dissipate into the sea breeze.

For golf enthusiasts in America, watching the Open is a ritual that begins in the predawn hours. While most of the country sleeps, dedicated followers brew their coffee in the dark and settle in to watch this event unfold across the Atlantic. Despite the distance, the connection feels immediate and profound. There's something about the

Open that feels unadulterated, even as modern commercial interests shape professional golf. Its northern setting offers a distinct advantage beyond the competition itself; with extended summer daylight, spectators can experience the championship's drama and play nearby links, many of which set aside tee times for visitors seeking to extend their connection to this game.

It's one of the very few tournaments where experience still matters. Success at the Open requires the same humbling as mastering any complex trade—setbacks and failures become teachers, gradually revealing the true way forward. How it's played speaks to how it endures; the Open Championship stands inviolate amid professional golf's current turbulence, maintaining its identity and prestige regardless of the broader disruptions reshaping the professional game.

That would be the major championships, and they are the unassailable winners of this struggle. Everyone else, to varying degrees, has lost.

After three years of turmoil in professional golf, the one incontrovertible takeaway is the four weeks that matter the most now matter more than ever. The rest of golf's landscape bears deep scars from this period of upheaval, leaving the major championships as beacons of competitive purity. The PGA Tour has surrendered pieces of its identity in its fight for survival. The DP World Tour struggles with financial uncertainty, the reputations of LIV players' stained for selling themselves out. Saudi Arabia's entry into golf's inner circle through financial force shows influence can be purchased, although legitimacy must be earned. Yet the major championships remain untouched by these currents of change, offering something precious in this fractured era: genuine merit. While victories in limited-field events like LIV's 48-player tournaments raise questions of competitive validity, achievement in the majors—The Masters, the PGA Championship, the U.S. Open, and The Open Championship—carries undiluted significance. These events continue to represent golf in its purest form, where success is earned through performance rather than arrangement.

This doesn't mean that what happens on the PGA Tour or LIV (or whatever entity comes next) is unimportant. The other 48 weeks of the year give a stage to golf's characters, building their backstory, adding context to their career and building a foundation for fan interest. But, with all due respect to the various leagues around the globe, history is not made there. It's why the PGA Tour's bet on legacy was a poor bet, for legacy can only be built at the four tournaments, where four rounds can be replayed forever.

The major championships offer something far more than competition: they are respites from golf's wider nonsense, moments when the essence of the game can shine through undimmed. In 2024 the Open visited Royal Troon on Scotland's west coast. It was the 152nd playing of the championship; it has survived two world wars, a pandemic, and John Daly. Whatever happens with the PGA Tour and Saudi Arabia, the Open will return next summer, and forever.

•   •   •

The PGA Tour had to do it to stop the bleeding. Only what they had to do looked a little like what cut them in the first place, while opening a new wound elsewhere.

In a direct response to LIV Golf's market entry, the PGA Tour overhauled its premium tournament structure. The Tour initially announced eight "elevated events," which really seemed like a reimagining of the World Golf Championships (WGCs) format. The Tour later expanded this series to 12 events, each boasting a $20 million purse and featuring carefully curated fields of 70-80 of the world's top players. The most significant departure from tradition came in the tour mandate that top players compete in these events. Beyond the enhanced purses, these tournaments carried increased FedEx Cup point allocations, raising their significance in the season-long championship chase.

"I think if you're trying to sell a product to TV and to sponsors and to try to get as many eyeballs on professional golf as possible, you need to at least let people know what they're tuning in for," McIlroy said at the 2022 Tour Championship. "When I tune into a Tampa Bay Buccaneers game, I expect to see Tom Brady throw a football. When I tune into a Formula 1 race, I expect to see Lewis Hamilton in a car."

The Tour's designated events—which would soon be renamed "signature"—are restricted to the top 50 finishers from last season's FedEx Cup, along with 15 others (10 from the current FedEx Cup standings and five from the full-field event standings between signature events). The 2023 season marked a pivotal shift in the Tour's competitive framework, reducing the playoff field from 125 to 70 players, while preserving full playing status for those finishing within the top 125 after the fall series. However, 2024 ushered in more transformation, as the Tour refined its fully exempt player pool from 125 to 100. It also reduced the number of Tour cards available via the Korn Ferry Tour from 30 to 20, reduced field sizes at most events, and decreased the number of spots available through Monday qualifying.

Prior to LIV Golf's emergence, industry observers had raised concerns about the Tour's organizational efficiency, particularly regarding the tenure of veteran players who consistently delivered unremarkable performances. However, these structural changes created significant professional uncertainty for a substantial segment of the Tour's membership: the middle-tier competitors who form its foundational base. These professionals' apprehension about the modifications was well-founded, as the changes appear primarily designed to accommodate and retain elite players rather than benefit the broader membership. The Tour's subsequent justification for its 2024 adjustments—citing pace of play improvements—struck many as particularly unconvincing, suggesting a disconnect between the stated rationale and the actual strategic motivations. This misalignment between communication and action only intensified the concerns of affected players regarding their professional futures.

The PGA Tour sells itself as a competition based firmly in meritocracy—where playing spots are earned, cuts must be made, and players only make what they earn—and it is this belief that has become a battle cry against LIV Golf, which essentially acts as a closed shop. These changes were meritocratic, alright; cannibalistic, absolutely, and unequivocally merciless. The problem for the tour is that the notion of meritocracy lacks a middle ground, no exceptions or special exemptions. Meritocracy is binary: it either *is*, or it *isn't*.

Spots for signature events are supposed to be earned by performance: an ethos that speaks to the Tour's true North Star. Except the Tour also gave each tournament four sponsor exemptions, and this is where it gets problematic, for the names those exemptions were used on compromise the very thing the Tour stands for.

Adam Scott and Webb Simpson served as player directors on the PGA Tour Policy Board during the 2024 season, positions that hold outsized importance as the Tour and its players attempt to secure the league's future in golf's civil war. Given that responsibility, you're forgiven for feeling like any sponsor exemptions bestowed upon them could be viewed as kickbacks for their dealings on the Tour board … especially when it happens more than once. Scott and Simpson each received five special invites to the restricted, $20 million fields. What's incredible is their first exemptions, used at the AT&T Pebble Beach Pro-Am, were under scrutiny; *Golfweek* posted a story with anonymous quotes from players during the AT&T Pebble Beach Pro-Am that called their exemptions "fishy," "shady," and "collusion." Those Pebble criticisms could have been couched because, ultimately, it was just one tournament. That it became a pattern shows the concerns were warranted.

That player leaders like Scott and Simpson were being rewarded is understandable. They sacrificed their time and energy to shape the Tour's trajectory and being. Compared to the motives behind other sponsor exemptions—which range from celebrity to nepotism to sponsor favoritism—bestowing spots to player advocates seemed downright noble. Yet, even with good intentions, cronyism is still that: cronyism. We expect that in other aspects of life; in golf, there is supposed to be no special treatment. The course, the opponent and those who come to watch only care about one question: can you golf your ball, or not?

Webb Simpson is respected by his peers and has enjoyed a prosperous career, with seven wins (highlighted by the U.S. Open and

JOEL BEALL

Players Championship) and over $45 million in earnings. It's also a career in the past tense, with Simpson logging just one top 5 finish in the past three years. For his part, Adam Scott remains a good player, someone that remains inside the top 50 of the OWGR; still, it's odd that Scott—who plays a limited schedule as is—rarely plays in tournaments he's exempt into on his own accord.

In their defense, there is not a laundry list of needle-movers who are on the outside looking in at these signature events. But there are certainly more players deserving of those spots, and perhaps worst of all are the optics. The rank and file don't view elevated tournaments as a chance to gather the game's best, instead believing they are a way for the blue bloods to stay where they're at—and get paid handsomely in the process—while curbing avenues for social mobility. A few seasons must play out before judging if that perception is reality; conversely, that a number of Korn Ferry Tour grads struggled to earn starts in 2024 amplifies the perception.

It's not just the internal message that is tainted. One of the reasons LIV Golf was denied ranking points was limited relegation and promotion into the league, which included two players (Lee Westwood and Martin Kaymer) keeping their status solely because they were team captains. For fans at home, you don't have to squint to see the symmetry between their plights and that of Simpson, who finished 141st in the FedEx Cup in 2023.

Of the myriad problems facing professional golf, sponsor exemptions are a low priority, but they're also a self-inflicted and unnecessary wound and speak to the larger, systemic issues plaguing the tour. Perhaps it's serendipity that the announcement of Scott and Simpson's sponsor exemptions at the Arnold Palmer Invitational coincided with Anthony Kim making his debut at LIV. Kim played as a wildcard in Saudi Arabia on LIV's version of a sponsor exemption. Given his hiatus, it's fair to question Kim's validity as a formidable golfer, but there's no questioning the curiosity around him as an entertainer. LIV is often knocked for being an exhibition; here, at least, there's value in being an exhibition vehicle. You ultimately must know what your core product is, and how it's presented. And just as importantly, what can confuse the messaging. Between the sponsor exemptions and eliminating playing opportunities, and the difficulty in cracking through to the signature series to the rest of the Tour playing regular events … the Tour was starting to become the closed shop it said it abhorred.

•   •   •

Most of my crooked media brethren had a Tuesday afternoon round scheduled at Western Gailes: a whimsy, magnificent links course nine miles north of Prestwick. I had to pass because of a drink date with Mark, a South African who has been coming to the Open Championship since the mid-1980s. Mark had been following my journey through social media's digital breadcrumbs and reached out, promising stories that could fill volumes. When he mentioned potentially colorful fan perspectives, I bit—though (initially) my enthusiasm would soon drain like a pint at last call.

We met at the T-Bar, a pub in Ayr where brick absorbed the late afternoon light and the floor bore the scars of countless spilled pints. Mark, blonde-haired and bright-eyed, had already claimed a tabletop and pushed a lager in my direction before I could properly settle in. There's no diplomatic way to frame this: Writers, by nature and necessity, are ruthless critics of narrative. We're perpetually hunting for the heart of a story, the thing that makes it matter beyond its moment. This trait is especially pronounced in me, and doubly so when I've sacrificed a round of golf during what feels like an endless work week. So when Mark's stories—though delivered with genuine warmth and charm—began to feel more like pleasant anecdotes than compelling yarns, I found my hand creeping toward my phone, preparing to manufacture an emergency exit. Then I glimpsed the time on the pub's ancient wall clock, and everything shifted.

Earlier, I briefly mentioned a brush with death. In fall 2022, at just 36, what started as a routine urgent care visit became a lights-and-sirens rush to the emergency room when a doctor suspected a heart attack. The memory remains visceral: the ambulance's sway, the shocking cold of the steel table, the choreographed chaos of the medical team swarming around me. The sound of my wife's prayers mixing with a priest's murmured responses somewhere beyond my field of vision. The crystal-clear thought: "Holy shit, I'm about to die." While it turned out to be a treatable heart defect rather than an attack, that moment—along with a hellish week of sleeplessness caused by a medication mix-up –rewired my perspective on life. Since then, I've developed an almost compulsive habit of clock-watching, not out of impatience but as a reminder of life's precious impermanence. Each glance serves as a meditation on presence, on making moments matter. Catching sight of my digital timepiece that afternoon, I realized I was failing my own philosophy. I pocketed my phone, flipped open my notebook, and signaled for another round.

Mark's stories, viewed through this new lens, took on different dimensions. Yes, they were personal: trailing South African heroes Ernie Els and Tim Clark through practice rounds, losing what he called "an embarrassing amount" on Sergio Garcia in the 2007 playoff heartbreak, catching the early sparks of Phil Mickelson's miraculous 2013 run. I suppose the real communal magic lay in a 2005 tale from St Andrews, where a chance meeting at a shawarma cart connected Mark with a Japanese golf enthusiast. From there they decided to find a drink together, which led to an introduction to two New Zealanders, spawning a transcontinental friendship that's produced Irish golf adventures and plans for a Scottish reunion next year.

These weren't just stories, they were testament to what brought Mark back—and who he was. To him, the Open Championship isn't just a tournament; it's an annual wandering that gives his life rhythm and meaning. Outside of the Masters, I can think of no other event in golf that has this gravitational pull on the soul.

I crossed paths with him again Friday afternoon as I left the media center. He stood with his wife Darlene, who offered me a steaming cup of hot chocolate against the Scottish chill. Though Mark never mentioned it during our pub session, his success as a currency trader was evident. But watching them together, I realized his true wealth wasn't in his portfolio. As Darlene put it, with the knowing smile of someone sharing an essential truth: "He is happiest when he is here."

Yes, I still feel a twinge of regret about missing Western Gailes. But Mark gave me something more valuable, reminding me that the richest stories aren't always the ones that shout the loudest.

•　　　•　　　•

The 2024 Open marked Martin Slumbers' final championship as the R&A's CEO. Unlike his counterparts at other major championships who carefully dodged questions about LIV Golf with diplomatic responses, Slumbers took a distinctly different approach. When faced with questions about the Saudi-backed league at the historic 150th Open at St Andrews in 2022, just weeks after LIV's debut, he didn't wait to be asked. Instead, he used his opening statement to deliver an unambiguous and forceful critique of the upstart tour.

"Professional golfers are entitled to choose where they want to play and to accept the prize money that's offered to them. I have absolutely no problem with that at all," Slumbers said. "But there is no such thing as a free lunch. I believe the model we have seen at Centurion and at Pumpkin Ridge is not in the best long-term interest of the sport as a whole and is entirely driven by money. We believe it undermines the merit-based nature and the spirit of open competition that makes golf so special."

"I would also like to say that in my opinion the continued commentary that this is about growing the game is just not credible and, if anything, is harming the perception of our sport that we are working so hard to improve. We believe the game needs to focus on increasing participation, achieving greater diversity and making sure that golf is truly open to all rather than this narrow debate involving a small number of players."

Slumbers' forthright stance stood in stark contrast to the cautious responses from other golf administrators, offering a rare moment of clarity in an increasingly murky landscape. While sources close to the PGA of America and USGA later revealed that their leaders had wanted to speak more candidly but were constrained by legal counsel—anticipating the litigation that would indeed follow—this context, though understandable, doesn't diminish the significance of Slumbers' courage. After all, he likely faced similar legal advisories yet chose to speak out anyway. There's something disheartening about watching principles yield to prudence, about witnessing conviction bow to caution. Conversely, there's something inspiring about those who choose to speak truth despite the consequences, recognizing silence itself carries a cost too heavy to bear.

This makes Slumbers' final address at Royal Troon particularly compelling, coming as it did after two years of seismic changes that had transformed the golf landscape that he had so boldly addressed at St Andrews. The golf world had shifted dramatically since that day at the Old Course, and I wondered whether his perspective had shifted with it.

"We have to make choices if we want to continue to build on the significant growth in participation that is essential for golf's future," Slumbers said that Monday. "We remain concerned about the impact substantial increases in men's professional prize money are having on the perception of the sport and its long-term financial sustainability. We are determined to act with the interests of the global game in mind as we pursue our goal of ensuring golf continues to thrive in 50 years' time."

Look no further than the financials of the Open: more than $3 million was tabbed for the 2024 champ and a total of $18 million for the field, yet the Open isn't even among the top 25 highest paying events in the sport. Speaking to the media later in the week at Troon, Slumbers reiterated his worry about what the ramifications of excess at the top can have on the rest of the sport.

"While we will always offer a very competitive prize fund for the Open, our wider focus is on increasing participation and improving pathways in golf," Slumbers said. "We have to make choices about how we allocate resources and make the resources we have go as far as they can. It takes financial resources to deliver projects of this kind, and we have to find ways to do more of this if we're to accelerate and maintain the upward trajectory of golf's participation curve. But perhaps the most important component of all to golf's future success is staying true to its values. What sets golf apart from other sports is its ability to maintain a unique value set. It's a value set defined by integrity, personal accountability, and respect. These are precisely the values that sponsors want their products or services to be associated with and that are fundamental to golf's appeal. These values are golf's secret weapon and we cannot afford to let them be diminished."

In his final act as R&A chief, Slumbers remained true to form, wielding his words with the same conviction that had defined his tenure. He chose resonance over retreat.

• • •

It was a slow week. It's fine, they happen, even at majors. But it does explain why one of the biggest headlines came from a tabloid interview.

"I hope people remember Tiger as Tiger was, the passion and the charismatic aura around him," Colin Montgomerie said in an interview with *The Times* of London prior to the week. "There is none of that now. At Pinehurst [for the U.S. Open], he did not seem to enjoy a single shot and you think, 'What the hell is he doing?' He's coming to Troon, and he won't enjoy it there either." Montgomerie later added, in response to Woods' comments a month earlier that his competitive days may be numbered, "Aren't we there? I'd have thought we were past there. There is a time for all sportsmen to say goodbye, but it's very difficult to tell Tiger it's time to go. Obviously, he still feels he can win. We are more realistic."

To various extents for the last decade, similar eulogies have been made about Woods' career—only for Woods to prove how much great golf he has left. Perhaps that's partly why Monty's remarks made the rounds. But as blunt as Montgomerie was, the collective response was just as telling, because there was little, if any, rebuttal. Montgomerie said what we all know to be true: In sports, everything ends badly. Otherwise, it wouldn't end.

A sober assessment of Woods' golf as he nears 50 would describe it as 'poor.' Since winning the 2019 Masters, he has failed to finish inside the top 20 at a major and has either missed the cut or withdrawn in five of the last seven. He's played four rounds of an official tournament just three times in the last four seasons. This is partly an upshot of the fact he hardly plays at all. The last time Woods teed it up at an event that wasn't a) a major, b) his Genesis Invitational or c) a silly-season event was in the summer of 2020. That is the profile of a ceremonial figure … which Woods was at the U.S. Open, in the field thanks to a special exemption from the USGA. He fought, but Pinehurst painfully illustrated it was a test he could not pass. Woods had become more celebrity than competitor.

Great athletes rarely know when to walk away. While Willie Mays is often used as the cautionary tale, his story is far from unique. Tom Brady played two seasons too many after his Tampa Bay Super Bowl victory. Michael Jordan's Washington Wizards' years dimmed the glow of his perfect Bulls finale. Muhammad Ali's fight against Larry Holmes was painfully one-sided. The list goes on—Jerry Rice, Shaq, Greg Maddux, Brett Favre, Chuck Liddell—all stayed past their prime. What makes this pattern so common is painfully ironic: the same competitive fire that drove these athletes to greatness also blinded them from seeing they were no longer what they were.

Golf is a different bird. There are no front offices making cuts or governing bodies ruling an athlete unfit for competition. Woods can play the Masters and PGA Championship as long as he wants and last year was gifted a lifetime exemption into PGA Tour signature events. The Open only recently implemented an age restriction at 55 years old, although Woods is grandfathered into the previous limit of 60. There's also the golden parachute that is the senior tour. Golfers don't retire, they fade into competitive irrelevance as the next generation emerges.

The problem is that Woods continues to be the sun this solar system revolves around, and why the finality of Woods' career is something of a third rail. Fans don't want it to be true, and collectively, no one quite understands what the end looks like, including Woods. That is at the heart of what Montgomerie was trying to convey. Woods has asserted he only tees it up when he thinks he can win. He doubled-down on the sentiment Tuesday at Royal Troon. "I'll play as long as I can play and I feel like I can still win the event," Woods said, the implication being that he feels that way about his chances this week in Scotland. The thing is, what Woods wants to do—what fans want him to do—he physically can't, his impressive physique belying a body fused together through more surgeries than you can count on two hands. And though the runway for those on the back-end of their careers has been extended, thanks to equipment gains and advancements in sports sciences such as training and recovery, professional golf is unequivocally a young man's game. Rory McIlroy is the only player older than 30 inside the world's top 10, and Adam Scott is the lone player older than 40 in the top 60.

Of course, this is ultimately Woods' legacy and his life, and Woods was clear Tuesday that he would not take directions from anyone but himself.

"Well, as a past champion, I'm exempt," Woods said. "Colin's not. He's not a past champion, so he's not exempt. So he doesn't get the opportunity to make that decision. I do." When pressed further if he's earned the privilege to continue, Woods responded, "When I get to his age, I get to still make that decision, where he doesn't."

Woods has earned the right. And the case can be made that there's something noble in battling a destiny we cannot escape yet refusing to surrender all the same. That he can conjure the magic that Phil Mickelson did at Kiawah, that 59-year-old Tom Watson did at Turnberry. The hope that, if only for one week or even one day, Woods can be as good as he once was. But the underlying heart of Monty's message was one of compassion. He's trying to tell Woods what he apparently can't see, and what Montgomerie doesn't want to see again.

And that's what we saw at Troon, with a 79 and 77. It's not about the golf, because in between his shots on the course and range, Woods was noticeably hobbling. (During his press conference, he wore shorts and a compression sleeve on his right leg from above the knee to his foot.) It is a gait hampered by injuries, functional only through an unshakable will and the belief that he can keep going because he's done it countless times before. However, at the end of Royal Troon, at the end of another lost year, golf fans were reminded there is no such thing as eternity.

The question is, how long will the sport be able to ignore the obvious, that Tiger's gait is no longer of a gladiator ready for combat, but of a man weighed down by the scars both suffered and inflicted from battles before? Or will the game continue to expect the same warrior until he puts down his shield for good?

The reckoning should have come by now. The popularity should have waned as his performance has, the crowds shrinking to those who have come to pay their respects rather than viewing him as the main—and to some, the only—attraction. There is no parallel in sports to a once-great athlete whose performance no longer lives up to its past still drawing as much attention. For a player who has spent more than a decade teetering on the precipice of no return, golf remains woefully unwilling to acknowledge a day will come when Tiger will no longer be capable of Tiger things. Most of the crowd still thinks—still hopes, still believes—that Woods remains Tiger Woods, for greatness radiates a magnetism that outlives the source.

To be fair, not all who come out expect the Woods of old. This was especially true in Scotland. Woods still commanded some of the largest galleries that week, but they knew who was and wasn't in front of them. They did not envision him making a run. There were no expectations, period. They just wanted to say they saw him, even if what they were watching was tough to watch.

•   •   •

I had picked the wrong day to forget my rain jacket. Showers had not only materialized that Saturday afternoon but had evolved into something uniquely, oppressively Scottish—possessing the ghostly omnipresence of highland mist yet delivering the relentless volume of a monsoon. This rain doesn't announce itself with drama; it simply becomes one with your clothes, transforming them into a second skin of cold weight. There's a peculiar brotherhood in this shared discomfort—a silent acknowledgment among journalists and fans who brave these elements for the love of the game, our wet shoulders badges of devotion. Yet beneath this notion of sporting dedication lay a more vulnerable truth: This was miserable. After an hour of this baptism by precipitation, my resolve finally dissolved. Troon's classic out-and-back links layout, typically a testament to golf course architecture, had become a cruel geometry problem—I was nowhere near shelter. Surrendering to both wisdom and weakness, I sought refuge in the merchandise tent, where at least the dripping of my clothes could harmonize with the gentle rustle of overpriced rainwear I now desperately coveted.

The R&A's merchandise pavilion rises from the links landscape like a monolith; a vast, hangar-sized monument to golf's material culture. I typically maintain a distance from retail spaces during tournament weeks, my reluctance born from professional principle and personal philosophy: there's something dissonant about wearing the emblems of events we're meant to observe with journalistic detachment, a blurring of the lines between witness and participant. That every event peddles identical gear, distinguished only by swapped logos, reinforces this hesitation. Yet I found unexpected insight in this commercial sanctuary as I was trying to get dry. Unlike the almost frenzied consumption at Augusta National—where patrons emerge laden with bags of treasure, their purchases driven by a complex web of social obligations and entrepreneurial calculations—the Open's commerce carries a more intimate resonance. Here, spectators move with purpose, selecting single items with thoughtful deliberation: a flag, cap, shirt, nothing more. These aren't just souvenirs; they're anchors to moments of personal pilgrimage, modest tokens that whisper "I was there" without needing to shout it.

What transpired next wasn't extraordinary in any conventional sense. From my vantage point, I watched two men extract hooded sweatshirts from crisp bags, their movements suggesting the ritual of preparation against the elements. But as one pushed open the door, letting in the sound of rain and a breath of cold air, the other hesitated—then carefully, almost reverently, returned his purchase to its plastic cocoon. I assumed, with the rain-soaked logic of someone who'd been out too long, that the weather had finally relented. When I pushed through those same doors moments later, the rain had intensified from steady drumbeat to full symphony. Thirty yards ahead, through the gray curtain, I watched a tale of two choices unfold: one man already wearing his new sweatshirt, shaking his head at his companion who sloshed alongside, shopping bag held close like precious cargo.

What struck me wasn't the apparent irrationality of leaving perfectly good rain gear unworn—it was the fierce intentionality behind the decision. Our sweatshirtless friend wasn't suffering from buyer's remorse but rather its inverse: he'd found something too precious to subject to mere utility, choosing to preserve it unsullied even at the cost of his own comfort. Later that night, as scalding shower water slowly rekindled feeling in my rain-numbed limbs, I realized certain logos aren't just screen-printed brand identifiers. Some, it seems, are worth catching a chill for.

• • •

The three words are plastered on every billboard and grandstand and awning, "Forged by Nature," not so much a slogan as it is the ethos at the British Open. It's golf how golf is supposed to be: without artifice or human intervention, nothing but a player against the earth and her elements. What's presented is a test and an education, an experience that's as romantic and religious as this game can get. That's the sell, at least. But marketing doesn't always match the product because *forged* was not the f-word that was used ad nauseam on Friday and Saturday at this Troon Open. This was not a test, something to weed out the pretenders from the contenders. And religious? Try biblical, Old Testament-style fire and brimstone, wrath from a divine power that cannot be conquered and only hoped to be survived, those left standing not by their own devices but by divine intervention or indifference or sheer dumb luck. It's why each man who stumbled off the course looked in serious need of a hug. Or a drink. Or perhaps both. The thing is, they had an idea that what happened would happen, yet knowing you're about to get punched doesn't make the blow any less painful.

And their pain was our pleasure. After Thursday's conditions delivered a tough-but-fair setup and Friday morning followed the same blueprint, Friday afternoon arrived and chose chaos, doing away with pleasantries and leaning into the mean that lied within, leaving those in the later Open wave looking on in dazed resignation.

"I need to lie down in a dark room. It's brutal out there," said Matthew Southgate after a 7-over 78. "That's one of the toughest experiences I've had on a golf course. It was crosswinds everywhere and pins on the same side where the wind was coming from. It's just so, so difficult. It was like survival golf really. It's so difficult just to make a par. The first nine holes ... you're sort of making the best educated guess you possibly can as to what club you need and where to aim. It was so tough."

The Open is notorious for one wave getting the business end of the weather while the other makes it out relatively unscathed, leading to the stigma that the claret jug requires a good deal of providence. That fear didn't come to fruition in Round 1: The morning shift posted an average score of +3.40 over par, the afternoon +3.50. But Friday proved the axiom true, as a mighty, consistent wind arrived off the Firth of Clyde, turning Troon's flags into those inflatable, arm-flailing tubemen erected at used car dealerships. The result was tee shots that looked good until they weren't, approach shots that wouldn't hold, and putts that couldn't be stopped. Parts of Troon you're supposed to avoid—the bunkers, the heather, the gorse—could not be avoided. The afternoon players were a whopping two strokes higher in average than their morning brethren.

Although storms can't be conveyed by numbers. It must be viewed by what's left in its wake. Justin Thomas finished his Thursday round with the Open lead. Nine holes and 45 shots later he was outside the cut. On the par-three 5th Thomas hit a 130-yard tee shot, which was a problem considering the hole measured over 210 yards, one of Thomas' hands on his club and the other on his hip, wondering what the hell was happening.

Robert MacIntyre, who won the Scottish Open the week before, walked off the 1st tee and directly into the heather, the Scotsman a whopping eight over through his first four holes. Joaquin Niemann made an 8 at the par-three Postage Stamp hole after finding three different bunkers on the 120-yard hole. Any hopes of a Rory McIlroy surge were kaput with a triple at the 4th, where McIlroy was only able to advance his second from the high stuff a few feet. He could only muster a sly smile, knowing that it wasn't his day and there was nothing he could do about it. Sahith Theegala had a triple, two doubles and four bogeys through his first 13 holes. Nicolai Hojgaard had to turn his hat around backwards to keep it from flying into the ether.

At one moment Friday evening the scoreboard showed that of the last 99 players who went out, only two—two!—were under par for the tournament. One of them was Brown, the former delivery truck driver turned Cinderella story, the other Justin Rose, who shot 68. However, Rose is facing the threat of disqualification, as there are rumors that he may have been playing a different course.

Then there is the tale of Aguri Iwasaki, who earned a spot in the field thanks to winning the Japan Open and, at 5-over through 29 holes, was inside the projected cutline. He proceeded to make a mess on the 12th, leading to double. Then he suffered three penalty strokes thanks to pumping a ball out of bounds with several unplayable lies, leading to a quintuple-bogey 9.

All of it was a trainwreck, and it was a delight. Because this British Open was what we want the U.S. Open to be. Where the best of the best are made to look like us, where there's not so much red and much more black, where "good bogey" is said in seriousness. It was a much-welcomed break from the onslaught of scoring we've seen in recent months in professional golf. In that same breath, this wasn't a mickey-mouse, gimmicky setup straight out of the USGA of yesteryear. Balls were not oscillating, putts did not roll endlessly off greens. To a man, no one directed blame at the R&A. The only blame could be to nature and no one wants to be the old man yelling at the sky. It was tough and unrelenting and diabolical. Troon is a nuanced challenge no matter the conditions. Add incessant gusts and ever-hardening surfaces to the recipe and what comes off the grill is a slab of charred golfers wondering if they should have gone into another profession.

It's here we should state this Open round coincided with the global release of *Twisters*, the sequel to the '90s film featuring tornados wreaking havoc for the better part of two hours. The new film was expected to rake in hundreds of millions at the box office, which made sense. The entertainment of a good disaster film is hard to beat.

•   •   •

I have a ritual on major championship Sundays, walking the course in the quiet hours before the tournament begins. These solitary morning walks serve multiple purposes—gathering thoughts, plotting coverage strategies, identifying storylines that could emerge depending on how the day unfolds. You learn the course's morning personality, discover the perfect viewing spots where drama might unfold later. This Sunday at Royal Troon began differently. My colleague and housemate Shane Ryan had misplaced his press credential, leading to a frantic search through the streets of Ayr. Relief came through an unexpected connection—a kind local reaching out via Facebook, having found the pass on the rain-slicked pavement outside our rental. Crisis averted, we made our way to the course. Instead of my usual wandering, I found myself drawn to the horseshoe of grandstands surrounding the 18th green. What I witnessed, to me at least, was remarkable: hours before any player would approach the final hole, in sideways rain that felt like needles against exposed skin, the stands were already filling with spectators. Even for Scots, who wear their weather-hardened reputation as a badge of honor, this level of dedication bordered on the sublime.

These weren't just golf fans—they were travelers who had come to worship. Watching those soaked figures huddled in anticipation, a bedrock certainty emerged: while we journalists spend countless words building monuments of those inside the ropes, it's the faithful beyond—braving storms, crossing oceans, passing their passion through generations—who transform this sport into scripture.

•   •   •

Twenty minutes, that's all it took. A quick in-and-out and mission complete before his British Open competitors knew what they were trying to capture could no longer be obtained. Two birdies, off beautiful approaches, the disappearance of the ensuing putts prodding the usually stoic Xander Schauffele to pump his fists as he willed what he wanted into existence. Twenty minutes when Thriston Lawrence began the 12th hole with a one-shot lead and left with a two-shot deficit, when the crowds—who had endured four days of wind and rain and more wind, and who were spiritedly behind Justin Rose's pursuit of a championship he could not quit—realized what Schauffele was doing was the one thing they could not weather. Twenty minutes that bookend two months of Schauffele erasing the story we wrote for him as he authored his own.

While 2024 had been a breakout for Schauffele, it's also been one of turmoil. Because he had so many strong showings at majors that ended without a trophy, there had been a belief that perhaps Schauffele was a little too level-headed for his own good, failing to recognize big-time golf calls for big-time emotion. Early-season stumbles at the Players Championship (when he faltered on the final two holes with a chance to win) and the Wells Fargo Championship (blinking as his one-shot lead evaporated into a seven-stroke deficit in a nine-hole stretch to finish a distant second to Rory McIlroy) only fueled the perception. There were also the optics of a poor Ryder Cup showing (1-3-0) made worse amid reports Schauffele was nearly kicked off the American team for demanding pay. On their own, each had an explanation or excuse. In the broader context, it reinforced a narrative that Schauffele, despite his undeniable talent, faltered in the moments that mattered most.

"Sometimes things go your way, and sometimes they don't," Schauffele said, about some of those past falls. "But for the most part, all those tough losses in the past or those moments where I let myself slip up and dream too early on that back nine, I was able to reel myself in today and make sure that didn't happen."

His win at the PGA Championship in May quieted that perception, although the game's scholars know one major is never enough, especially for someone of Schauffele's caliber. Their talents beget more summits to reach. Failing to add to that total is seen as squandered potential. On Sunday, in a voice so loud and clear it can never be silenced again, Schauffele made no doubt about it: He is that dude.

What followed was not necessarily theater, not in the classical sense. Schauffele safely found the green at the 17th, Lawrence unable to give himself viable looks at birdie. Schauffele even passed on marking his ball for the final putt, instead tapping in what remained and conferring the stage to Rose, who drained his putt and raised his hat to the crowds as if he was the victor. But as Rose walked off ,Schauffele turned to the grandstands on the left and right sides of the green and pounded his hands in their directions, and they returned the favor.

It lacked the tenor of love that Rose was given, but the gestures from Schauffele and the galleries were baked in respect. And the winning description goes to Rose's caddie Mark 'Fooch' Fulcher, who was irritated that on top of being such a good player that Schauffele is a good guy. "I kind of wish he was a wanker."

So, what do we make of Schauffele? Now two major championships, nine career wins, an argument to be made against Scheffler for Player of the Year honors. The type of performance that cements Schauffele as a certified alpha and begs questions of where he can go from here. Schauffele, of course, had no appetite for such conjecture.

"Pretty much that's you guys' job to speculate on those things," Schauffle said. "I'm just trying to win as many of these things as I can and play the best golf as I can and be a decent guy."

For years, Schauffele had dreamed of the walk up the 18th, to be surrounded by the blue stands and yellow leaderboards and know they were bowing to him. It was a dream that was shared, so it was apropos that the man Xander shared it with was there to relish it too.

That would be Stefan Schauffele, Xander's dad. The Ogre, as he's affectionately known. For the better part of Xander's career, Stefan was known as more than just a father or teacher, but a shadow, following his son wherever he went. It was Stefan that gave his son a sense of direction, the conviction and backing to know where he was going wasn't a wish but a reality that could be attained. Their bond was visceral and true, but also one that drew criticism. As Xander's shortcomings became numbered, there was talk that perhaps the son needed a little separation to deliver on his potential.

Following the Ryder Cup—where Stefan had given several interviews, confirming the noise of payments and exclusion—father and son had a talk. It was time for Stefan to take a step back and bestow Xander space. Stefan obliged, which is why when Xander lifted the Wanamaker trophy in Louisville, the father was watching 5,000 miles away in Hawaii.

"It's mature of [Stefan] to just step back and say, 'Hey, we need something else here and we need to try something else to get you over that top,'" explained Schauffele's caddie Austin Kaiser. "His dad's accepted that. [Stefan's] in Hawaii now, building things and he's happy. That's all Xander cares about. He just wants his dad happy."

Maybe that's why one of the first people Xander greeted in celebration was his father, who was tucked behind the clubhouse, watching the reality only he and Xander envisioned. Golf is a lot of things. At its heart, is a game of fathers and sons. To see Xander and Stefan embrace—Xander holding on tight, Stefan's sunglasses unable to conceal the tears that flowed from behind—was a reminder of the spell this beautifully dumb game has on so many of us.

"I sat down with my dad when I was maybe 15 and 16, and we started to really hash out some goals and dreams of what I'd like to do," Schauffele said. "I was on the couch with my dad a lot watching other guys win majors and win big tournaments. My dad and I, we've definitely talked about this. We've watched that walk up 18 pretty much every year until I've played in the Open."

Only those two know the toll of all the previous shortcomings, of the weight that comes with unmet expectations and what it's like when that weight has been lifted. Xander joked he would allow Stefan to choose what they would drink first from the trophy, although he was deadly serious when insisting Stefan would get the first sip. It's ridiculous, of course, to distill what Schauffele did to 20 minutes. It took a lifetime of work and effort and disappointment and doubt to allow him to do what he did in those 20 minutes, and because of it, Xander Schauffele's name is on the claret jug, now and forever.

•　　•　　•

The Low Green sprawls between Ayr Bay and the town's administrative heart, where Edwardian edifices of local government loom like displaced fragments of Edinburgh. This vast expanse, punctuated by weathered monuments, serves as the community's stage for concerts and festivals. Today though, it's an impromptu dog park where Bruiser and I decompress in the Open's wake.

The morning after always aches with the peculiar emptiness that follows intensity. While golf journalism may lack the physical toll of mining coal, major weeks consume us in 16-hour marathons of observation and creation. We pour ourselves into the coverage because we understand what these moments mean to the fans. It's exhilarating and depleting in equal measure, leaving us hollow by Monday. Yet even in exhaustion, the game's magnetic pull remains—which is why the solitary figure practicing pitch shots at the green's edge drew me in.

He was an adolescent, caught in that liminal space between boy and man, answering my queries with the economic language of youth: grunts, nods, and clipped phrases. His swing bore the hallmarks of Scottish ingenuity—slightly handsy, played from the inside, designed to pierce wind and control trajectory. His demeanor suggested he wanted to be left alone, but as I turned to leave, he broke his reserve: "You were at the Open, were you?" I nodded, and shared fragments of Troon and Schauffele, offering enough to satisfy his curiosity. He resumed his practice, murmuring "It's fun to see what it's all about."

Local pride underpins this championship, although their relationship with the Open transcends mere hosting duties. It's not their defining moment but rather their gift to the game—a demonstration of golf in its purest form, stripped of all the unnecessary BS. Here was their legacy, quietly practicing in the salt air, carrying forward an ancient conversation between player and land. They understand what we don't, that our search does not have to be complicated, and there's nothing to be caught. It's here, open to all.

CHAPTER 11

Home

St Andrews with friends • The price of greed •
Permanence

I am looking at my phone, then up at the sky, then back to my phone, muttering a prayer I know won't be heard. They are the movements of cornered prey, each glance carrying the weight of dwindling options. This must be what it feels like to be a fugitive, to see the border that promises freedom on the horizon become blocked out by the red-and-blue lights of the closing in law enforcement. I begin to acknowledge what cannot be changed: We are not going to make it.

I'm back in St Andrews, with company. Two fellow scribes from the Athletic, Brendan Quinn and Brody Miller, have made the pilgrimage north from Edinburgh. They're more co-conspirators than colleagues, my reliable companions for long nights in hotel bars across the world. This will be their baptism at the Open, and they've arrived early to visit me in St Andrews, partly to witness golf's holiest ground, partly to discover what force keeps pulling me back to Scotland.

Alex Cowie, my friend and our shepherd for the day, has secured us a late tee time at the Old Course. In Alex, we've drawn the perfect guide. A former military police officer who traded his badge for a more contemplative life in St Andrews when he retired in 2012, he carries himself with the corkscrew athleticism of someone who's outrunning time. At first glance, his build suggests someone who enforces debts rather than golf etiquette, but the impression dissolves as soon as he speaks. Alex is a raconteur whose commentary weaves seamlessly between tactical advice ("Take it just left of that gorse bush") and historical color ("Faldo stood right here in '90 when ... "). He has the gift of making each insight feel like a secret shared between friends.

It was an inauspicious start. Let's just say Brody's opening salvo challenged traditional notions of golf ball trajectory—a topped tee shot and ensuing lateral shot at the first that I've been explicitly instructed to omit from the record. Lesser men would have walked into the North Sea; Brody has shouldered his bag, onward. Though Brendan and Brody are relatively new converts to golf, they possess the capacity for awe. Their jaws drop at greens big enough to land planes on and bunkers that seem placed by mischievous gods. Walking these fairways, they drift between awe and joy, like travelers who've found something even better than they imagined. Brendan is playing well, we are having fun, life is good.

But there's an uncomfortable truth about the Old Course: its pace of play is glacial. With a stream of visitors—many overwhelmed by the course's demands and uncertain about its numerous blind shots— rounds regularly stretch beyond five hours. While this timeline poses little concern for most of the day's tee sheet, it presents a significant challenge for our midsummer 6 p.m. start, with sunset approaching at 10 p.m. Our position relative to our remaining holes creates an increasingly problematic equation. After walking off the 9th green at 7:50 p.m., we encounter a severe bottleneck at "The Loop" —a notorious sequence of five intersecting holes beginning at the 7th. This section, which typically impedes play under normal circumstances, has devolved into complete gridlock. By the time we reach the 11th tee, 40 minutes have elapsed. Though Brendan and Brody maintain their optimism, Alex and I exchange knowing glances. The calculations of daylight over distance leaves little room for interpretation and suggests an outcome neither of us wishes to voice.

Brendan and Brody are two of the best sportswriters in the game. This should be the first of many Opens for them. But you never know. Our industry is a fickle one. Same with life. They are here, and I want them to reach the end. Selfishly, I do too. My two-week stay—filled with rounds on the Old Course, quiet observations from beside the 18th green, countless steps across these grounds—is drawing to a close. Each visit feels like a beginning rather than an end, but experience has taught me the cruelty of assumption. The privilege of returning is never guaranteed, making each moment more precious than the last.

Similarly, the ability to finish—for something to reach its good end—is also a privilege. We concede to reality on the 15th, making our way back so they can glimpse the Road Hole and 18th in the fading light. The historic Swilcan Bridge emerges through the gathering darkness, illuminated only by the warm glow of town windows—a scene that echoes with its own cinematic beauty, like wanderers discovering a mystical baseball diamond at dusk.

Still, regret weighs as we walk off the course and into the pub. These friends have traveled across an ocean only to experience an abbreviated round. My apology tumbles out as we walk, but Brody's response carries genuine wonder: "Are you kidding? This is incredible."

In the corner booth at Dunvegan's, Brendan's reassuring hand finds my shoulder. "It was awesome, brother," he says with quiet conviction. "Don't worry; that course ain't going anywhere."

•   •   •

The next day, on our final evening in St Andrews, Alex and his wife Kathryn welcome us into the St Andrews Golf Club, housed in one of the distinguished stone edifices that stands along the 18th hole of the Old Course. The interior fulfills every expectation of traditional Scottish elegance: crimson carpets and drapes frame dark wooden fixtures, historical black-and-white photographs chronicling the legacy of those who've graced these halls. A game room crowns the upper floor.

Yet we find ourselves drawn to a diminutive balcony, accessed through one of the towering windows, suspended several stories above the 18th green. From this perch, we observe the parade of golfers below completing their pilgrimage. I turn to Alex, curious if this magnificent vista ever becomes commonplace, but he halts mid-response, caught in a moment of reflection.

"For some reason I was going to say 'Yes,' but honestly, this always feels special," Alex says. "I would say 'comfortable.' There's a warmness to it that grows the more you come. But this never becomes background. What brought us here is still what brings us back."

A few moments later I spot fellow media members Sean Zak, James Colgan, Alex Miceli, and Darren Riehl coming up the 18th. They too have come to pay their respects to St Andrews before heading west to Troon. I was told not to mention that James, after barely keeping his drive in-bounds—proceeds to top his approach.

We watch my buddies finish out and shake hands, with Sean playfully shaking James after what appears to be a rough day.

"That?," Alex says from the balcony, nodding to Sean and James below. "You'll see that at other courses. But not from every group like you do here. That is why this never gets old."

• • •

It is almost Thanksgiving. The PGA of America's recent announcement regarding ticket prices for the 2025 Ryder Cup at Bethpage Black represents the latest middle finger to the common golf fan. The organization has established a baseline price of $750 per ticket, with additional fees exceeding $200, creating a total cost that approaches $1,000 per attendee. This pricing strategy appears particularly discordant at Bethpage Black: a municipal facility that has long stood as a symbol of golf's accessibility to the public. This pricing structure effectively transforms what has historically been celebrated as golf's premier team competition—one focused on national pride rather than commercial interests—into another corporate sell-out. The irony is acute given that the Ryder Cup's atmosphere and moments are often better captured by the fans it is now trying to milk. But that's what the civil war has reduced professional golf to: profit over the people that make it matter. What the players want, rather than what the game deserves.

Saudi Arabia's analysis of professional golf's ecosystem demonstrated an understanding that eluded industry veterans, media observers, and governing bodies alike. Their assessment revealed the fundamental principle that had been obscured by tradition and mythology: at its elite level, the game had transformed into a sophisticated commercial platform where competition served as packaging. Saudi Arabia's motivation, rooted in geopolitical objectives rather than conventional return on investment metrics, meant they could sustain losses that would be untenable for traditional golf businesses. Yet strength was not its financial power. It did not create weaknesses in golf's model. It just accelerated them, dismantling a house that lacked the structural integrity to withstand a crisis in the first place.

Professional golf's perpetuation is assured by the sheer magnitude of monetary interests, personal ambitions, and institutional agendas embedded within its framework. The ecosystem has grown too vast, too intertwined with media empires, corporate sponsorships, and global business interests to evaporate. But what endures bears a superficial resemblance to the game's essential nature. The designation of "professional" has become more than a mere qualifier—it represents a transformation that separates this realm irrevocably from golf's true spirit. Their failure isn't merely one of business strategy; it reflects an inability to grasp why golf has endured for centuries as more than mere entertainment. There is a valley between what they think about golf, and what we feel about golf, and they don't have the brains or vision or desire or character to bridge the divide.

Because real golf exists in a realm beyond manufacture or manipulation, dwelling in spaces where corporate strategy holds no dominion. What matters in golf—truly matters—exists beyond transaction. The game marks its passage through rounds with aging parents whose swings grow shorter but whose stories grow richer, in matches with friends we see often or rarely, but with whom the ease remains the same. These precious hours, these accumulated moments of truth and beauty and occasional heartbreak, form the foundation of golf's enduring power. True golf can't be bought, because neither can memories or values.

It can't buy the quiet triumph in the eyes of the man I met at Leven: a golfer who had come to Scotland 17 times, yet his first since suffering a stroke five years before. He found delight in shooting above 100 because, "It's hard to make a backswing in a coffin."

It can't buy the ineffable bond between the sister and brother I encountered at Golspie. Fresh from their 120-hole marathon the weekend before, they were out there again, their laughter carrying across the links.

It can't buy the brotherhood I witnessed among those boys in Elie's car park, or the way Ru Macdonald's voice sparks when he speaks of Cruden Bay—not just as home, but as the keeper of his heart. It can't buy the crisis of conscience I saw in that young Bostonian in North Berwick, his voice heavy with worry: "I really don't know how I can go back to American golf after this."

It can't buy those exchanges in Scotland's pubs, where the simple recognition between golfers transforms strangers into confidants, where stories flow as freely as the whisky, and where the boundaries between "them" and "us" dissolve into the embrace of shared passion. You can't buy this connection between nation and game, between player and land—a romance written in centuries of swings and swears and steps across the links, in the wind-worn faces of locals who live and breathe this game, in the silent prayers of golfers who come seeking something they often cannot name but always seem to find.

You can't buy my memory of my dad taking me to Scotland for the first time. His careful saving wasn't just about the expenses of a golf trip. It was an act of love, a father's determination to open a door through which his son might glimpse something larger than himself, something worth orienting a life around.

When summer surrendered to autumn, my wife, our dog, and I boarded the ferry to Northern Ireland—the first leg of our long journey back to America. The vessel's engine thrummed beneath my feet as I stood alone on the top deck, watching Scotland recede into a grey smudge on the horizon. The panic hit without warning: a visceral, hollow ache as I realized that this chapter—these precious months of belonging—was ending. The thought of turning to face our westward journey felt like a betrayal of something essential, as if breaking eye contact with the Scottish coast would sever an umbilical cord of belonging I wasn't ready to relinquish.

I'm no stranger to leaving places behind—it's the tax we pay for exploration, for seeking out new horizons. But Scotland had worked its way beneath my skin in ways I hadn't anticipated. There, I had found a rare acceptance that asked nothing of me but presence.

Some places simply know us, hold us, welcome us back with a wordless understanding that defies explanation. Places that strip away our carefully maintained veneers, not to expose us, but to remind us who we are beneath the accumulated layers of who we pretend to be. Places that realize the true meaning of home has nothing to do with a billing address.

I can't predict where professional golf's fractured landscape will settle—in five weeks or five decades—and my feelings about its uncertain future remain as complex and frustrating as my short game. But there is one gospel truth from my summer, and it is this: Quinn was right. I don't know when I will be back, but I will, and the Old Course and St Andrews and Scottish golf will be there. They have secured the right to endure, if only to stand as testament that certain truths rise above the fleeting prejudices of man and time.

THE 12*

Well, technically 13. The Old Course has to stand alone, as it's impossible to decouple the links from the extracurriculars from the town, the Open, what it means to golf, et cetera. Anyway, these are not necessarily what I think are the best courses in Scotland; it's merely the list of my favorites, a mix of what I think speaks to the Scottish golf experience, and the places I desperately want to revisit on my return.

Old Course

North Berwick	Prestwick
Cruden Bay	Machrihanish
Brora	Dunaverty
Nairn	Dunbar
Elie	Castle Stuart
Dornoch	Crail

Honorable Mentions: Gullane 1, Kilspindie, Troon, Murcar Links, Lundin, St Andrews New, Royal Aberdeen, Panmure, Carnoustie

N/A—Western Gailes, Shiskine: No grade at the moment, as I've yet to visit or play these courses.

Muirfield, Turnberry, Ardfin: Muirfield and Turnberry are among the five best links in Scotland, but the money and exclusivity aren't copacetic with true Scottish golf.

Kingsbarns, Dumbarnie, Castle Course: Extremely good, even great. Some of the best hospitality. They just feel slightly American-ized. And yes, I realize the same could be said for Castle Stuart, but Stuart is that good.

Fine Nines: Anstruther, Carradale, and Durness.

Acknowledgments

This book, in this form, doesn't exist without Jim Sitar. To have a publisher that is invested in the subject, that understands and cares about the subject, is a luxury authors don't have. In an era when the written word continues to get watered down, to have a warrior like Jim on the front lines making sure meaningful golf literature still gets out to the masses gives hope that this industry, while hurting, is not going anywhere.

My agent, Nick Mullendore at Vertical Ink, recognized the importance of this book and how much it meant to me. Thank you for shepherding me through the process, for polishing the vision, and helping bring it to fruition.

Everything in journalism needs a break. I got mine from Tom Zentmeyer. Tom, I'm eternally grateful you were willing to give a college kid a shot at a national publication.

Meeting Jake Westrich proved to be one of the seminal moments of my life. An incredible person that facilitated most of the significant friendships I have in my life, who remains one of the best editors I've had. Almost makes up for Jake being such a mess after Mardi Gras that he had to lay down in the backseat as myself and our buddy John had to navigate the 15-hour ride home from New Orleans. Sarah you are a saint for putting up with him.

Speaking of friends, thank you to John and Kate, EJ and Kait, K-Mac and Jon, Vince and Julie, Tommy and Clare, Jay, Kyle, Mean Joe, Sundergod and the rest of my Athens-centric family. I'm extremely blessed to have you in my life, even though I am cursing your names after our All-Star Weekends together.

Same goes for my Cincinnati brothers: Brian, Corey, Pat, Jared, RJ, Bryan, the BPST05 crew. I remain doubtful we will see a Reds or Bengals championship but can't think of anyone else I'd rather be stuck in fandom purgatory with. To all my relatives, which is essentially half the West Side of Cincinnati, thank you for fostering such a tight-knit clan.

To Brian and Jenny, Dan and Laura, Alex and Michelle, John and Sarah, the Scullys and Collins families, thank you for making Connecticut feel like home.

Being an Elder Panther shaped who I am. What makes that place special is the strength of the community, although I have to give specific thanks to basketball coach Joe Schoenfeld, golf coach Mike Trimpe and *Purple Quill* editor Dave Reiring. Thank you for being leaders of men.

Jamie Kennedy was my Scottish golf whisperer. He took time out of his life to make this project come true, and to make it better. My only regret is we didn't get a chance to play more rounds together.

Writing can be isolating, yet I'm lucky to be surrounded by a village of talented, decent men and women in this industry: Sean, Brendan, Kyle, KVV, Bacon; Brody, Quinn and Gabby; James, Dylan, Sean and Claire; Lav, Brentley, Rex; Eamon, Damon, Raps and Adam; the teams at No Laying Up and Fried Egg. A special shoutout to Doug Ferguson, who has been a mentor to me and goes out of his way to make sure other writers, especially the younger ones, are taken care of.

I'm only in this world thanks to *Golf Digest*. Alex Myers was one of the first guys to make me feel welcomed, that I was part of a team when my world was spinning. While I maintain your hole-in-one was illegal, you're a good husband, father and dude. Steve, CP, and Keely are like siblings to me, and I cherish getting to work with talented people like Iooss, Meredith, Peter, Drew, Will, Daria, Jared, Greg,

Billy, Sneds, & Sneeds and countless others. Ben Walton, thank you for finally making yourself useful by designing this awesome book cover.

A writer is only as good as their editor. I am always in safe hands with Tod Leonard, John Strege and Jay Coffin. Mike O'Malley and Alan Pittman were instrumental in making my prose readable for the magazine.

To Chris Reynolds, thank you for fighting for us. To Max Adler, thank you for letting us take on the hard stories, often because we think they are the right thing to do. To Jerry Tarde, thank you for setting an example.

Shane Ryan and Luke Kerr-Dineen were voluntarily enlisted as sounding boards for this project, and the book is better off for it. Shane and Luke, I've enjoyed our growing friendships and times on the road together. Shane wanted me to mention how handsome he is to the readers, so there you go.

When I took the job at *Golf Digest*, I was halfway across the country from friends and family. Mike Johnson and Mike Stachura gave me a semblance of stability and belonging. They are father figures to me and the type of people I strive to be.

Ryan Herrington has been my direct boss for a decade. He's trusted me, defended me, given me the freedom to pursue tough topics. He's one of the hardest working people I know, and more importantly, someone whose sense of right and wrong serves as a compass for my own life. I can't ask for a better boss. Sam Weinman took a chance on me at a time when I was looking to quit the industry. He has put in hours upon hours of work behind the scenes to make me better as a writer and person. He genuinely cares about the people under his watch in a way that is unfortunately all too rare in modern times. I would follow Sam into battle any day. I won't be able to ever repay the debts I owe to Ryan and Sam.

To my grandparents—Betty, Rita, Joe, Justin—thank you for being anchors.

I've played golf with thousands of people in my life. My favorite partner remains my brother, Ben. His creativity and heart are things

I wish everyone had. To my sister Jenna, thank you for being a model of toughness, even if I'm jealous that you are the better writer.

To my mom, Wendy, who was there to dust me off when I fell, who kept me sane during health battles, who always went out of her way for others. To my dad, Roger, for introducing Scotland and golf to me, who helped with the editing process not as a father but as an avid golf reader to make sure it made sense.

To all the people and towns that were so welcoming during my stay in Scotland. I apologize I couldn't fit all your stories in, but know everyone I came across in my journeys left a mark on this book.

Most of all, thank you to my wife, Zahya. She is a beach girl, so I had to pitch her hard that Scotland's weather wasn't as bad as people make it out to be. It did not help that our summer turned out to be one of the wettest on record in 50-something years. She is genuinely the best person I know and probably the smartest, too; why she spends her time with me remains unclear. Zay, you are my rock, and my love. Just behind North Berwick and Brora.